MICKEY'S
Gourmet Cookbook

The Most Popular Recipes from
Walt Disney World® and Disneyland®

HYPERION
New York

Library of Congress Cataloging-in-Publication Data

Mickey's gourmet cookbook: the most popular recipes
from Walt Disney World and Disneyland. —1st ed.
p. cm.
Includes index.
ISBN 0-7868-8016-3
1. Cookery. 2. Walt Disney World (Fla.)
3. Disneyland (Calif.) 4. Mickey Mouse (Fictitious
character)
TX714.M52 1994
641.5—dc20   93-38706
                                                   CIP

FIRST EDITION
10 9 8 7 6 5

Contents

FOREWORD

Welcome to Disney's world of culinary delights!

With this book, you can recreate many of the memorable meals you enjoyed as a Disney guest. You'll also discover hundreds of other dishes, including some of Walt Disney's own personal favorites.

From spicy to sweet and simple to sophisticated, for the novice or gourmet cook, the recipes on these pages are the ones most requested from the thousands of menu items prepared daily at the Disney theme parks, resorts, and restaurants. The menus from which they have been selected vary to reflect our chefs' creativity, as well as our guests' preferences, the changing seasons, holidays, and other special occasions we celebrate.

These recipes are as unique as the settings in which they are served, and as varied as the cultures and eras they represent. Many have been created by our award-winning chefs, and each has been tested for accuracy and dining satisfaction.

Whether you remember the lemony tang of seafood savored by a starry lagoon, the silky richness of a chocolate mousse relished in Victorian elegance, or the good-morning heartiness of a fragrant muffin enjoyed by a bustling, sunny square, each culinary memory is as much a part of the Disney experience as Mickey's smile.

We've enjoyed gathering these taste experiences for you, and hope that each one brings you pleasurable new discoveries and fond recollections of your time with us.

Bon appétit!

A Special Acknowledgement

We wish to thank all of the Disney chefs for
their contributions to this book. We appreciate the time,
skills, and talent they have shared to make this
volume a very special collection.

BEVERAGES

BEVERAGES

CAFÉ DANOIS
(Danish Coffee)
Special Events
Walt Disney World Resorts

Yield: 1 serving

1 ounce cognac
½ ounce cherry liqueur
Coffee

Whipped cream
Cinnamon stick

In a lemon-rimmed glass dipped in sugar, add cognac, cherry liqueur, and coffee. Top with whipped cream.
Serve with cinnamon stick.

CAFÉ ESPAGNOL
(Spanish Coffee)
Special Events
Walt Disney World Resorts

Yield: 1 serving

1 ounce Spanish cognac
½ ounce coffee liqueur

Coffee
Whipped cream

In a lemon-rimmed glass dipped in sugar, add Spanish cognac, coffee liqueur, and coffee. Top with whipped cream.
Serve immediately.

CAFÉ FRANÇAIS
(French Coffee)
Special Events
Walt Disney World Resorts

Yield: 1 serving

1 ounce French cognac
½ ounce orange liqueur
Coffee

2 whole cloves
Cinnamon stick
Whipped cream

In a lemon-rimmed glass dipped in sugar, add French cognac, orange liqueur, and coffee. Add cloves and stir with cinnamon stick. Top with whipped cream.
Serve immediately.

CAFÉ HOLLANDAIS
(Dutch Coffee)
Special Events
Walt Disney World Resorts

Yield: 1 serving

**1½ ounces chocolate mint
  liqueur
Coffee**

**Whipped cream
Mint leaves, fresh**

Combine chocolate mint liqueur and coffee in a stemmed glass and top with whipped cream. Garnish with fresh mint leaves.
Serve immediately.

CAFÉ IRLANDAIS
(Irish Coffee)
Special Events
Walt Disney World Resorts

Yield: 1 serving

**1½ ounces Irish whisky
Coffee**

Whipped cream

In a lemon-rimmed glass dipped in sugar, add Irish whisky and coffee, and top with whipped cream.
Serve immediately.

CAFÉ LAC BELLE VUE
(Lake Buena Vista Coffee)
Special Events
Walt Disney World Resorts

Yield: 1 serving

**1¼ ounces almond-based
  liqueur
¾ ounce brandy**

**Coffee
Whipped cream
Maraschino cherry**

In a lemon-rimmed glass dipped in sugar, combine almond-based liqueur, brandy, and coffee. Top with whipped cream and cherry.
Serve immediately.

GIN FIZZ BEVERAGE
Rose & Crown Pub & Dining Room
United Kingdom   EPCOT Center

Yield: 1 serving

¾ ounce gin
4 ounces lemon bar mix

Ice cubes
1 split champagne, chilled

Combine gin and lemon bar mix with ice. Strain into a 10-ounce glass and add chilled champagne.

LAGUNA SPRAY
Outer Rim
Disney's Contemporary Resort

Yield: 1 serving

Ice cubes
1¼ ounces dark rum
¾ ounce blackberry brandy
2 ounces pineapple juice

2 ounces orange juice
¼ ounce grenadine
Pineapple wedge

Fill a 12-ounce cocktail glass with ice cubes. Add rum, brandy, pineapple juice, orange juice, and grenadine. Pour into a shaker and shake. Return to the original cocktail glass.
Garnish with pineapple wedge.

LEMON SHERBET PUNCH
Liberty Tree Tavern
Liberty Square   MAGIC KINGDOM Park

Yield: 1 quart

4 cups lemon sherbet
1 cup frozen lemonade
    concentrate, thawed

3 cups warm water
Ice cubes
Lemon slices

Place sherbet in mixing bowl. Using electric mixer on low speed, add lemonade concentrate and water. Mix well (about 5 minutes). Refrigerate.
Serve in tall glasses with ice and garnish with lemon slices.

MARGARITA BEVERAGE
San Angel Inn Restaurante
Mexico   EPCOT Center

Yield: 1 serving

Lemon juice
Kosher salt
Crushed ice
7 ounces water
1¼ ounces lemon bar mix

2¼ ounces tequila
1½ ounces clear orange
  liqueur
Lime slice

Dip the rim of a 16-ounce margarita glass in lemon juice, then in kosher salt. Fill with ice and set aside.

In a blender, combine water and lemon bar mix. Add tequila and clear orange liqueur and blend until foamy. Pour over crushed ice.

Garnish with slice of lime.

Note: For a frozen margarita, add ice to blender with other margarita ingredients and blend until thick and smooth.

MATSU BEVERAGE
Mitsukoshi Restaurant
Japan   EPCOT Center

Yield: 1 serving

½ ounce gin
1 ounce melon liqueur
2 ounces pineapple juice

1 ounce lemon bar mix
4 ounces crushed ice

Mix all ingredients in a blender until frothy.
Serve in a tall glass with a straw.

MONORAIL PINK
Top of the World
Disney's Contemporary Resort

Yield: 1 serving

1¼ ounces gin
1¼ ounces pineapple juice
1¼ ounces orange juice
1 ounce grenadine
½ ounce lemon bar mix

1½ ounces heavy cream
¾ cup crushed ice
Orange slice
Maraschino cherry

Mix gin, fruit juices, grenadine, lemon bar mix, and heavy cream in a blender with ice. Blend for 10 seconds. Pour into a tall glass.
Garnish with orange slice and cherry.

MONORAIL RED
Top of the World
Disney's Contemporary Resort

Yield: 1 serving

1¼ ounces tequila
¾ ounce sweet licorice-
flavored liqueur
¾ ounce grenadine

2½ ounces lemon bar mix
2 ounces pineapple juice
¾ cup crushed ice
Maraschino cherry

Combine tequila, licorice liqueur, grenadine, lemon bar mix, pineapple juice, and ice in a blender. Blend for 10 seconds and pour into a tall glass.
Garnish with maraschino cherry.

MONORAIL YELLOW
Top of the World
Disney's Contemporary Resort

Yield: 1 serving

1½ ounces rum
3 ounces orange juice
¾ ounce coconut cream
2½ ounces pineapple juice

¾ cup crushed ice
Maraschino cherry
Orange slice

Combine rum, orange juice, coconut cream, pineapple juice, and ice in a blender. Blend for 10 seconds and pour into a tall glass.
Garnish with maraschino cherry and orange slice.

NARCOOSSEE'S SPICED TEA BASE
Narcoossee's
Disney's Grand Floridian Beach Resort

Yield: 2 quarts (with tea)

1 lemon, sliced
4 whole cloves
Cinnamon stick
½ cup sugar

1 quart orange juice, fresh
Ice cubes
Lemon wedge
Mint sprig, fresh

Simmer sliced lemon, cloves, cinnamon stick, sugar, and orange juice for 15 minutes in a 2-quart saucepan. Do not allow mixture to boil. Strain juice and discard other ingredients. Refrigerate until well chilled.

To serve the spiced tea, prepare a mixture of 50% juice base and 50% cool brewed tea over ice. Garnish with lemon wedge and fresh mint sprig.

Note: Always allow tea to cool before adding to juice base, or tea will discolor. Keep refrigerated.

PIÑA COLADA
Outer Rim
Disney's Contemporary Resort

Yield: 1 serving

1¼ ounces rum
4 ounces pineapple juice
2 ounces coconut cream

1 ounce heavy cream
1½ cups crushed ice
Pineapple wedge

In a blender, combine rum, pineapple juice, coconut cream, heavy cream, and ice. Blend on high speed for about 1 minute. Strain into a 14-ounce cocktail glass.

Garnish with pineapple wedge.

PINK LEILANI
Coral Isle Cafe
Disney's Polynesian Resort

Yield: 1 serving

2 cups strawberries, fresh
  if possible (or 2 cups of
  frozen unsweetened
  berries if fresh are not
  in season)

3 cups orange juice
1 tablespoon grenadine
Crushed ice
Orange wheel
Strawberry

Puree berries in a blender. Add orange juice and grenadine. Pour into a tall glass over crushed ice.

Garnish with orange wheel and strawberry.

SMOOTH SAILING
Tambu Lounge
Disney's Polynesian Resort

Yield: 1 serving

Cracked ice
1 ounce vodka
½ ounce clear orange
  liqueur
¼ cup orange juice

¼ cup cranberry juice
¼ cup sour mix
½ ounce cherry brandy
Orange slice
Maraschino cherry

Put cracked ice in an 8-ounce glass. Add vodka, clear orange liqueur, orange juice, cranberry juice, and sour mix. Stir lightly. Float cherry brandy on top.

Garnish with orange slice and cherry.

STRAWBERRY MARGARITA
Outer Rim
Disney's Contemporary Resort

Yield: 1 serving

Lemon juice
Kosher salt
Crushed ice
1 cup strawberries, fresh
  or frozen

1 ounce tequila
1 ounce strawberry tequila
2 ounces lime juice
Lime wedge

Dip the rim of a 12-ounce margarita glass in lemon juice, then in kosher salt.

Combine strawberries, tequilas, and lime juice in a blender with 4 ounces of crushed ice. Blend thoroughly, adding more ice until mixture is thick. Pour into prepared glass.

Garnish with lime wedge.

SUNRISE
Grand Floridian Cafe
Disney's Grand Floridian Beach Resort

Yield: 10 cups

3 whole eggs
¼ cup honey

1 cup lime juice
2 quarts orange juice

Blend eggs, honey, and lime juice in a blender. Mix with orange juice.

Serve over crushed ice.

SUNS UP BREAKFAST
Chef Mickey's Village Restaurant
Disney Village Marketplace

Yield: 1 serving

2 ounces mixed berry yogurt
2 ounces plain yogurt
3-4 strawberries, fresh
1 small banana, fresh
2 teaspoons honey

4 ounces orange juice, fresh
½ teaspoon cinnamon, ground
2 egg whites
1 strawberry, fresh

Place all ingredients in a food processor or blender and mix well. Pour into chilled goblet.

Garnish with whole fresh strawberry and serve immediately.

SUN-KISSED MARGARITA
Outer Rim
Disney's Contemporary Resort

Yield: 1 serving

Lemon rind
Kosher salt
1½ ounces 80°
  oak-aged tequila
¾ ounce brandy-based
  orange liqueur

¾ ounce orange liqueur
4 ounces sour mix
Crushed ice
Lime wheel
1 ounce orange juice

Rub the rim of a cocktail glass with lemon rind and dip into kosher salt.

Combine tequila, liqueurs, and sour mix in a shaker filled with ice. Shake well and strain into salt-rimmed cocktail glass. Top with orange juice.

Garnish with lime wheel.

Variation: Seven Seas Sunset is prepared by substituting cranberry juice for orange juice.

TANGAROA TEASER
Tangaroa Terrace
Disney's Polynesian Resort

Yield: 4 servings

3 cups orange juice
1 cup pineapple juice
1 tablespoon coconut
  cream

½ cup papaya juice
Crushed ice
Pineapple wedge
Paper parasol

Place all ingredients in a blender with ice. Blend until smooth. Pour into a glass.

Garnish with pineapple wedge and paper parasol.

NOTES

APPETIZERS

APPETIZERS

BAKED BRIE CHEESE WITH JALAPEÑO CHUTNEY
Special Events
Disneyland Hotel

Yield: 4 servings

1 cup mango chutney
1½ tablespoons jalapeño
  pepper, minced
¼ cup cilantro, minced

1 12″ x 12″ sheet puff pastry,
  thawed if frozen
1 6-inch wheel Brie cheese
1 egg, beaten

Preheat oven to 375 degrees.

In a small bowl, combine chutney, pepper, and cilantro. Mix well. Cover and refrigerate until ready to use.

On a clean, dry work surface, lay out sheet of puff pastry. Place Brie in center of pastry and bring edges of the pastry to the center of cheese, covering cheese completely. Trim off any excess pastry and seal seams of pastry with beaten egg. Place wrapped cheese, seam side down, on a lightly greased cookie sheet and brush entire pastry with egg.

Bake for 12 to 15 minutes, or until crust is golden brown. Remove from oven and allow cheese to stand for 10 minutes before serving.

Serve with jalapeño chutney.

Note: Puff pastry is available at most supermarkets.

CRANBERRY CHUTNEY
50's Prime Time Cafe
Disney-MGM Studios Theme Park

Yield: 4 servings

½ cup cranberries, frozen,
  thawed
3 tablespoons sugar
1 tablespoon brown sugar
½ teaspoon cinnamon
½ teaspoon ginger

½ teaspoon cloves
¼ cup water
¼ cup celery, finely diced
¼ cup onion, finely diced
1 medium apple, peeled, diced
2 tablespoons raisins

In a medium-size saucepan, bring water to a boil. Add all above ingredients except apples and raisins. Simmer for 15 minutes. Add apples and simmer for an additional 10 minutes, or until apples are soft. Remove from heat and stir in raisins while sauce is still hot. Cool thoroughly.

Serve as an accompaniment to turkey burgers or carved turkey.

DEEP FRIED CALAMARI
Flagler's
Disney's Grand Floridian Beach Resort

Yield: 2 servings

4 ounces baby calamari,
   thinly sliced
2 tablespoons flour,
   seasoned with a dash each
   of basil, garlic, oregano,
   salt, and pepper

¼ cup marinara sauce
½ lemon, wrapped in cheese
   cloth

Soak calamari in cold water for 30 minutes. Drain and pat dry with paper towels. Coat with seasoned flour. Deep-fry in hot oil until golden brown.

Arrange on a plate with marinara sauce on the side. Garnish with wrapped lemon.

DEEP FRIED MOZZARELLA
Caffe Villa Verde
Disneyland Hotel

Yield: 4 servings

1 pound whole mozzarella
   cheese
3 eggs, beaten
½ cup flour

1 cup bread crumbs
¼ cup parsley, chopped
4 cups vegetable oil, for frying
Marinara sauce

Cut mozzarella cheese into 3-inch sticks about ½ inch thick. Combine bread crumbs and chopped parsley in a small bowl and set up beaten eggs in another. Place flour on a plate. First thoroughly dust cheese sticks in flour, shaking off any excess. Dip in beaten egg, coating thoroughly, and then in bread crumbs. Press lightly to ensure an even coating. Refrigerate 15 minutes to allow breading to set up.

In the meantime, heat oil in a heavy skillet just large enough to allow for 2 inches of oil. When oil is hot, fry a few cheese sticks at a time to a golden brown. Drain on paper towels. Repeat until all cheese has been fried.

Serve hot with marinara sauce on the side for dipping.

FRIED CAMEMBERT CHEESE
Disney-MGM Studios Theme Park

Yield: 4 servings

4 4.5-ounce wheels	2 cups bread crumbs
Camembert cheese	3 eggs
8 teaspoons lingonberries	2 tablespoons water

Preheat oven to 300 degrees.

Unwrap cheese and place on a cutting board. Cut a cone-shaped circle about the size of a fifty-cent piece in the center of the top of each cheese. Remove the cone-shaped pieces of cheese and fill the openings with lingonberries. Press berries into cavities and replace tops.

Whisk eggs and water. Dip cheese in egg mixture, coating thoroughly. Coat with bread crumbs and fry in hot oil until golden brown. Remove from pan and drain on absorbent paper. Repeat process until all cheese has been fried. Place cheese on a baking sheet and bake for 8 to 10 minutes until hot.

Serve immediately with additional lingonberries.

JAMAICAN HOT WINGS
Captain's Hideaway
Disney's Caribbean Beach Resort

Yield: 40–50 wings

1 pound butter	5 pounds chicken wings (or
8 ounces Jamaican jerk spice	drumettes), fresh, not
½ ounce Tabasco sauce	frozen
8 ounces tomato juice	Oil for frying
8 ounces flour	

Melt butter in a 2-quart sauce pot over low heat. Add jerk spice, Tabasco sauce, and tomato juice. Mix well. Set aside.

Rinse wings under cold running water and pat dry with paper towels. Dust wings with flour and deep-fry in a heavy pot or skillet in about 2 inches of hot oil until done. Place cooked wings in sauce mixture and allow to marinate just a few minutes. Drain off any excess liquid.

Serve immediately.

Note: Jamaican jerk spice may be found in specialty food stores.

LOBSTER COCKTAIL
Narcoossee's
Disney's Grand Floridian Beach Resort

Yield: 1 serving

2 lobster tails, about
5 ounces each
½ cup lettuce, shredded

¼ cup cocktail sauce
2 lemon wedges

Remove shells from lobster tails and clean under cold running water. Place lobster tails in boiling water for 7 to 10 minutes, depending on size. Cook long enough for the flesh to turn white and firm. Remove from pot and cool thoroughly.

Set up plates with lettuce. Place lobster tails on top of lettuce and garnish with lemon wedges. Serve with cocktail sauce on the side.

MARINATED MUSHROOMS
Concourse Grille
Disney's Contemporary Resort

Yield: 2 quarts

2 pounds mushrooms, fresh
⅓ cup lemon juice, fresh
1¼ cups vinaigrette dressing
2 medium bay leaves
⅔ cup red wine vinegar

salt, to taste
1½ cups bermuda onion,
   julienne
4 tablespoons pimiento, diced

Choose medium-size mushrooms, about 34 to a pound. Two pounds makes about 10 cups.

Trim stems and put mushrooms in a large bowl. Add lemon juice. Strain vinaigrette dressing and put solids in a cheese-cloth square. Tie shut and put in a 3-quart container. Combine vinaigrette liquid, bay leaves, and vinegar in a saucepan and bring to a boil. Add mushrooms and simmer 1 minute.

Pour into 3-quart container and add salt, onions, and pimientos. Let mushroom mixture cool before refrigerating overnight.

NACHO CHEESE DIP
Fiesta Fun Center Snack Bar
Disney's Contemporary Resort

Yield: 3 cups

½ pound provolone cheese, grated
½ pound American cheese, grated
¾ cup heavy cream
8 ounces cream cheese

¼ teaspoon garlic powder
¾ teaspoon Worcestershire sauce
⅛ teaspoon cayenne pepper
⅛ teaspoon yellow food coloring

Melt provolone cheese in top of a double boiler over boiling water. Add American cheese and stir in heavy cream. Add cream cheese and stir until all cheese is melted. Remove from heat and whip in seasonings and food coloring.

Serve warm with crackers, chips, or fresh vegetables.

NACHOS
Sgt. Preston's Yukon Saloon and Dance Hall
Disneyland Hotel

Yield: 4 servings

1 8-ounce bag tortilla chips
½ cup refried beans
½ cup cheese sauce
¼ cup jalapeño peppers, sliced
½ cup ripe olives, sliced
½ cup onion, diced
½ cup tomatoes, diced

2 cups cheddar cheese, shredded
2 cups Monterey Jack cheese, shredded
½ cup scallions, chopped
½ cup sour cream
½ cup guacamole
½ cup salsa

Preheat oven to 400 degrees.

In a 9-inch baking dish, spread an even layer of tortilla chips. Pour cheese sauce and refried beans evenly over chips. Sprinkle with jalapeños, olives, onions, and tomatoes. Top with shredded cheese and bake for 5 minutes, or until cheese melts. Remove from oven and garnish with chopped scallions.

Serve with sour cream, guacamole and salsa.

MAUI OYSTERS
Tangaroa Terrace
Disney's Polynesian Resort

Yield: 4 servings

24 oysters, shucked and on
   the half shell
¼ cup green bell pepper,
   finely diced
¼ cup pineapple, chopped
¼ cup bacon, finely diced
¼ cup celery, finely diced

¼ cup butter, melted
1 teaspoon cayenne pepper
¼ teaspoon Tabasco sauce
⅛ cup Parmesan cheese
⅛ cup fresh bread crumbs
Rock salt

Preheat oven to 350 degrees.

Mix pepper, bacon, celery, and pineapple with melted butter. Season with cayenne pepper and Tabasco. Portion evenly among oysters. Mix Parmesan cheese and bread crumbs and lightly sprinkle over oysters, using all the mixture.

Pour rock salt onto a cookie sheet with sides and place oysters on rock salt. Bake for 8 to 10 minutes.

Serve immediately.

MUSSELS MARINIERE
Shipyard Inn
Disneyland Hotel

Yield: 4 servings

4 pounds fresh mussels,
   in the shell
¼ cup olive oil
3 cloves garlic, crushed
3 whole shallots, chopped
5 stalks scallions, chopped
¼ cup parsley, chopped

¼ cup dill, chopped
1 cup white wine
½ cup sherry
1 lemon, juiced
1 cup water
Lemon crowns
Parsley, chopped

Scrub and clean mussels in fresh water and set aside.

In a pot large enough to hold mussels, heat olive oil. Add garlic, shallots, and scallions and sauté for 5 minutes over medium heat. Add remaining ingredients and bring to a simmer. Add mussels and cover pot. Simmer until all mussels have opened. Remove mussels from pot and discard any that did not open. Keep mussels warm and bring cooking liquid to a boil. Reduce sauce by half and spoon over warm mussels.

Garnish with lemon crowns and additional chopped parsley.

MINI CHICKEN BROCHETTES WITH SWEET AND SOUR SAUCE
Special Events
Disneyland Hotel

Yield: 12 skewers

12 5-inch bamboo skewers
1½ pounds boneless chicken breast, cut into ½-inch cubes
1 10-ounce can pineapple chunks; reserve juice

1 6-ounce jar cocktail onions
1 large green bell pepper, cut into 24 small squares
Sweet and sour sauce (recipe follows)

Soak bamboo skewers in cold water for 30 minutes to prevent burning when cooked.

Assemble brochettes in this order: chicken, onion, pepper, chicken, pineapple, chicken, onion, pepper, and chicken. Repeat the process until all brochettes are complete.

Broil, bake, barbecue, or sauté brochettes, as desired, until fully cooked.

Serve immediately, topped with sweet and sour sauce.

Sweet and Sour Sauce

½ cup onion, chopped
½ cup green bell pepper, chopped
2 ounces butter
Reserved juice from pineapple can
2 cups tomato ketchup

2 tablespoons red wine vinegar
1 cinnamon stick
1 teaspoon ginger, ground
1 teaspoon cloves, ground
1 tablespoon brown sugar
½ cup orange juice

Melt butter in a medium-sized skillet. Add onion and pepper and sauté until tender. Add all remaining ingredients and mix well. Bring to a boil and reduce heat to simmer.

Cook for 8 to 10 minutes.

PASTA WITH WILD MUSHROOMS
Disney-MGM Studios Theme Park

Yield: 4 servings

1 cup shiitake mushrooms
1 cup oyster mushrooms
1 cup button mushrooms
2 tablespoons butter
1 tablespoon garlic,
 chopped
2 teaspoons onion, chopped

¾ teaspoon vegetable
 seasoning
¼ teaspoon salt
¾ cup heavy cream
2 cups angel hair pasta,
 cooked

Rinse mushrooms under cold running water and pat dry. Slice as desired and set aside.

Melt butter in a large skillet. Add garlic and onion and sauté until tender (about 5 minutes). Add mushrooms and continue cooking until mushrooms are tender but not mushy. Season with vegetable seasoning and salt and add heavy cream. Bring mixture to a simmer and cook until sauce thickens slightly (3 to 5 minutes). Add cooked pasta to mushrooms and sauce and cook only long enough to heat pasta.

Serve immediately.

Note: Any combination of mushrooms may be used.

PIÑA COLADA DIP
Special Events
Disneyland Hotel

Yield: 1 pint

1½ cups cream cheese
¾ cup piña colada mix
½ cup sour cream

1¼ cups pineapple chunks
½ cup maraschino cherries,
 halved

In a blender or food processor, combine cream cheese, piña colada mix, and sour cream and blend until smooth. Remove from blender to a mixing bowl and fold in pineapple chunks and maraschino cherry halves. Refrigerate 1 hour.

Serve with other fresh fruit or dried fruit and nuts.

POLYNESIAN EGG ROLLS
Tangaroa Terrace
Disney's Polynesian Resort

Yield: 8 egg rolls

4 ounces pork shoulder
4 ounces salad shrimp, cooked
1¼ cup white cabbage, shredded
¼ cup celery, diced
1 medium carrot, shredded
2 teaspoons garlic powder
½ teaspoon ginger powder
¼ teaspoon white pepper
¼ teaspoon salt
1 tablespoon sesame oil
1 egg
8 egg roll wrappers
3 cups vegetable oil, for frying
Pork marinade (recipe follows)

Cut pork into matchstick-size pieces.

Prepare pork marinade and add to pork. Marinate 1 hour.

Drain marinade from pork and cook pork in small sauté pan on medium high heat for about 5 minutes. Allow to cool, or refrigerate while you prepare the rest of the ingredients.

Place cabbage, carrot, and celery in a mixing bowl with garlic powder, ginger powder, white pepper, salt, and sesame oil. Mix well. In a large sauté pan, cook cabbage mixture for 3 to 5 minutes on high heat. Spread out on a large plate and allow to cool.

When both the pork and cabbage mixtures are cool, combine with cooked salad shrimp and blend well.

Crack egg into a shallow dish and whisk with a fork. Place egg roll wrapper with point facing you. Place ⅛ of the mixture ⅓ of the way up from bottom of wrapper. Fold bottom point up and over mixture and roll egg roll halfway up. Brush top corner of wrapper with beaten egg. Fold corners toward middle and continue rolling. Set on a wire rack with seam side down. Repeat until all egg rolls are complete.

Deep-fry egg rolls in oil 5 to 6 minutes, or until golden brown. Drain on paper towels.

Serve with duck sauce and hot mustard.

Pork Marinade

½ teaspoon ginger powder
1 teaspoon sherry
3 tablespoon hoisin sauce
1 tablespoon sugar
¼ teaspoon salt

QUESO FUNDIDO
(Cheese and Sausage Dip)
San Angel Inn Restaurante
Mexico   *EPCOT Center*

Yield: 4 servings

½ pound Muenster cheese   6 flour tortillas
¼ pound chorizo sausage

Slice or grate Muenster cheese. Set aside.

Peel chorizo sausage and cut into large chunks. Sauté in a small frying pan until nicely browned. Break up sausage into small pieces while browning and drain any excess fat.

Lightly butter an oven- and broiler-proof casserole dish. Arrange half the sliced or grated cheese in bottom of casserole dish. Top with cooked sausage and remaining cheese. Broil sausage and cheese until cheese melts and lightly browns.

Warm tortillas and cut into quarters. Spoon sausage-cheese mixture onto tortilla pieces and serve immediately.

SEAFOOD DIP
Special Events
Disneyland Hotel

Yield: 6 cups

1½ cups cream cheese
1½ cups sharp cheddar
  cheese, grated
½ cup scallions, chopped
1½ cups mayonnaise
½ cup frozen chopped
  spinach, thawed, drained
¼ cup parsley, chopped

½ teaspoon garlic powder
½ teaspoon sugar
1½ teaspoons tarragon
¼ cup water
¼ cup red wine vinegar
½ teaspoon white pepper
1½ cups bay shrimp, cooked,
  cleaned, diced

Combine all above ingredients in a food processor or blender, except shrimp. Blend until smooth and well mixed. Fold in shrimp and chill 30 minutes.

Serve with fresh vegetables, crackers, or chips.

TUNA FISH DIP
Concourse Grille
Disney's Contemporary Resort

Yield: 4 cups

⅓ cup onion, diced
¼ cup parsley, coarsely chopped
1 2-ounce can anchovies, drained
2 teaspoons tarragon leaves
2 tablespoons vinegar
1 tablespoon prepared horseradish
1 clove garlic
2 6½-ounce cans tuna fish, drained
2 tablespoons lemon juice

1¾ cups mayonnaise
4 ounces cream cheese, room temperature
¼ cup blue cheese (about 2 ounces), room temperature
¼ teaspoon Worcestershire sauce
½ teaspoon curry powder (more if desired)
Salt
Pepper

In a food processor with a steel blade, combine onion, parsley, anchovies, tarragon, vinegar, horseradish, garlic, tuna fish, and lemon juice. Process until mixed thoroughly. Transfer into a 2-quart mixing bowl and add remaining ingredients. Mix well and adjust seasoning with additional curry, salt, and pepper, if desired. Chill overnight to thicken and blend flavors.

Serve with assorted crackers.

TUNA MOUSSE
Special Events
Disneyland Hotel

Yield: 10 servings

9 ounces cream cheese
⅔ cup sour cream
¾ cup mayonnaise
⅓ cup red onion
1 teaspoon salt
1 teaspoon white pepper
1 teaspoon Tabasco sauce

8 ounces white tuna in water, drained
2 teaspoons plain gelatin
¼ cup warm water
Lemon slices
Olives
Parsley sprigs

In a blender or food processor with a steel blade, combine first 7 ingredients. Add drained and flaked tuna and blend 15 seconds.

Combine warm water and gelatin and allow gelatin to soften. Add to tuna mixture and mix until well incorporated. Pour into a standard-size loaf pan and refrigerate until set (about 2 hours).

Very quickly dip loaf pan in hot water and invert pan to remove mousse. Refrigerate until ready to use.

Garnish with lemon slices, olives and parsley.

SNAILS CALIFORNIA
Disney-MGM Studios Theme Park

Yield: 4 servings

2 tablespoons vegetable oil
1 teaspoon garlic, chopped
fine
1 teaspoon shallots,
chopped fine
1 cup red bell pepper, diced
small
24 medium snails, canned

1¼ cups tomatoes, canned,
diced, drained
½ cup Burgundy wine
1 cup cut corn, frozen
1 cup heavy cream
Salt
Pepper

Heat vegetable oil in a medium-size sauté pan. Add garlic and shallots. Sauté 2 to 3 minutes. Add bell pepper and continue to cook for another 2 to 3 minutes. Add snails, tomatoes, corn, and Burgundy wine. Bring to a boil and reduce the liquid by half. Add heavy cream and simmer about 5 minutes. Reduce sauce to consistency of gravy. Do not reduce too much, or liquid will separate. Add salt and pepper to taste.

To serve, divide snails equally among 4 bowls and top with sauce.

SOUTHWESTERN STUFFED PEPPER
The Land Grille Room
The Land   EPCOT Center

Yield: 4 servings

8 mild green banana
peppers (or 4 small green
bell peppers)
1 cup stuffing (recipe
follows)

1½ cups pepper sauce
(recipe follows)
1 cup grated part-skim
mozzarella cheese

Roast banana peppers over open flame or under broiler until skins turn black on all sides. Peel under cold running water and slit one side to remove seeds and pulp.

Preheat oven to 375 degrees.

Divide stuffing mix evenly among roasted peppers, filling each pepper cavity. Place stuffed peppers in a baking dish and cover each with grated mozzarella cheese. Bake for 10 to 15 minutes, or until cheese melts and peppers are hot.

Remove from oven and serve with pepper sauce.

30

(continued on next page)

SOUTHWESTERN STUFFED PEPPER
(continued from previous page)

Stuffing

¼ cup turkey, skinless
  breast meat, diced
¼ cup green bell pepper,
  diced
¼ cup red bell pepper,
  diced
½ cup tomato, fresh, diced

¼ cup onion, diced
1 teaspoon vinegar
¼ cup feta cheese,
  crumbled
⅛ teaspoon basil
Pinch cumin

Sauté turkey meat, peppers, tomato, and onion in a non-stick skillet with vegetable spray for 3 to 4 minutes until turkey is cooked and vegetables are tender. Add vinegar, basil, and cumin and mix well. Remove from heat and add feta cheese. Set aside until ready to use.

Pepper Sauce

¼ cup red bell pepper,
  finely diced
1 cup tomato, fresh, finely
  diced
1 tablespoon leek, finely
  diced
¼ teaspoon basil, fresh,
  chopped
⅛ teaspoon rosemary, fresh,
  chopped

⅛ teaspoon thyme, fresh,
  chopped
½ cup chicken stock
1½ teaspoons white
  vinegar
½ cup corn, frozen,
  thawed
Salt
Pepper

In a large skillet or sauté pan, add vegetables and herbs and sauté for 3 to 5 minutes. Add chicken stock, vinegar, and corn and bring to a boil. Season with salt and pepper to taste and remove from heat until ready to use.

YACHT CLUB CLAMS
Yacht Club Galley
Disney's Yacht Club Resort

Yield: 24 clams

2 cups white bread crumbs, fresh
1 teaspoon thyme leaves
½ teaspoon rosemary leaves, chopped

1 teaspoon garlic, chopped
1 teaspoon parsley, chopped
24 cherrystone clams
12 ounces butter

Combine bread crumbs, thyme, rosemary, garlic, and parsley and mix well. Open clams, reserving each clam on the half shell, and place about one teaspoon of herb bread-crumb mix over each clam. Top each clam with ½ ounce of butter.

Broil clams 2 to 3 minutes until butter melts and bread crumbs are lightly browned.

SOUPS

SOUPS

ALBONDIGAS WITH MUSHROOMS, EN CROUTE
Special Events
Disneyland Hotel

Yield: 10 servings

1 cup onion, chopped
1 clove garlic, crushed
2 tablespoons cooking oil
1 pound mushrooms,
    assorted, sliced (shiitake,
    oyster, and Chanterelle)
½ cup white wine
5 cups beef broth
4 beef bouillon cubes
1 pound ground beef

1 egg, beaten
2 tablespoons cilantro,
    chopped
½ teaspoon oregano
1 teaspoon salt
½ teaspoon pepper
Puff pastry for 10 individual
    oven-proof soup bowls
1 egg, beaten

In a medium-size skillet, heat oil and sauté onion and garlic until tender. Add mushrooms and white wine and bring to a boil. Reduce heat and cook 1 minute. Remove from heat and set aside.

Combine beef broth and bouillon cubes in a large soup pot and bring to a boil.

Combine ground beef, egg, cilantro, oregano, salt, and pepper and form into ½-inch meatballs. Drop into boiling broth and cook for 5 minutes. Remove from broth after 5 minutes with a slotted spoon and set aside.

Preheat oven to 400 degrees.

To assemble, evenly divide the meatballs among 10 oven-proof soup bowls. Top each with an equal amount of mushroom mixture and add enough broth to cover. Cut puff pastry to fit top of each soup bowl and crimp edges to seal bowl. Brush with beaten egg and bake for 20 to 25 minutes, or until crust is golden brown and filling is hot.

Remove from oven and allow to cool for 5 minutes before serving.

ALPHABET SOUP
50's Prime Time Cafe
Disney-MGM Studios Theme Park

Yield: 6 servings

¼ cup carrots, diced
¼ cup rutabaga, diced
¼ cup celery, diced
¼ cup onion, diced
1 cup tomatoes, crushed
¼ cup peas, frozen
¼ cup cut green beans, frozen
2 tablespoons pearl barley,
   cooked, cooled

¼ cup alphabet noodles,
   cooked, cooled
3 cups water
2 chicken bouillon cubes
2 beef bouillon cubes
2 tablespoons cornstarch,
   dissolved in ¼ cup water

In a 4-quart soup pot, add water and bouillon cubes. Bring to a boil and simmer, covered, for 15 minutes.

Add carrots, rutabaga, celery, and onions to soup pot. Simmer 15 minutes, or until tender but not mushy.

Separately cook, rinse, drain, and cool pearl barley and alphabet noodles and set aside.

After vegetables are tender, add tomatoes, peas, and green beans. Simmer an additional 5 minutes and stir in cornstarch mixed with ¼ cup water. Allow soup to thicken slightly and add pearl barley and alphabet noodles. Heat only long enough to warm all ingredients.

Serve immediately.

BEEF BARLEY SOUP
Steerman's Quarters
Disney Village Marketplace

Yield: approximately 1 gallon

1 cup carrots, diced small
1 cup celery, diced small
1 cup onion, diced small
2 tablespoons beef base (or
   4 bouillon cubes)
2 tablespoons chicken base
   (or 4 bouillon cubes)

6½ ounces pearl barley
3 quarts water
½ pound ground beef
2 tablespoons butter
Salt
Pepper

Sauté all vegetables in butter until tender.

In a separate pan, cook ground beef. Drain any excess fat. Add drained ground beef to vegetables. Add bases, water and barley. Simmer for 30 minutes. Season with salt and pepper to taste.

BLACK BEAN SOUP
Fisherman's Deck
Disney Village Marketplace

Yield: 2½ quarts

1¼ cups black beans
1 quart water
3 tablespoons bacon fat
1 cup onion, diced
1 cup celery, diced
½ cup green bell pepper, diced
2 quarts chicken broth

1 large ham hock
½ cup white long-grain rice, uncooked
¾ teaspoon cumin
¼ cup red wine vinegar
Salt
Pepper

Rinse beans and soak overnight in 1 quart of water.

Heat bacon fat in a large saucepan and sauté onion, celery, and green pepper until tender. Add chicken broth, ham hock, and drained beans. Cook until beans are almost done (about 1 hour). Add rice and cook an additional 20 minutes, or until rice is tender.

Remove ham hock and cool. If there is meat on ham hock, dice in small pieces and return to soup. Discard fat, skin, and bone.

Season soup with cumin and red wine vinegar. Add salt and pepper to taste.

CHEESE, LEEK AND ONION BISQUE
Grand Floridian Cafe
Disney's Grand Floridian Beach Resort

Yield: 2 quarts

1 cup leeks, peeled, cleaned and chopped
1 cup celery, chopped
1 cup onion, chopped
1 clove garlic, chopped
2 tablespoons butter
¼ cup white wine

6 cups chicken stock
¼ cup sour cream
¼ cup cream cheese
¼ cup heavy cream
Salt
Pepper

Sauté leeks, celery, onion and garlic in butter until tender. Add white wine and chicken stock and simmer for 30 minutes. Remove from stove and puree in a food processor. Add sour cream, cream cheese, and heavy cream and blend well. Strain through a fine sieve and return to pot. Bring back to a simmer and add salt and pepper to taste.

CHICKEN TORTELLINI SOUP
Tony's Town Square Restaurant
Main Street, U.S.A. *Magic Kingdom Park*

Yield: 8 cups

1 cup chicken breast meat, diced
1 tablespoon butter or margarine
⅔ cup carrots, diced
1 cup celery, diced
1 cup onion, diced
5 chicken bouillon cubes
5½ cups water

1 tablespoon parsley, chopped
⅛ teaspoon thyme, ground
¼ teaspoon garlic powder
Salt
White pepper
½ pound tortellini, cooked according to package directions

In a 3-quart saucepan, melt butter or margarine. Add carrots and sauté 2 to 3 minutes. Add diced chicken meat and cook another 5 minutes until chicken is done. Add celery and onions and continue to cook another 4 to 5 minutes. Dissolve chicken bouillon cubes in water and add to soup with all remaining ingredients except tortellini. Simmer soup until all vegetables are tender. Add salt and pepper to taste. Add cooked tortellini and serve.

CLAM CHOWDER
50's Prime Time Cafe
Disney-MGM Studios Theme Park

Yield: 4 servings

1 stick margarine or butter
2 stalks celery, diced (about 1½ cups)
1 small onion, diced (about 1 cup)
⅛ teaspoon thyme
½ cup flour

3 cups milk
½ teaspoon clam base or clam juice
2 cups chopped clams, canned, with juice
Salt
White pepper

Melt margarine or butter in a 4-quart sauce pot. Add celery and onion and sauté 3 to 5 minutes. Add thyme and continue to sauté another 1 to 2 minutes. Add flour and mix well, cooking for 3 to 5 minutes to form a roux. Slowly add milk and bring mixture to a boil. Stir constantly to prevent burning. Add clam base and chopped clams and season with salt and pepper to taste.

COUNTRY WEDDING SOUP
Liberty Tree Tavern
Liberty Square   Magic Kingdom Park

Yield: 10 6-ounce servings

6 cups chicken broth
½ cup carrots, cut in ½-inch dice
½ cup celery, cut in ½-inch dice
½ cup onion, cut in ½-inch dice
½ cup tomatoes, fresh, seeded and diced
1 clove garlic, chopped

2 cups red leaf lettuce, roughly chopped
½ cup smoked ham, cut in ½-inch dice
¼ cup scallions, chopped
1½ cups white rice, cooked
Salt
Pepper
16 turkey meatballs (recipe follows)

In a 4-quart soup pot, add chicken broth, carrots, celery, onion, tomatoes, and garlic. Bring to a boil and simmer 20 minutes until vegetables are tender but not mushy. Add lettuce, ham, scallions, and rice. Season with salt and pepper to taste. Add turkey meatballs.
Serve immediately.

Turkey Meatballs

Yield: 16 meatballs

½ pound turkey meat, ground
2 tablespoons onion, finely diced
⅛ teaspoon garlic powder

¼ cup bread crumbs, unseasoned
⅛ teaspoon salt
⅛ teaspoon pepper

Preheat oven to 350 degrees.
Combine all ingredients in a small bowl and mix well. Form into ½-inch meatballs and place on a greased baking sheet. Bake for 10 to 12 minutes until firm and fully cooked. Remove from oven and add to soup.

CREAM OF SHRIMP WITH LEEKS
Coral Reef Restaurant
The Living Seas   EPCOT Center

Yield: 8 to 10 servings

2 quarts chicken stock or
  broth
1 pound small shrimp
  (40-50 count)
8 slices bacon, diced small
2 cups leeks, finely diced
½ cup carrots, chopped
½ cup shallots, chopped
¼ cup butter
½ cup dry white wine

2 bay leaves
1 sprig thyme
4-5 parsley stems
4-5 peppercorns
1 cup heavy cream
Salt
Pepper
¼ cup leeks, blanched,
  julienne

Bring chicken stock to a boil. Add shrimp and cook until tender. Remove shrimp and cool in cold water to stop cooking process. Save stock.

In a heavy pot, cook bacon until tender. Drain most of the fat. Add butter, leeks, carrots, shallots, herbs, and peppercorns. Cook until tender. Add wine and reduce by half. Add chicken stock and simmer for 45 minutes.

Place everything in a food processor and puree. Strain back into pot through a fine-mesh strainer and bring back to a boil. Add cream and salt and pepper to taste. Cut shrimp in half and add back into soup.

Garnish individual cups of soup with blanched leeks.

CUCUMBER YOGURT SOUP
Garden Gallery
The Disney Inn

Yield: 4 servings

2 cups plain yogurt
1 cup cucumber, peeled,
  seeded, grated
2 teaspoons white vinegar
1 teaspoon olive oil

2 teaspoons mint leaves,
  fresh, finely cut (or 1
  teaspoon dried mint)
½ teaspoon dill, fresh,
  finely cut (or ¼ teaspoon
  dried dill weed)

In a deep bowl, stir yogurt with a wire whisk or large spoon until smooth. Gently beat in grated cucumber, vinegar, olive oil, and herbs. Add salt to taste.

Served chilled.

GERMAN POTATO SOUP
Plaza Inn
Main Street, U.S.A.   DISNEYLAND Park

Yield: 6 servings

¾ cup onion, diced
¼ cup butter
3 medium leeks, sliced,
    white part only (about
    2 cups)
2 pounds potatoes, peeled
    and cut in ½-inch cubes
1 ham bone, any size

¼ teaspoon thyme, dried
6 cups chicken stock or
    broth
1 cup heavy cream
Salt
Pepper
Croutons

In a 3-quart saucepan, sauté onions in butter until golden brown. Add leeks, potatoes, ham bone, thyme, and chicken stock and bring to a boil. Cover and simmer until potatoes are very soft. Remove ham bone and discard.

Cool potato/leek mixture slightly and put through a fine sieve or puree in a food processor using a steel blade. Return to pan and add cream. Cook an additional 2 to 3 minutes and add salt and pepper to taste.

Serve hot with croutons.

GERMAN POTATO SOUP
Concourse Grille
Disney's Contemporary Resort

Yield: 1 gallon

1 cup onions, diced small
1 cup celery, diced small
1 cup carrots, diced small
2 cups potatoes, diced small
4 tablespoons bacon fat
4 cubes chicken bouillon

⅓ cup leeks, diced
1 teaspoon marjoram
1½ cups instant potatoes
4 quarts water
Salt
White pepper

Sauté onions, celery, and carrots in bacon fat about 5 minutes. Slowly add water, bouillon cubes, leeks, and potatoes and cook at a rolling simmer for about 20 minutes. Add instant potatoes, marjoram, and salt and pepper to taste. Simmer 15 minutes.

GINGER EGG DROP SOUP
Papeete Bay Verandah
Disney's Polynesian Resort

Yield: 5 servings

1 quart chicken stock or
 broth
1 teaspoon ginger powder
¼ teaspoon white pepper
1 teaspoon egg shade food
 coloring (or yellow food
 coloring; optional)

1 egg, beaten
2 ounces cornstarch
1 tablespoon salt

Heat chicken stock, add ginger powder, pepper and food coloring. Bring to a simmer. Dilute cornstarch with water and add to stock slowly to avoid lumps. Whip mixture if lumps appear. Add beaten egg around edge of hot pot. Egg will surface when done. Add salt and pepper to taste.

KALTSCHALE SOUP
(Cold Fruit Soup)
Club 33
New Orleans Square   DISNEYLAND Park

Yield: 6 servings

2 cups peaches, peeled and
 sliced
2 cups pineapple, fresh,
 peeled, diced
½ cup watermelon or
 honeydew melon, pulp
½ cup red and white
 currants

1 cup strawberries, pureed
2 cups white wine
⅛ teaspoon cinnamon
¾ cup sugar
Zest of one lemon
3 cups champagne, chilled

In a medium-size saucepan, combine all ingredients except champagne. Bring to a boil and simmer for 1 minute. Cool completely and drain juice from fruit. Combine fruit juice and champagne. Equally divide fruit into 6 serving bowls. Pour juice and champagne over fruit.
 Serve immediately.

Note: If currants are unavailable, substitute ½ cup seedless red currant jelly.

LOBSTER BISQUE
Coral Reef Restaurant
The Living Seas   EPCOT Center

Yield: 10 servings

1 cup carrots, diced
¼ cup onion, diced
¼ cup butter
1 sprig thyme, fresh
1 bay leaf
3-4 stems parsley
1 lobster (2 to 2½ pounds)
¼ cup sherry

1 cup dry white wine
¾ cup short-grain white
  rice
1 teaspoon salt
6 cups fish stock or bouillon
1 cup heavy cream
Pinch cayenne pepper
1 teaspoon chervil, chopped

In a heavy saucepan, sauté carrots and onion in butter until tender. Add thyme, bay leaf, and parsley and continue cooking until carrots and onion are light brown.

Cut lobster into 8 to 10 pieces. Remove stomach and rinse lobster. Add to vegetables and sauté until shells begin to turn red and meat is firm. Add sherry and white wine. Reduce heat and simmer for 10 minutes. Remove lobster and clean meat from shells. Set meat aside and return shells to pot.

In a separate pot, cook rice in fish stock with salt for 20 minutes. After 20 minutes, add fish stock and rice to vegetables and lobster shells and simmer for 45 minutes. At this time rice will be fully cooked and broth will be slightly thickened.

Remove shells from pot and strain broth through a fine sieve. Discard bay leaf. Press rice and vegetables through sieve and discard any remains left in sieve.

Add heavy cream to broth and simmer 3 to 5 minutes.

Dice reserved lobster meat and season with cayenne pepper and chervil. Add to bisque last.

Serve immediately.

LOUISIANA STYLE CORN AND CRAB CHOWDER
Concourse Grille
Disney's Contemporary Resort

Yield: 3 quarts

½ cup onion, diced
½ cup celery, diced
½ cup red bell pepper, diced
1 stick margarine
4 tablespoons flour
10 cups milk
4 fish bouillon cubes

10 ounces imitation crab legs, cut in ½-inch cubes
1½ cups whole-kernel corn
1½ cups potatoes, cooked, diced
Salt
Pepper
Cayenne pepper

In a 4-quart saucepan, melt margarine and sauté onion, celery, and bell pepper until tender. Add flour and cook an additional 5 minutes. Slowly add milk and fish bouillon cubes, stirring occasionally until thickened. Add imitation crab and potatoes and simmer for 10 minutes. Season to taste with salt, pepper, and cayenne pepper.

LOW-CALORIE CAULIFLOWER SOUP
Disneyland Hotel

Yield: 1 quart

3 cups water
2 cups cauliflower, cored, chopped
1 cup carrots, sliced
¼ cup onions, chopped

1 tablespoon parsley, chopped
2 chicken bouillon cubes
Salt
White pepper

In a 2½-quart saucepan, add all ingredients but salt and pepper. Cover and simmer until vegetables are tender (about 20 minutes). Strain off and reserve most of the liquid. Place vegetables in a food processor and puree. Add vegetables and reserved liquid back into the pot, add salt and pepper to taste, and reheat.

MINESTRONE SOUP
L'Originale Alfredo di Roma Ristorante
Italy   EPCOT Center

Yield: 8 servings

1½ cups red kidney beans, dried
Water
4 tablespoons olive oil
2 ounces prosciutto, chopped (about ½ cup)
4 cups spinach, fresh, chopped, tightly packed
1 cup cabbage, shredded
1 leek bulb, thinly sliced (about ½ cup)

1 cup carrots, diced
1 cup zucchini, diced
1 cup celery, diced
1½ cups yellow onion, chopped
1 cup potatoes, peeled and diced
2 teaspoons salt
½ teaspoon black pepper, freshly ground

Rinse beans well and soak overnight in cold water.

Drain beans and rinse well. Place beans in a saucepan large enough to hold beans with enough water to cover beans by 1 inch. Simmer beans for approximately 2 hours until tender. Drain and reserve cooking liquid and set aside.

Heat olive oil in a large sauce pot or dutch oven and sauté prosciutto for 2 minutes. Add all vegetables and drained beans to sauce pot with prosciutto and sauté for an additional 5 minutes. Add enough water to liquid in which beans were cooked to equal 2 quarts. Add to vegetables and bring to a boil. Reduce heat to a simmer and season with salt and pepper. Simmer for 1 hour, adding more boiling water if necessary.

NARCOOSSEE'S FAMOUS CLAM CHOWDER
Narcoossee's
Disney's Grand Floridian Beach Resort

Yield: 6 servings

1 tablespoon olive oil
1 cup onion, finely diced
1 cup green bell pepper,
  finely diced
1 clove garlic, minced
⅔ cup white wine
1 teaspoon basil, fresh,
  minced
1 teaspoon thyme, fresh,
  minced

⅛ teaspoon red pepper
  flakes
1 cup plum tomatoes,
  canned, diced
1½ cups tomato juice
2 cups clam broth, canned
10 ounces clams, canned,
  chopped

In a medium-size saucepan, heat olive oil. Add onion, green bell pepper, and garlic and sauté about 5 minutes. Add white wine, spices, and herbs and cook an additional 5 minutes. Add diced tomatoes, tomato juice, and clam broth and bring to a boil. Add clams and simmer 20 to 30 minutes.

NEW ENGLAND CLAM CHOWDER
Liberty Tree Tavern
Liberty Square   MAGIC KINGDOM *Park*

Yield: 6 servings

½ cup celery, diced small
½ cup onions, diced small
½ cup green bell pepper,
  diced small
½ cup butter or margarine
½ cup flour
24 ounces clam juice

1 12-ounce can chopped
  clams, with juice
1 quart milk
⅛ teaspoon thyme
¼ teaspoon salt
⅛ teaspoon white pepper
2 cups potatoes, cooked, cut
  in ½-inch cubes

In a 4-quart saucepan, melt butter or margarine. Add celery, onions, and green peppers. Sauté about 5 minutes until tender. Add flour and cook an additional 5 minutes to form a roux. Stir in clam juice, chopped clams, and milk and bring to a boil. Reduce heat immediately and simmer for 15 minutes. Continue stirring while chowder thickens. Season with thyme, salt, and pepper and add cubed, cooked potatoes.

When potatoes are hot, serve immediately.

NORTHERN BEAN SOUP
Concourse Grille
Disney's Contemporary Resort

Yield: 1 gallon

1 pound northern beans	1 gallon water
¾ cup onion, diced	¼ teaspoon cumin
⅔ cup celery, diced	¼ teaspoon garlic,
⅔ cup carrots, diced	granulated
¼ cup bacon fat	1 teaspoon paprika
½ pound ham, diced	½ teaspoon thyme
1 12-ounce can tomatoes,	½ teaspoon oregano
diced	1 teaspoon salt
3 beef bouillon cubes	⅛ teaspoon pepper

Soak beans overnight in cold water in the refrigerator.

Drain beans and place in a 2-gallon soup pot with water, bouillon cubes and spices. Cook 30 to 40 minutes or until tender.

Meanwhile, sauté onions, celery and carrots in bacon fat until tender. When beans are tender, add cooked vegetables, ham and diced tomatoes. Simmer 15 to 20 minutes.

ONION CHEESE SOUP
Yacht Club Galley
Disney's Yacht Club Resort

Yield: 4 cups

3 large Spanish onions	½ teaspoon pepper
4 tablespoons butter	½ teaspoon mace
4 tablespoons flour	1 egg yolk, beaten
2 cups milk	1 cup mild cheddar cheese,
2 cups chicken stock or	grated
broth	
½ teaspoon salt	

Melt butter in a 4-quart sauce pot on medium heat. Add onions and sauté until lightly browned. Add flour and cook an additional 5 minutes until butter and flour are well blended. Slowly add milk and chicken stock, stirring constantly to prevent lumps. Season with salt, pepper, and mace and continue to cook until soup thickens. Whisk in egg yolk slowly and add grated cheese. Simmer for another 5 to 10 minutes, stirring occasionally to prevent burning. Remove from heat.

Serve immediately.

OYSTER BRIE SOUP
Disney-MGM Studios Theme Park

Yield: 3 quarts

6 ounces Brie cheese
7 cups half and half
½ cup butter
½ cup flour
2 cubes fish bouillon

1 cup champagne
1 16-ounce can oysters,
   drained, juice reserved
Salt
Pepper

In a 3-quart saucepan, melt butter. Add flour and cook for 5 to 8 minutes. Do not brown. Add half and half slowly and whip until smooth. Simmer approximately 5 minutes. Dissolve bouillon cubes in oyster juice and add to half and half with champagne. Season with salt and pepper and continue cooking another 5 minutes. Add Brie cheese and stir until melted. Add drained oysters and continue cooking only long enough to heat oysters.

Serve immediately.

Note: If using fresh oysters, poach 12 medium-size oysters in a liquid of fish bouillon and water and use the cooking liquid to equal 16 ounces with oysters.

POLYNESIAN SEAFOOD CHOWDER
Coral Isle Cafe
Disney's Polynesian Resort

Yield: 6 servings

2 ounces bay shrimp,
   cooked
2 ounces crab meat, cooked
2 ounces albacore tuna,
   cooked
¼ cup butter
½ cup carrots, diced
¼ cup celery, diced
½ cup onion, diced
¼ cup green bell pepper,
   diced
1 teaspoon garlic, fresh,
   chopped

½ cup potatoes, diced
4 cups clam juice
½ cup tomato, fresh, diced
1 teaspoon thyme
1 teaspoon basil
1 bay leaf
1 tablespoon fish bouillon
Tabasco sauce
Dash Worcestershire sauce
Pepper
2 teaspoons filé powder

In a large soup pot, sauté carrots, celery, onions, bell pepper, and garlic in butter until tender. Add clam juice and bring to a boil. Add potatoes, tomatoes, and spices and simmer for 15 minutes. Stir in fish bouillon and season with Tabasco, Worcestershire, and pepper. Add filé. Stir well and add cooked seafood.

SCOTCH BARLEY SOUP
Rose & Crown Pub & Dining Room
United Kingdom   EPCOT Center

Yield: 5 quarts

¼ cup butter
1 cup leeks, diced
1 cup onion, chopped
1 cup carrots, diced
1 cup celery, chopped
1 cup white turnip, diced
1 pound mutton or lamb,
   neck or breast (or ½
   pound coarse-ground
   lamb)

1 cup pearl barley
4 quarts chicken broth
3 tablespoons cornstarch
1½ cups half-and-half
Salt
Pepper

In a large skillet, heat butter and sauté leeks and onion for 5 minutes. Add carrots, celery, and turnip and continue cooking for an additional 10 minutes.

Remove fat and skin from lamb and grind meat in a food processor with a steel blade or put through a meat grinder. If using ground lamb, do not regrind.

Add ground lamb to vegetables. Cook and stir meat until lightly browned, breaking up any chunks of meat as it cooks.

Meanwhile, cover barley with boiling water and let stand 10 minutes. Drain and rinse with cold water. Add to meat and vegetables with 1 cup of chicken broth. Cover and let steam over low heat for about 10 minutes. Add remaining chicken broth and bring to a boil. Reduce heat and simmer 1 to 1½ hours, or until barley is tender. Blend cornstarch and half-and-half and stir into soup. Bring to a boil and allow to thicken (2 to 4 minutes). Add salt and pepper to taste.

SOPA AZTECA
(Traditional Tortilla Soup)
San Angel Inn Restaurante
Mexico   EPCOT Center

Yield: 4 servings

3 tablespoons olive oil, divided
⅓ cup onion, chopped
1⅓ cups tomatoes, peeled, seeded, chopped
1 teaspoon garlic
1 quart rich chicken broth
2 tablespoons dill, fresh, chopped (or 2 teaspoons dried dill, chopped)
2 whole red chili peppers, fresh
4 soft corn tortillas
½ cup avocado, ripe, cubed
4 tablespoons sour cream
¼ cup Monterey Jack cheese, shredded

Heat 2 tablespoons of the oil in a large sauce pot. Sauté onion, tomatoes, and garlic until tender (about 5 minutes). Add chicken broth and dill. Cover and simmer for 20 minutes.

Remove seeds and stems from peppers and cut each in 2 pieces lengthwise. Cut tortillas in ⅓-inch strips and set aside. Heat remaining tablespoon of olive oil in a small skillet and sauté peppers for 1 to 2 minutes. Remove peppers and drain on a paper towel. Add tortilla strips to skillet and cook until golden brown. Remove tortilla strips and drain separately on paper towels.

Divide peppers, tortilla strips, and avocado cubes among 4 heavy ceramic or clay soup bowls. Pour hot chicken broth into bowls.

Garnish with sour cream and Monterey Jack cheese.

SOUNDSTAGE GREAT NORTHERN BEAN SOUP
Soundstage Restaurant
Disney-MGM Studios Theme Park

Yield: 10 to 12 servings

½ pound great northern
   beans, dry
10 cups water
4 chicken bouillon cubes
¾ cup celery, diced small
1 cup onion, diced small
1 cup carrots, diced small
1 cup smoked ham, diced
   small

¾ cup tomato, diced small
¼ teaspoon salt
¼ teaspoon white pepper
¼ teaspoon thyme, ground
¼ cup cornstarch, diluted
   in ⅔ cup water

Soak beans in cold water overnight.

Drain beans, rinse well, and place in a large soup pot with 10 cups fresh water and bouillon cubes. Bring to a boil and reduce heat to a simmer. Cook beans for approximately 1 hour until tender but still firm on the inside. Add celery, onions, and carrots and cook an additional 30 minutes until vegetables are tender. Add ham, tomato, salt, pepper, and thyme and mix well. Cook for 10 minutes. Add cornstarch mixed with water and simmer for 5 to 10 minutes until mixture thickens. Remove from heat and let soup cool for 10 to 15 minutes.

Mix well and serve.

TOMATO FLORENTINE SOUP
Liberty Tree Tavern
Liberty Square   *MAGIC KINGDOM Park*

Yield: 6 cups

1 tablespoon butter or
  margarine
½ cup carrots, diced small
½ cup celery, diced small
¼ cup onion, diced small
½ cup plum tomatoes, diced
2 cloves garlic, chopped
2 12-oz cans chicken stock
  or broth
2 12-oz cans tomato juice
⅛ teaspoon white pepper
1 tablespoon sugar
1 bay leaf

1 teaspoon red pepper
  flakes
⅛ teaspoon oregano
1 teaspoon Worcestershire
  sauce
1 12-oz package frozen,
  chopped spinach
1 pound turkey meat,
  ground
1 8-ounce package pasta of
  choice, cooked (small
  shells work well)

Melt butter or margarine in a 4-quart saucepan and sauté carrots, celery, onions, tomatoes, and garlic until tender (about 5 minutes). Add remaining ingredients, except turkey and pasta. Simmer for 15 to 20 minutes.

Cook pasta according to package directions.

Sauté turkey separately, breaking up into as small pieces as possible until done. Drain any excess fat and add to soup. Drain pasta and add it also. Remove bay leaf and add additional seasoning if necessary.

SPLIT PEA AND HAM SOUP
Garden Gallery
The Disney Inn

Yield: 6 servings

1 pound green split peas, dried
5 cups chicken broth, fresh or canned
5 cups water
1 meaty ham bone (or 2 smoked ham hocks)
2 stalks celery, diced medium
3 tablespoons parsley, fresh, chopped
½ teaspoon tarragon leaves
1 cup carrots, diced medium
1 cup onions, diced medium
1 leek, white part only, rinsed and sliced
2 tablespoons dry sherry
½ teaspoon black pepper, freshly ground

Soak and rinse peas for 20 minutes. In a 6-quart pot, combine water, chicken broth, and peas. Bring to a boil. Add ham bone, carrots, celery, onions, leek, tarragon, and 1 tablespoon of parsley. Reduce heat to medium low and simmer, partially covered, stirring occasionally for 1 hour. Remove from heat.

Remove ham bone and shred meat from bone. Remove any excess fat and return meat to pot. Add sherry, pepper, and remaining 2 tablespoons of parsley. Heat through.

Serve immediately.

STEAK AND BEAN SOUP
Yachtman's Steakhouse
Disney's Yacht Club Resort

Yield: 1 gallon

1 pound bottom round steak, cut in ½-inch cubes
2 tablespoons vegetable oil
1 cup onion, coarsely chopped
¼ cup celery, coarsely chopped
¼ cup carrots, coarsely chopped
¼ teaspoon garlic, fresh, minced
3 quarts beef stock or broth
1 cup kidney beans
1 cup pinto beans
Dash Tabasco sauce
Salt
Pepper
¼ cup tomato paste

Soak beans in cold water overnight. Rinse and drain well and drain again until quite dry.

Heat vegetable oil in a 6-quart soup pot and add cubed beef. Sauté 4 to 5 minutes until lightly browned on all sides. Add onion, celery, carrots, and garlic and sauté until tender. Add beef stock and beans and simmer for 45 minutes, or until beans are tender. Add Tabasco and season with salt and pepper to taste. Stir in tomato paste and simmer an additional 5 minutes.

Serve hot.

TUCKERNUT GUMBO
Ariel's
Disney's Beach Club Resort

Yield: 8 servings

¼ cup butter
1 tablespoon garlic, chopped
¼ cup onion, diced
¼ cup celery, diced
2 tablespoons leeks, diced, whites only
3 tablespoons flour
2 tablespoons white wine
2 cups tomatoes, diced
2 cups chicken stock or broth
2 cups fish stock
1 teaspoon filé powder
1 teaspoon Old Bay Seasoning

¼ teaspoon tarragon, chopped
¼ teaspoon basil, chopped
1 cup sweet sausage, cut in ½-inch cubes
½ cup small shrimp, peeled and cleaned
½ cup tiny bay scallops
1 tablespoon topneck clams, roughly chopped
1 cup okra, frozen, sliced
Salt
Pepper

In a large saucepan, melt butter and add garlic, onions, celery, and leeks. Sauté until tender (about 8 minutes). Add flour and cook an additional 3 to 5 minutes. Add wine, tomatoes, chicken stock, fish stock, spices, and herbs and bring to a boil. Reduce heat and simmer for 10 to 15 minutes.

In a separate pan, sauté cubed sausage until fully cooked and browned. Remove from pan and discard grease. Add to gumbo.

Combine seafood and okra and add to gumbo and continue to simmer for 5 minutes, or until the seafood is fully cooked. Add salt and pepper to taste.

Serve hot.

TURKEY VEGETABLE SOUP
King Stefan's Banquet Hall
Fantasyland   MAGIC KINGDOM Park

Yield: 8 servings

1 cup onion, peeled, diced
1 cup carrots, peeled, diced
2 stalks celery, diced
2 quarts water
4 chicken bouillon cubes
2 cups leeks, peeled,
    washed, diced

1 cup potatoes, diced
¾ pound turkey meat,
    cooked, diced
Salt
Pepper

Clean, peel and dice onion, carrot, and celery into ½-inch cubes.
In a large pot, bring water to a boil. Add onion, carrots, celery, and bouillon cubes. Simmer for 30 minutes. Add leeks, diced potatoes, and turkey meat. Simmer an additional 10 to 15 minutes, or until potatoes and leeks are tender. Season with salt and pepper if necessary.
Serve hot.

WONTON SOUP
Coral Isle Cafe
Disney's Polynesian Resort

Yield: 4 servings

1 quart chicken consommé
    (or strong clarified broth)
½ teaspoon sesame oil
¾ ounce scallions, diced
    (about ½ cup)

Salt
White pepper
8 wontons, frozen, steamed

Combine consommé, sesame oil, and scallions. Bring to a boil and simmer 5 minutes. Season with salt and pepper if necessary. Add steamed wontons.

NOTES

BREADS

BREADS

BANANA BREAD
Monorail Cafe
Disneyland Hotel

Yield: 2 large loaves

2 sticks butter
2 cups sugar
2 eggs
2 teaspoons water
2 cups bananas, mashed

¼ teaspoon vanilla extract
3 cups flour
½ teaspoon salt
2 teaspoons baking soda
1 cup walnuts, chopped

Preheat oven to 350 degrees.

Sift together flour, salt, and baking soda. Set aside.

Melt butter on the stove or in the microwave. Mix butter and sugar until well blended. Add eggs, one at a time, mixing well after each. Add bananas and vanilla. Fold in flour mixture and walnuts and blend until all flour is moist.

Grease 2 loaf pans and divide batter equally between the 2 pans.

Bake for 1 hour or until center of loaf is firm and a toothpick inserted in center comes out clean.

BLUEBERRY MUFFINS
Farmers Market
The Land   EPCOT Center

Yield: 12 muffins

¾ cup bread flour
¾ cup cake flour
½ cup sugar
¾ teaspoon salt
2 tablespoons dry milk
   powder

3 teaspoons baking powder
¼ cup shortening
½ cup water
2 egg whites
½ cup blueberries, fresh or
   frozen

Preheat oven to 350 degrees.

In a bowl, sift together flours, sugar, salt, dry milk powder, and baking powder. Cut in shortening with a pastry cutter and blend until lumps are about the size of peas.

Combine water and egg whites with a fork; do not whip. Add to dry ingredients and mix only long enough to moisten. Batter will be lumpy.

Spoon into paper-lined muffin tins and bake for 20 to 25 minutes, or until nicely browned.

BOSTON BROWN BREAD
Yacht Club Galley
Disney's Yacht Club Resort

Yield: 3 1-pound loaves

4 ounces molasses
2 cups milk
1 egg
1 cup all-purpose flour
1 cup rye flour

1 cup whole wheat flour
¾ cup corn meal
2 teaspoons salt
½ cup milk
1 tablespoon baking
   powder

In a large mixing bowl with an electric mixer, combine molasses, milk, and egg. Mix on medium speed for about 4 minutes. Sift together flours, corn meal, and salt and add to molasses and blend for 1 minute. Dissolve baking powder in half cup of milk and add to flour mixture. Blend well, scraping down sides of bowl and mixing until well incorporated.

Using 3 canning jars with tight-fitting lids, or 3 1-pound coffee cans, spray inside of jars or cans with non-stick vegetable spray. Divide batter evenly among jars and close lids. Place closed jars in a large pot of boiling water, standing upright, and cover pot. Reduce heat to a simmer and steam bread for approximately 1 hour, 45 minutes. Check pot frequently and replenish water as necessary. Do not let pot go dry, or jars may break. When bread is done, remove from pot and allow to cool for 2 hours.

Refrigerate any unused bread.

BRAN MUFFINS
Farmers Market
The Land   EPCOT Center

Yield: 1 dozen

2 cups bran flakes
1 cup milk
½ cup brown sugar
½ cup vegetable oil
½ cup honey

3 eggs
1 cup all-purpose or bread
   flour
⅛ teaspoon salt
1 teaspoon baking soda
½ cup raisins

Preheat oven to 400 degrees.

In a large mixing bowl, combine all ingredients. Using an electric mixer, blend at medium speed for 5 to 7 minutes. Pour into paper-lined muffin cups.

Bake for 20 minutes.

CHEESE BREAD
Farmers Market
The Land   EPCOT Center

Yield: 4 loaves

3½ to 4 cups bread flour, divided
2 tablespoons sugar
1½ teaspoons salt
1 package active dry yeast
1 cup very warm water (120 to 130 degrees)
2 tablespoons margarine, melted
1 cup natural Swiss cheese, shredded (4 ounces)
½ cup Parmesan cheese, grated (2 ounces)
1 egg, lightly beaten

In a large bowl, combine 2 cups of bread flour with sugar, salt, and yeast. Mix well. Gradually add water and margarine. Mix until a soft dough forms. Combine the cheese in a separate bowl and reserve ¼ cup. Add remaining cheese mixture, egg, and 1 cup of flour to dough. Mix again and turn out onto a floured board. Knead dough 8 to 10 minutes and add as much of the remaining flour as dough will incorporate. Place dough in a lightly greased bowl, turning once to coat dough, and let rest 20 minutes.

After 20 minutes, knead dough again and divide into 4 equal pieces. Let rest 15 minutes and roll each piece into a rectangle. Roll dough, jelly-roll style, sealing bottom seam, and place on a lightly greased baking sheet or in loaf pans.

Allow dough to rise in a warm place for about 50 minutes, or until double in bulk. Cut a ¼-inch-deep slit in top of each loaf and sprinkle an equal amount of remaining cheese on each.

Bake in a preheated 375-degree oven for 20 to 30 minutes, or until golden brown.

Remove from pans immediately and brush with margarine.

CINNAMON SUGAR FRENCH TOAST
Contemporary Room Service
Disney's Contemporary Resort

Yield: 4 servings

¼ cup sugar
1 teaspoon cinnamon
4 slices sourdough bread,
    ½ inch thick
4 eggs, well beaten

Soy bean oil
Confectioners' sugar, if
    desired
Butter, whipped
Maple syrup, warm

Mix sugar and cinnamon and set aside.

Cut bread slices in half diagonally. Dip in beaten eggs, soaking bread well with egg. Heat oil in a skillet and fry bread, turning to brown both sides. Roll at once in sugar and cinnamon, and dust with confectioners' sugar, if desired.

Serve with butter and syrup.

CONTEMPORARY FRENCH TOAST
Concourse Grille
Disney's Contemporary Resort

Yield: 4 servings

1 cup milk
½ teaspoon sugar
2 eggs
1½ teaspoons cinnamon,
    divided
⅛ teaspoon salt

1 loaf sourdough bread, or
    any bread desired
Butter or oil
¼ cup confectioners' sugar
Maple syrup and butter, if
    desired

Combine milk, sugar, eggs, ½ teaspoon of cinnamon, and salt and mix until blended.

Cut bread into ¾-inch slices. Dip in milk/egg mixture long enough to soak through. Place in a hot skillet with melted butter or oil and fry until golden brown on both sides. Remove from pan and roll in confectioners' sugar mixed with the remaining cinnamon.

Serve with syrup and butter, if desired.

CORN MUFFINS
Farmers Market
The Land   EPCOT Center

Yield: 18 muffins

⅔ cup sugar
1 teaspoon salt
⅓ cup shortening
1 teaspoon vanilla extract
2 eggs

2 cups all-purpose or bread
  flour
2 teaspoons baking powder
¾ cup yellow corn meal
1⅓ cups milk

Preheat oven to 400 degrees.

In a medium-size mixing bowl, combine sugar, salt, shortening, and vanilla. With an electric mixer, blend about 5 minutes until slightly creamed. Add eggs, one at a time, and mix well after each addition.

In a separate bowl, combine flour, baking powder, and corn meal and mix well. On low speed, add half flour mixture alternately with half milk until all ingredients have been added.

Spoon into paper-lined cupcake pans and bake for about 20 minutes, or until lightly browned.

CRACKED WHEAT RYE BREAD
Biergarten
Germany   EPCOT Center

Yield: 30 small loaves

2 cups cold milk
2 tablespoons sugar
4 tablespoons vegetable oil
2 tablespoons salt

3 eggs
2 cups coarse rye meal
5½ cups bread flour
2 packages active dry yeast

Combine all ingredients in a large mixing bowl with an electric mixer equipped with a dough hook. Blend well for about 10 minutes. Remove dough hook and allow dough to rest 20 minutes.

Turn dough out onto a floured board and knead lightly into a long roll. Cut into 30 equal pieces and form into balls. Flatten slightly and place on a large, lightly greased baking sheet. Cover and let rise in a warm place until double in bulk.

Bake in a preheated 400-degree oven for 20 minutes, or until lightly browned.

Serve warm.

FRENCH BREAD AND ROLLS
Ariel's
Disney's Beach Club Resort

Yield: 4 loaves

3 cups water, warm
1 ounce active dry yeast
8½ cups flour

1 ounce salt
1½ ounces honey

In an electric mixer with a dough hook, add water and yeast. Allow yeast to soften. Stir in honey. Sift flour and salt together and add to yeast mixture. Mix on low speed 1 minute, then on medium for 2 minutes. When dough pulls away from sides of bowl, remove bowl and cover dough with a cloth. Let dough rise until double in bulk (about 1 hour).

Place dough on a clean and floured work surface and knead lightly. Form dough into desired shapes (baguettes, petit pan rolls, or pan loaf).

Preheat oven to 200 degrees and turn off.

Score tops of dough with a razor blade just enough to break the skin (about ⅛ inch deep). Place dough in oven until double in bulk.

Remove from oven while it preheats to 400 degrees.

Bake bread to a golden brown (about 20 to 25 minutes).

FROCACCIE BREAD
Flagler's
Disney's Grand Floridian Beach Resort

Yield: 10 small or 4 regular loaves

1½ cups water
¾ ounce active dry yeast
¾ cup milk
¼ cup olive oil
2 eggs
9 cups all-purpose flour

2 tablespoons honey
1 tablespoon salt
1 teaspoon pepper
1½ teaspoons thyme
1½ teaspoons basil

Dissolve yeast in warm water and let stand 5 minutes.

Mix milk, olive oil, eggs, and yeast mixture together and blend for 1 minute. Add remaining ingredients and mix until dough pulls away from sides of bowl (about 3 minutes). Turn dough out onto a floured board and knead for 5 minutes. Return dough to bowl and lightly rub with olive oil. Let rise in a warm place until doubled in bulk (about 1 hour).

Knock down and knead again. Divide dough into 10 small loaves or 4 regular loaves. Let rise until double in bulk.

Bake in a preheated 350-degree oven for 40 minutes, or until nicely browned and hollow to the touch.

ITALIAN BREAD
L'Originale Alfredo di Roma Ristorante
Italy   EPCOT Center

Yield: 7 small loaves

3 cups water, ice-cold
7 cups bread flour, divided

2 packages quick-rise yeast
1 tablespoon salt

In an electric mixer with a dough hook, add ice water. Sift together 5 cups bread flour and quick-rise yeast. Add to ice water and mix well. Blend until a sticky dough forms. Sift together remaining 2 cups of flour and salt and add to sticky dough mixture. Blend on medium speed for approximately 5 minutes until a drier dough forms. Remove from bowl and knead dough for 2 to 3 minutes. Let dough rest for 30 minutes, covered, in a warm place.

Divide dough into 7 equal pieces and knead each piece, forming into small oval or round loaves. Place formed dough on a lightly greased baking sheet and let rise till double in bulk (30 to 40 minutes).

Bake in a preheated 400-degree oven for 30 to 40 minutes until nicely browned.

JAMAICAN BUNS
Cinnamon Bay Bakery
Disney's Caribbean Beach Resort

Yield: 2 dozen

3½ cups flour
½ cup sugar
2 teaspoons baking powder
½ teaspoon salt
2 tablespoons lemon rind
(or 1 tablespoon lemon
extract)

1 cup butter or shortening
3 eggs
¾ cup milk
1 cup raisins
1¼ cups shredded coconut
2 egg whites, lightly beaten

Preheat oven to 350 degrees.

In a large mixing bowl, combine flour, sugar, baking powder, salt, and lemon rind. Cut in butter until mixture is crumbly in texture. Beat eggs with milk and add to flour mixture. Blend until just moistened. Do not over mix. Add raisins and coconut and mix again, just enough to incorporate. Using an ice-cream scoop or tablespoon, portion dough onto a greased cookie sheet. Brush the tops of each bun with beaten egg whites and sprinkle with sugar.

Bake for about 25 minutes. Buns should be golden brown and firm to touch.

OATMEAL MACADAMIA MUFFINS
Papeete Bay Verandah
Disney's Polynesian Resort

Yield: 12 medium-size muffins

1 cup oatmeal
1 cup milk
½ cup butter or margarine,
  melted
1 egg
¼ cup brown sugar

½ cup raisins
½ cup macadamia nuts
1 cup whole wheat flour
1½ teaspoons baking soda
1½ teaspoons baking
  powder

Preheat oven to 400 degrees.

In a large bowl, soak oatmeal in milk for 30 minutes. Add melted butter or margarine, egg, brown sugar, and raisins. Stir until well blended. Combine nuts, flour, baking soda, and baking powder and add to oatmeal mixture. Blend only enough to moisten flour. Batter will remain lumpy. Line a muffin tin with paper liners or spray with vegetable spray and fill each cup two-thirds full with batter.

Bake for 15 to 20 minutes.

SOUTHERN SPOON BREAD
1900 Park Fare
Disney's Grand Floridian Beach Resort

Yield: 8 servings

2½ cups water
½ cup butter
¼ cup sugar
1 teaspoon salt

1¼ cups yellow corn meal
1½ cups milk
5 eggs
2 teaspoons baking powder

Preheat oven to 350 degrees.

Combine water, butter, sugar, and salt in a 1½-quart saucepan. Bring to a boil, add corn meal slowly, and stir until thick. Remove from heat. Place mixture in a large bowl. Blend in milk, then eggs, then baking powder. Pour batter into a 9x13x2-inch greased cake pan.

Bake for 45 minutes, or until golden brown.

TOP OF THE WORLD PANCAKES
Top of the World
Disney's Contemporary Resort

Yield: 12 5-inch pancakes

1 egg
4 tablespoons oil
⅓ cup milk
⅓ cup water
2 teaspoons vanilla extract

2 cups buttermilk pancake
  mix
4 tablespoons sugar
1 teaspoon baking powder

With a whisk, mix egg, oil, milk, water, and vanilla in a bowl.
In another bowl, blend pancake mix, sugar, and baking powder. Gradually add dry ingredients to liquid mixture, mixing well with a whisk.

Cook pancakes on a lightly greased griddle over medium heat, using about ¼ cup batter for each pancake. When top of pancake is dry, turn and cook 1 to 2 minutes longer.

Note: This recipe makes thick pancakes. For a thinner batter, increase water as needed.

WHEAT PESTOLEROS
Special Events
Disney's Yacht and Beach Club Resorts

Yield: 3 dozen 2-ounce rolls or 4 loaves

4 1-ounce packages active
  dry yeast
4 cups warm water
4 cups all-purpose flour

4 cups pastry flour
4 cups whole wheat flour
2 tablespoons honey
6 teaspoons salt

In a large bowl, combine warm water and yeast. Allow yeast to soften about 5 minutes. Add remaining ingredients, salt last. Mix with a dough hook or by hand until well blended Allow dough to rest 30 minutes.

Place dough on a clean pastry board and knead 10 minutes. Divide into 4 loaves, or any combination of breads and rolls. Shape as desired. Score tops of dough with a sharp knife, just enough to break skin. Allow dough to rise until double in bulk (about 1 hour and 15 minutes, depending on size of loaf).

Bake in a preheated 400-degree oven until golden brown.

Remove from oven and allow to cool completely before cutting.

SALADS
AND SALAD
DRESSINGS

SALADS

ANTIPASTO ALL'ITALIANA
Flagler's
Disney's Grand Floridian Beach Resort

Yield: 1 serving

2 slices Genoa salami
2 slices prosciutto
2 slices provolone cheese
2 slices pepper salami
2 slices Coppacola ham

1 whole artichoke heart, cut
  in quarters
13 black olives
3 radicchio leaves
Peperoncini
Basil, fresh, julienne

Thinly slice meats and arrange them on a round salad plate in a circular design. Place artichoke hearts and black olives in radicchio leaves and place in center of plate.

Garnish with peperoncini and basil.

BEEFSTEAK TOMATO AND BERMUDA ONION SALAD
with Mustard Basil Vinaigrette
Granville's Steak House
Disneyland Hotel

Yield: 4 servings

4 large beefsteak tomatoes
2 medium Bermuda onions

1 head butter lettuce
Mustard basil vinaigrette
  dressing (recipe follows)

Slice tomatoes into ½-inch slices. Peel and slice onions into about ¼-inch slices. Separate lettuce leaves and wash thoroughly. Pat dry on paper towels. Place 2 lettuce leaves on a chilled salad plate and top lettuce with alternating slices of tomato and onion. Evenly distribute the tomato and onion among four salads.

Serve with Mustard Basil Vinaigrette Dressing.

Mustard Basil Vinaigrette Dressing

2 tablespoons Dijon®
  Mustard
½ lemon, juiced
2 tablespoons red wine
  vinegar

1 whole egg
2 tablespoons basil, fresh,
  chopped
1 cup olive oil

In a small mixing bowl, combine all ingredients except oil and mix well. Slowly add oil in a steady stream while mixing to incorporate. Spoon over salad.

BEEFSTEAK TOMATO SALAD
Yachtman's Steakhouse
Disney's Yacht Club Resort

Yield: 1 serving

1 vine-ripe beefsteak
   tomato, sliced
1 Spanish onion, peeled,
   sliced

1 leaf romaine lettuce
1 leaf radicchio
1 ounce alfalfa sprouts
Vinaigrette dressing

Arrange lettuce on a chilled salad plate. Shingle onion and tomato together and place on top of lettuce.
Garnish with alfalfa sprouts and serve with vinaigrette dressing.

BELGIAN ENDIVE AND WATERCRESS SALAD
with Feta Cheese and Walnut Dressing
Special Events
Disneyland Hotel

Yield: 4 servings

1 pound Belgian endive
2 bunches watercress
1 red bell pepper, julienne

¼ pound feta cheese,
   crumbled
Walnut dressing (recipe
   follows)

Wash and prepare above ingredients and pat dry on paper towels. Arrange Belgian endive around perimeter of chilled salad plates with points toward edge of plates. Place watercress in center of endive and garnish with red pepper strips. Crumble feta cheese over each salad.
Serve with walnut dressing.

Walnut Dressing

1 cup walnut oil
¾ cup rice vinegar
¼ cup walnuts, chopped
1 bunch chives, chopped

1 teaspoon Worcestershire
   sauce
Pinch salt
Pinch pepper

Combine all ingredients in a small bowl and blend well.

BUTTERMILK COCONUT DRESSING
Coral Isle Cafe
Disney's Polynesian Resort

Yield: 1 gallon

1 cup oil
¾ cup sugar
1 cup red wine vinegar
6 cups buttermilk
1 teaspoon black pepper

½ teaspoon salt
2 cups sour cream
2 cups mayonnaise
1 6-ounce can coconut
cream

In a blender or food processor with a steel blade, combine all ingredients and blend well.
Refrigerate any unused portion.

CAESAR SALAD
Club 33
New Orleans Square   *DISNEYLAND Park*

Yield: 2 servings

1 clove garlic, crushed or
put through a press
1 teaspoon Worcestershire
sauce
3 tablespoons red wine
vinegar
1 egg, coddled (cooked in
shell for 1 minute)

¾ teaspoon Dijon® Mustard
1 head romaine lettuce, torn
into 2-inch pieces
½ cup croutons
½ lemon
Parmesan cheese
Pepper, freshly ground

In a small bowl, combine crushed garlic, Worcestershire sauce, vinegar, and egg. Add a grind or two of fresh pepper and mix well. Clean and dry lettuce on paper towels and add to mixing bowl with dressing. Toss lettuce, coating each piece well. Add croutons and sprinkle entire salad with Parmesan cheese.
Toss again and serve immediately.

CHEFS DE FRANCE HOUSE DRESSING
Chefs de France
France   EPCOT Center

Yield: 1 cup

1 tablespoon Dijon®
  Mustard
2 tablespoons red wine
  vinegar

½ teaspoon salt
White pepper
1 egg
⅔ cup vegetable oil

In a small stainless steel bowl, using an electric mixer, beat mustard, vinegar, salt, pepper, and egg at high speed until frothy. On medium speed, gradually add oil until well blended. Mixture should resemble thin mayonnaise.

CHICKEN, TUNA, AND EGG SALAD MEDLEY
Grand Floridian Cafe
Disney's Grand Floridian Beach Resort

Yield: 1 serving

1 piece leaf lettuce
½ cup iceberg lettuce,
  shredded
⅓ cup egg salad
⅓ cup tuna salad
⅓ cup chicken salad

4 cantaloupe wedges
2 tomato wedges
2 black olives
3 cucumber slices
1 strawberry

Place leaf lettuce on a chilled salad plate. Place shredded lettuce in middle of leaf lettuce. Scoop tuna, egg, and chicken salads separately across plate in a row.
Garnish plate with remaining ingredients.
Serve chilled.

CHICKEN ORIENTAL SALAD
Narcoossee's
Disney's Grand Floridian Beach Resort

Yield: 2 large servings

2 chicken breasts, cooked,
　sliced, chilled
4 ounces pea pods
¼ cup celery, diced
¼ cup tomatoes, diced
¼ cup carrots, julienne
½ cup chow mein noodles

1 head lettuce, romaine,
　iceberg, or Bibb
Oriental dressing
Sesame seeds, toasted
Oriental dressing (recipe
　follows)
Scallions, sliced, for garnish

Toss first 7 ingredients together and top with dressing, sesame seeds and scallions.

Oriental Dressing

1 cup soy bean oil
½ cup sesame oil
½ cup rice vinegar
½ cup oyster sauce
¼ cup sugar
¼ cup scallions, sliced

2 tablespoons ginger,
　minced
1 teaspoon red pepper
　flakes
1 teaspoon sesame seeds,
　toasted

Mix soy bean oil, sesame oil, and rice vinegar. Add oyster sauce and sugar and blend well. Add remaining ingredients.

CHICKEN SALAD
Chef Mickey's Village Restaurant
Disney Village Marketplace

Yield: 4 servings

1 pound chicken meat,
　cooked, diced
½ cup mayonnaise
1 apple, peeled, cored,
　diced
1 tablespoon apple juice

¼ cup celery, diced
½ teaspoon spicy brown
　mustard
Salt
Pepper
Pineapple spears, fresh

Mix first 6 ingredients and season with salt and pepper to taste. Chill one hour.

Serve with fresh pineapple spears or other fresh fruit of your choice.

CINDERELLA SALAD
King Stefan's Banquet Hall
Fantasyland   *MAGIC KINGDOM Park*

Yield: 4 to 6 servings

2 heads Boston lettuce
1 head red leaf lettuce
1 small head Belgian endive
1 small head radicchio
1 cup watercress, stems
  removed
2 plum tomatoes, sliced
1 cup button mushrooms,
  whole
1 small cucumber, peeled,
  sliced in half moons
6 black olives

½ pound mozzarella cheese,
  cut in ½-inch cubes
1 cup cauliflower, cut in
  ½-inch pieces
1 cup broccoli, cut in
  ½-inch pieces
¾ cup alfalfa sprouts
Stir-fried chicken (recipe
  follows)
Dill vinaigrette dressing
  (recipe follows)

Wash Boston and red leaf lettuce, Belgian endive, radicchio, and watercress and pat dry. Tear greens and toss together in a large salad bowl. Arrange tomatoes, mushrooms, cucumber, black olives, mozzarella cheese, cauliflower, broccoli, and sprouts around outside of salad bowl on top of greens.

Place stir-fried chicken in center of salad and toss with dill vinaigrette dressing.

Stir-Fried Chicken

2 tablespoons olive oil
½ tablespoon Cajun spice

2 pounds chicken breast,
  boneless

Cut chicken breasts into ¼-inch strips. Heat olive oil in a large skillet and add chicken. Sprinkle with Cajun spice and sauté chicken until tender and fully cooked.

Serve immediately.

(continued on next page)

CINDERELLA SALAD
(continued from previous page)

Dill Vinaigrette Dressing

½ cup water
½ cup red wine vinegar
½ cup white wine vinegar
¼ cup lemon-lime soda
   or ginger ale
1 teaspoon Worcestershire
   sauce
¼ teaspoon lemon juice
2 tablespoons Dijon®
   Mustard

¼ teaspoon sugar
Dash salt
Pinch pepper
Dash vegetable seasoning
2 tablespoons red onion,
   diced
2 tablespoons dill weed,
   fresh, minced

In a stainless steel or glass mixing bowl, combine first 8 ingredients and mix well. Season with salt, pepper, and vegetable seasoning. Add diced red onion and fresh dill and refrigerate until ready to use.

CLUB GALLEY SALAD
Yacht Club Galley
Disney's Yacht Club Resort

Yield: 1 serving

2 leaves radicchio
2 leaves Bibb lettuce
½ head baby red oak
   lettuce
1 cup iceberg lettuce,
   chopped
3 chives, chopped
3 slices cucumber
2 Greek peppers
1 artichoke heart, halved

3 green olives, stuffed
1 heart of palm, sliced
1 radish, sliced
2 slices cheddar cheese
4 slices tomato
4 slices salami
4 slices ham
3 slices mortadella
2 slices smoked turkey

On a chilled dinner plate, place chopped iceberg lettuce in center of plate. Arrange radicchio, Bibb, and baby red oak lettuce around iceberg lettuce. Form meats and cheeses into cones and arrange around rim of plate.

Garnish center of plate with remaining ingredients, as desired, using all items.

Serve with dressing of choice.

CUCUMBER SALAD
Garden Gallery
The Disney Inn

Yield: 4 servings

2 cucumbers, peeled,
  seeded
½ teaspoon coarse kosher
  salt
1 cup plain yogurt
1 tablespoon extra-virgin
  olive oil
2 teaspoons white wine
  vinegar

Salt
Pepper
2 tablespoons dill, fresh,
  chopped
Scallions, sliced, for
  garnish

Peel cucumbers, cut in half lengthwise and remove seeds with a spoon. Slice 2 halves into thin crescents. Lay them on paper towels, sprinkle with coarse salt and refrigerate, uncovered, for 1 hour.

Remove cucumbers from refrigerator and pat dry. Combine yogurt, oil, vinegar, salt, pepper, and dill in a small bowl. Blend thoroughly and toss with cucumbers.

Garnish with scallions and serve.

EGG SALAD FOR RIVER BELLE TERRACE
River Belle Terrace
Frontierland   DISNEYLAND Park

Yield: 6 servings

12 eggs, hard-boiled, peeled
1 cup mayonnaise
1 tablespoon prepared
  mustard
1 teaspoon seasoning salt

1 teaspoon pepper, freshly
  ground
1 tablespoon lemon juice,
  fresh

Rinse peeled eggs and pat dry with paper towels. In a glass or stainless steel bowl, or a food processor with a steel blade, chop eggs to a medium-fine consistency. Fold in mayonnaise and seasonings, mixing well.

Refrigerate until ready to use.

FLYING FRUIT FEAST
Hurricane Hanna's Grill
Disney's Beach Club Resort

Yield: 4 servings

8 strawberries, hulled,
   fanned
1 apple, cored, diced
½ honeydew melon, peeled,
   seeded, diced
2 oranges, peeled, diced

1 cantaloupe, peeled,
   seeded, diced
1½ cups seedless grapes
4 leaves leaf lettuce
4 sprigs mint, fresh

Mix apples, melons, oranges, and grapes together. Place one leaf of lettuce on each plate. Divide fruit equally onto each plate.

Garnish each salad with two fanned strawberries and a sprig of fresh mint.

Serve chilled.

FRESH FRUIT SALAD
Fisherman's Deck
Disney Village Marketplace

Yield: 4 servings

4 bunches grapes
1 pineapple ring, fresh
8 strawberries
2 kiwi fruit
2 oranges

1 honeydew melon
1 cantaloupe
Raspberry yogurt sauce
   (recipe follows)

Skin and slice all fruit except grapes and strawberries. Arrange orange sections and melon slices around bowl. Garnish center with pineapple, grapes, strawberries, and kiwi.

Serve with raspberry yogurt sauce.

Raspberry Yogurt Sauce

2 cups low-fat yogurt

3 cups raspberries, whole,
   fresh

Place raspberries in a food processor or blender and blend until smooth. Force raspberries through a fine sieve and discard seeds.

Blend pureed raspberries with yogurt and chill.

GINGER DRESSING
Mitsukoshi Restaurant
Japan   EPCOT Center

Yield: 2 quarts

2 ounces ginger root (about ½ cup)
1 medium onion, cut in quarters
3 cups vegetable oil
1 cup vinegar

1¾ cups soy sauce
1½ tablespoons tomato paste
¼ lemon, juiced
1 clove garlic
1¾ cups water

Soak ginger root in cold water for a few minutes to make it easier to remove outer skin. Remove skin and cut into quarters.

Combine all ingredients in a food processor with a steel blade and blend until smooth. (Divide ingredients in half and blend each half separately if food processor will not handle entire recipe.)

Refrigerate.

GINGER DRESSING HAWAIIAN
Tahitian Terrace
Adventureland   DISNEYLAND Park

Yield: 1½ cups

7 tablespoons red wine vinegar
5 tablespoons vegetable oil
3 tablespoons fresh ginger root, peeled, chopped

1 tablespoon garlic salt
8 tablespoons pineapple, crushed
3 tablespoons sugar

In a blender, combine vinegar, oil, and fresh ginger. Blend well on high speed for 15 seconds. Add salt, pineapple, and sugar. Blend another 15 seconds.

Refrigerate until ready to use.

GREEN GODDESS DRESSING
King Stefan's Banquet Hall
Fantasyland   MAGIC KINGDOM Park

Yield: 4 cups

2 cups mayonnaise
½ cup sour cream
½ cup half and half
1 tablespoon scallions,
  chopped
1 tablespoon parsley,
  chopped
¼ cup green bell pepper,
  chopped

2 anchovy fillets
¼ teaspoon lemon juice
Dash Worcestershire sauce
Dash Tabasco sauce
½ teaspoon garlic,
  granulated
⅛ teaspoon salt
⅛ teaspoon white pepper
Green food coloring

Combine scallions, parsley, green pepper, anchovy fillets, and lemon juice in a food processor with a steel blade and puree until smooth. Place mixture in a large bowl with all remaining ingredients, except food coloring, and blend until smooth. Add one drop of food coloring at a time until dressing resembles color of celery.

Refrigerate until ready to use.

HONEY MUSTARD DRESSING
Blue Bayou Restaurant
New Orleans Square   DISNEYLAND Park

Yield: 1 cup

1 cup mayonnaise
1 tablespoon honey
1 tablespoon prepared
  mustard
2 teaspoons lemon juice

1 tablespoon sugar
Salt
White pepper
Tabasco sauce, if desired

Combine all ingredients in a small stainless steel mixing bowl and whip with a wire whisk until well blended (about 5 minutes).

Refrigerate until ready to use.

HOT CAESAR SALAD
50's Prime Time Cafe
Disney-MGM Studios Theme Park

Yield: 4 servings

Salad

1 head romaine lettuce
4 leaves radicchio, chopped
¼ cup Parmesan cheese,
  grated

½ cup croutons
½ cup hot Caesar dressing
  (recipe follows)

Clean and chop romaine lettuce and combine with radicchio.
Prepare hot Caesar dressing.
Add dressing to lettuce and toss well, coating all lettuce.
Divide salad evenly among 4 salad plates and top each salad with croutons and Parmesan cheese.
Serve immediately.

Hot Caesar Dressing

5 egg yolks
1 teaspoon lemon juice
1 teaspoon water
1½ cups butter, melted
1 tablespoon anchovy paste
1 clove garlic, finely
  chopped
1 teaspoon Worcestershire
  sauce

1 teaspoon Dijon® Mustard
1 teaspoon red wine
  vinegar
1 drop Tabasco sauce
Pinch salt
Pinch white pepper
¼ cup Parmesan cheese,
  freshly grated

In a stainless steel bowl over hot, not boiling water, add egg yolks, lemon juice, and water. Whip constantly until light and fluffy and yolks are warm, not hot. Too much heat will scramble eggs. Remove from heat and add melted butter in a steady stream, whipping constantly to incorporate. When all butter has been added and mixture is consistency of thin mayonnaise, add remaining ingredients slowly and blend well to incorporate.

HONEY-LIME DRESSING
Hollywood & Vine
Disney-MGM Studios Theme Park

Yield: 1 cup

4 tablespoons honey
2 teaspoons lime juice, fresh
1 teaspoon lemon juice, fresh

1 tablespoon red wine vinegar
½ cup low-fat plain yogurt

Combine honey, lime juice, lemon juice, and vinegar and blend well. In a separate bowl, place yogurt and slowly whisk in honey mixture in a steady stream. Whip well and refrigerate.

Note: This dressing can also be served as a cold sauce with grilled chicken or fish.

TONY'S HOUSE DRESSING
Tony's Town Square Restaurant
Main Street, U.S.A.   MAGIC KINGDOM Park

Yield: 1 quart

2 tablespoons Dijon®
Mustard
¾ cup red wine vinegar
2½ cups extra-virgin olive oil
2 teaspoons garlic, fresh, chopped
¼ cup plus 2 tablespoons sugar

½ teaspoon Cajun seasoning
3 tablespoons pimientos, diced
½ teaspoon pepper, freshly ground
¼ teaspoon salt

Blend all ingredients well in a large bowl with a wire whisk. Store in a glass or plastic container.
Keep refrigerated.

THE LAND GRILLE ROOM SALAD
The Land Grille Room
The Land   EPCOT Center

Yield: 6 servings

½ cup real mayonnaise
½ cup dairy sour cream
¼ teaspoon salt
⅛ teaspoon pepper, freshly
  ground
1 cup apple, chopped
1 teaspoon lemon juice

¾ cup beets, cooked,
  chopped
¼ cup red onion, chopped
6 ½-inch wedges iceberg
  lettuce
6 red bell pepper rings, cut
  in half

In a 2-quart mixing bowl, combine mayonnaise, sour cream, salt, and pepper. Toss apple with lemon juice and add to mayonnaise mixture with beets and onion. Blend well and refrigerate.

To serve place lettuce on a plate. Spoon a serving of apple/beet mixture on lettuce and garnish with pepper.

TOP OF THE WORLD CHICKEN SALAD
Top of the World
Disney's Contemporary Resort

Yield: 4 servings

2 pounds chicken breast
  meat, boneless, cooked
1 cup mayonnaise
2 tablespoons peach juice
½ cup heavy cream,
  whipped
Salt

White pepper
2 cups peaches, canned,
  drained, diced
Iceberg or romaine lettuce
4 lime wedges

Cut cooked chicken breast meat into ½-inch cubes and set aside.

Blend mayonnaise and peach juice in a 2-quart mixing bowl and fold in whipped cream. Season with salt and pepper as needed. Add cubed chicken meat and diced peaches and mix lightly, coating chicken. Stir gently until blended. Refrigerate for 1 hour.

Portion onto dinner plates lined with lettuce and garnish with lime wedges.

KEY WEST CAESAR SALAD
Disney Village Resort Club
Disney Village Resort

Yield: 4 servings

1 head romaine lettuce, cleaned and cut into 2-inch pieces (about 12 ounces)
1 cup Key West Caesar salad dressing (recipe follows)
1 cup bay shrimp, cooked
2 oranges, peeled, segmented
1 cup croutons
4 teaspoons Parmesan cheese, grated

Clean and trim lettuce and cut into 2-inch pieces. Drain well in a colander and pat dry with paper towels, if necessary.

In a large bowl, combine lettuce, dressing, shrimp, orange segments, and croutons. Toss gently and place on chilled salad plates. Sprinkle with grated Parmesan cheese.

Serve immediately.

Key West Caesar Salad Dressing   Yield: 1 cup

2 tablespoons Dijon® Mustard
2 teaspoons garlic, finely minced
1 tablespoon anchovy, mashed
1 teaspoon brown sugar
4 teaspoons Parmesan cheese, grated
1/8 teaspoon black pepper
1/2 cup olive oil
1 teaspoon red wine vinegar
1 tablespoon orange juice

In a 1-quart stainless steel or glass mixing bowl, add mustard, garlic, anchovy, brown sugar, and Parmesan cheese. Whisk in olive oil slowly until fully incorporated. Whip in vinegar and orange juice and refrigerate.

TAVERN SALAD DRESSING
Liberty Tree Tavern
Liberty Square   MAGIC KINGDOM Park

Yield: 4 cups

5 egg yolks
1 tablespoon Dijon®
   Mustard
3 cups salad oil
1 cup red wine vinegar
1 tablespoon
   Worcestershire sauce

1 teaspoon lemon juice,
   fresh
⅛ teaspoon white pepper
½ teaspoon dill, fresh,
   chopped
1 tablespoon sugar
⅓ cup water

Place egg yolks in an electric mixing bowl and whip until pale yellow and light. Slowly add mustard and oil until completely incorporated. Add remaining ingredients and continue to mix to a creamy consistency. Dressing should be thick enough to coat a spoon.
   Refrigerate unused portion.

LOBSTER SALAD
Ariel's
Disney's Beach Club Resort

Yield: 6 servings

2 pounds lobster meat,
   cooked
½ cup yellow squash,
   julienne
½ cup zucchini, julienne
¼ cup red bell pepper,
   julienne
¼ cup yellow bell pepper,
   julienne
4 green peppercorns

2 teaspoons Dijon® Mustard
Pinch thyme, fresh,
   chopped
Pinch basil, fresh, chopped
Pinch chives, fresh,
   chopped
Salt
Pepper
1 iceberg lettuce bowl

Cut lobster meat into ¾-inch cubes. Add peppercorns, mustard, and spices. Mix gently and refrigerate for 6 to 8 hours.
   Prepare lettuce bowl by cutting head of lettuce in half and gently pulling out center of head. Remove all but 3 to 4 layers of lettuce leaves to be filled with lobster salad.
   To serve, place lobster salad in lettuce bowl and garnish with julienne vegetables. Serve chilled.

MAPLE DIP DRESSING
Le Cellier Restaurant
Canada   EPCOT Center

Yield: 2 cups

¼ cup maple syrup
2 tablespoons light brown
  sugar

1¼ cups sour cream
2 tablespoons whipping
  cream

Mix maple syrup and sugar together. Blend in sour cream and whip on low speed with an electric mixer until smooth. Add whipping cream and whip on high until mixture is light and creamy. Serve with fresh fruit. Keep any unused portion refrigerated.

MEXICAN CLUB SANDWICH
The Crystal Palace
Main Street, U.S.A.   MAGIC KINGDOM Park

Yield: 1 serving

1 13-inch flour tortilla
¼ cup cheese spread, your
  choice
4 thin slices smoked ham
1 cup iceberg lettuce,
  shredded
2 jalapeño peppers, finely
  diced
⅛ cup tomato, diced

1 tablespoon onion, diced
1 tablespoon black olives,
  chopped
2 teaspoons Thousand
  Island dressing
2 2-ounce slices turkey
  breast
½ cup salsa

Lay tortilla on a cutting board. Spread with cheese spread and top with sliced ham, evenly covering cheese and tortilla. Add even layers of remaining ingredients in order listed. Fold in two sides of tortilla and roll up from bottom like a log. Secure with toothpicks and cut into 3 equal pieces.
Serve with salsa.

MAUI NIÇOISE SALAD
Coral Isle Cafe
Disney's Polynesian Resort

Yield: 1 serving

½ cup green beans,
  blanched, cooled
2 small red-skin potatoes,
  cooked, quartered
2 cups spinach, fresh,
  chopped
½ cup radicchio, chopped

¼ cup mushrooms, sliced
¼ cup bean sprouts
1 3-ounce tuna fillet
1 teaspoon olive oil
Salt
Pepper
Bacon vinaigrette dressing
  (recipe follows)

Wash spinach and radicchio and pat dry on paper towels. Chop lightly and place on a dinner plate. Arrange blanched green beans, quartered potatoes and mushroom slices around rim of plate. Sprinkle sprouts over entire salad.

Brush tuna fillet with olive oil and season with salt and pepper. Broil 3 to 5 minutes on each side, until lightly browned and firm to the touch. Place tuna in center of salad.

Serve with bacon vinaigrette dressing.

Bacon Vinaigrette Dressing

1 cup prepared vinaigrette
  dressing
1 cup water
¼ cup bacon bits

3 tablespoons sugar
2 teaspoons cornstarch,
  mixed with 1 teaspoon
  water

In a small saucepan, combine prepared vinaigrette dressing, water, bacon bits, and sugar. Bring to a boil and reduce heat. Whisk in cornstarch mixed with water and simmer until sauce thickens.

Cool slightly and refrigerate.

NEPTUNE SALAD
Papeete Bay Verandah
Disney's Polynesian Resort

Yield: 6 servings

½ pound crab meat
⅔ cup celery, diced
¼ cup onion, diced
½ cup red bell pepper, diced
1 cup cucumber, peeled, seeded, diced
1 cup pea pods, fresh, cut in half

2 cups mayonnaise
1 tablespoon vegetable seasoning
½ package cellophane noodles (about 2 cups)
Salad greens

Crumble crab meat into a large bowl. Add all diced and cut vegetables and toss lightly. Blend mayonnaise and vegetable seasoning and add to crab/vegetable mixture. Mix well.

Cook cellophane noodles according to package directions and drain well. Cut twice and mix with crab salad. Refrigerate.

Serve on a bed of salad greens.

PAPEETE BAY SALAD
Papeete Bay Verandah
Disney's Polynesian Resort

Yield: 4 servings

½ head leaf lettuce, sliced
½ head iceberg lettuce, sliced
2 leaves red cabbage, shredded
½ head romaine lettuce, sliced
¼ cup carrots, grated

4 leaves radicchio
16 small baby shrimp, cooked
4 pieces pickled okra
4 cherry tomatoes
4 small mushrooms, sliced
Ginger dressing

Wash and rinse all lettuce and cabbage and combine in a salad bowl with grated carrot. Evenly portion mixed salad greens among four salad plates. Place leaf of radicchio in center of each plate and fill with 4 shrimp.

Garnish with remaining ingredients and serve with ginger dressing.

PAN FRIED CHICKEN SALAD
Fisherman's Deck
Disney Village Marketplace

Yield: 4 servings

4 5-ounce chicken breasts
2 whole tomatoes, sliced
1 head radicchio
½ head iceberg lettuce
½ head romaine lettuce

1 cup crayfish tails
¼ cup Cajun seasoning
Honey vinaigrette dressing
(recipe follows)

Dust chicken breast in Cajun seasoning and blacken in a hot cast-iron skillet with a small amount of hot oil (about 8-10 minutes). Remove from heat and cool.

Toss crayfish in flour and shake off any excess. Deep-fry 3 to 6 minutes in hot oil.

Chop radicchio, iceberg, and romaine lettuce and divide among 4 dinner plates. Slice chicken breast and place on bed of lettuce. Place fried crayfish opposite chicken.

Garnish with sliced tomatoes and serve with honey vinaigrette dressing.

Note: Substitute shrimp or lobster tails if crayfish are not available. Prepare the same as crayfish.

Honey Vinaigrette Dressing

1 cup honey
⅓ cup white vinegar

1 cup olive oil
2 whole lemons, juiced

Mix vinegar, lemon juice, and honey. Add oil slowly and chill.

THE DISNEY INN PASTA SALAD
Garden Gallery
The Disney Inn

Yield: 4 servings

½ cup salami, julienne
1 cup smoked trout or
  mackerel
¼ cup red onion, slivered
¼ cup green bell pepper,
  1-inch julienne
¼ cup herbs, fresh,
  chopped (thyme, basil,
  dill)

½ cup light sour cream
2 tablespoons white wine
  vinegar
2 tablespoons olive oil
½ teaspoon salt
Pepper, freshly ground
½ pound pasta (shells,
  spirals, or fusilli)

Toss salami, smoked fish, onion, pepper, and fresh herbs in a large bowl. Set aside.

Stir sour cream and vinegar in a bowl, whisk in oil, salt and pepper until smooth and thick.

Bring a 2-quart pot of water to a boil and add pasta. Cook at a rolling boil until tender. Drain, rinse, and toss with salami mixture and dressing until well coated. Refrigerate 1 hour.

Serve cold.

PASTA SALAD
Disney-MGM Studios Theme Park

Yield: 3½ cups

1½ cups tricolor rotini
  pasta
¼ cup cabbage, shredded
¼ cup onion, diced
½ cup tomato, diced
¼ cup celery, diced
½ cup cucumber, peeled,
  seeded, diced

2 teaspoons herb seasoning
1 teaspoon dill, fresh,
  chopped
1 teaspoon basil, fresh,
  chopped
¾ cup plain yogurt
4 tablespoons vinaigrette
  dressing, divided

In a 2-quart saucepan, boil pasta until tender and rinse with cold water. Toss with 2 tablespoons vinaigrette dressing and set aside.

In a large bowl, combine shredded cabbage, onion, tomato, celery, and cucumber. Mix well and season with dill, basil, and herb seasoning. Add cooked pasta, yogurt, and remaining vinaigrette dressing. Blend well and refrigerate at least 1 hour.

Serve chilled.

PEKING JADE SALAD
Coral Isle Cafe
Disney's Polynesian Resort

Yield: 1 serving

1 6-ounce chicken breast	1 black olive
2 cups mixed salad greens, your choice	1 hard-boiled egg, peeled, quartered
¼ cup carrots, shredded	¼ cup alfalfa sprouts
¼ cup snow peas, fresh	Salt
2 slices tomato	Pepper

Lightly season chicken breast with salt and pepper. Broil chicken approximately 5 minutes on each side, until lightly browned and cooked.

Place mixed salad greens on a large salad plate or bowl. Arrange carrots, snow peas, tomato slices, black olive, and egg around sides of plate or bowl. Slice broiled chicken on bias and place in center of salad.

Garnish with alfalfa sprouts and serve with your choice of dressing.

P.M. CITRUS SALAD
Narcoossee's
Disney's Grand Floridian Beach Resort

Yield: 1 serving

¼ cup Parmesan cheese, freshly grated	¼ cup tomato, chopped
	2 slices avocado
4 orange sections, peeled	2 cups salad greens, fresh
4 grapefruit sections, peeled	Citrus salad dressing (recipe follows)
¼ cup pecan meats	Lime wedges

Toss all ingredients lightly with fresh salad greens. Refrigerate. Serve with citrus salad dressing and lime wedges.

Citrus Salad Dressing   Yield: 1 quart

½ cup mayonnaise	6 tablespoons dry mustard
2 cups Key lime juice	1 cup pineapple vinegar

Blend all ingredients until smooth and refrigerate.

RED SKIN POTATO SALAD
Garden Gallery
The Disney Inn

Yield: 8 cups

3 pounds red-skin potatoes, cut in 1-inch cubes
¼ cup white wine vinegar
¼ cup virgin olive oil
½ teaspoon salt
¼ teaspoon pepper, freshly ground
½ cup red onion, finely diced
½ cup celery, finely diced

½ cup pickle relish
1 cup mayonnaise (more if necessary)
3 tablespoons Dijon® Mustard
6 eggs, hard-boiled, peeled, chopped
½ cup Italian parsley, fresh, chopped

In a 4-quart sauce pot, cook diced potatoes covered with water until fork-tender (about 15 minutes). Drain potatoes and place in a large mixing bowl. Sprinkle still-hot potatoes with vinegar, olive oil, salt and pepper. Add remaining ingredients and adjust seasoning. Refrigerate 1 hour.

SEAFOOD COBB SALAD
Yacht Club Galley
Disney's Yacht Club Resort

Yield: 1 salad

3 ounces white fish, cooked
3 ounces scallops, cooked
2 ounces shrimp, cooked, cleaned
3 tablespoons pesto, divided
1 large leaf iceberg lettuce
1 leaf radicchio
1 cup iceberg lettuce, torn
½ avocado, ripe

4 strips bacon, cooked, crumbled
⅛ cup blue cheese, crumbled
¼ cup tomato, diced
3 ripe olives
Scallions, chopped, for garnish
Lemon wedges

In 3 small bowls, separately blend white fish, scallops, and shrimp with 1 tablespoon of pesto each. Refrigerate until ready to use.

On a chilled dinner plate, place leaf of iceberg lettuce. Place radicchio on top of that and fill center of plate with torn iceberg lettuce. In even rows on top of lettuce, arrange white fish, scallops, and shrimp.

Garnish plate with remaining ingredients and serve with lemon wedges and dressing of choice. Blue cheese dressing is recommended.

YACHTMAN'S STEAKHOUSE HOUSE SALAD
Yachtman's Steakhouse
Disney's Yacht Club Resort

Yield: 1 serving

1 leaf radicchio
1 leaf Belgian endive
¼ head iceberg lettuce
3 wedges tomato
1 ounce alfalfa sprouts

2 black olives
1 leaf red oak lettuce
2 ounces house dressing
  (recipe follows)

Combine radicchio, Belgian endive, iceberg, and red oak lettuce. Place on a chilled salad plate. Garnish the plate with sprouts, tomato wedges and black olives.

Serve with house dressing.

Yachtman's Steakhouse House Dressing   Yield: ½ gallon

4 eggs
3 cups soy bean oil
1 tablespoon Dijon®
  Mustard
1 tablespoon cider vinegar
¾ tablespoon
  Worcestershire sauce
Dash Tabasco sauce

1 tablespoon lemon juice
¼ cup onion, minced
1 tablespoon anchovy paste
½ teaspoon white pepper
½ teaspoon salt
4 cups mayonnaise
½ cup Parmesan cheese

Start with eggs at room temperature. Crack into a large mixing bowl and with either a wire whisk or electric mixer, beat eggs. Slowly pour oil in a steady stream into eggs with mixer running at low speed. Mix until all oil is incorporated. Blend in all remaining ingredients but mayonnaise and Parmesan cheese. Fold in mayonnaise and Parmesan cheese. Mix until well blended.

Refrigerate until ready to use.

STEAKHOUSE SALAD
Yachtman's Steakhouse
Disney's Yacht Club Resort

Yield: 6 servings

1 head iceberg lettuce,
   cored, wedged in sixths
6 radicchio cups
6 leaves Belgian endive
6 leaves baby red oak
   lettuce

2 cups alfalfa sprouts
1 large beefsteak tomato
6 ripe olives, pitted
Yachtman's Steakhouse
   house dressing (recipe on
   previous page)

On 6 chilled salad plates, place a wedge of iceberg lettuce each. Next to each wedge, place 1 radicchio cup. In radicchio, place a leaf of Belgian endive and baby red oak lettuce. Divide sprouts in sixths and place one sixth in center of radicchio cup. Cut tomato into 12 equal wedges and garnish each plate with 2 tomato wedges and a ripe olive.

Serve well chilled with Yachtman's Steakhouse house dressing.

STEERMAN'S SALAD
Steerman's Quarters
Disney Village Marketplace

Yield: 2 servings

2 large pieces leaf lettuce
1 large beefsteak tomato,
   sliced
1 red onion, peeled, sliced
1 ripe avocado, sliced
1 tablespoon tarragon
   vinegar

3 tablespoons extra-virgin
   olive oil
2 sprigs thyme, fresh
Pinch salt
Pinch pepper
Pinch garlic powder

Slice and shingle alternately tomato and onion. Sprinkle with a pinch of salt, pepper, and garlic powder. Let stand, covered, in refrigerator for 1 hour.

Peel and slice avocado. Place 1 leaf of lettuce each on 2 plates. Place half of tomatoes and onions on one side of each plate and half avocado on the other.

Garnish with sprig of thyme and drizzle with tarragon vinegar and olive oil.

SUN COAST FRESH FRUIT PLATE
Grand Floridian Cafe
Disney's Grand Floridian Beach Resort

Yield: 1 serving

4 ½-inch honeydew melon
  wedges
3 1-ounce watermelon sticks
½ cantaloupe crown (fluted)
1 kiwi fruit, peeled, sliced

2 slices orange
1 bunch grapes
2 whole strawberries
1 large piece leaf lettuce
Raspberry yogurt

Line a medium-size oval salad plate with lettuce leaf. Place cantaloupe crown in center of plate with honeydew wedges on right and watermelon sticks on left. Fan kiwi and orange slices across bottom of plate and garnish with grapes and strawberries.

Fill center of cantaloupe with raspberry yogurt, or place yogurt in a bowl on the side.

KARTOFFELSALAT
(German Potato Salad)
Biergarten
Germany   EPCOT Center

Yield: 3 cups

⅓ cup olive oil
2 teaspoons mixed herbs,
  (tarragon, parsley, sorrel)
½ cup beef broth
1 tablespoon wine vinegar
1 tablespoon Dijon®
  Mustard

2 teaspoons sugar
3 teaspoons onion, grated
4 large baking potatoes
Salt
Pepper

In a small bowl combine olive oil, herbs, beef broth, vinegar, mustard, sugar, and onion. Set aside.

Steam potatoes until tender. Peel and slice potatoes into ¹⁄₁₆-inch slices while still warm. Add to oil mixture and mix carefully. Let stand 1 hour, or until potatoes have absorbed most of the liquid. Mix again without breaking potatoes and season to taste with salt and pepper.

Refrigerate until ready to use.

TOP OF THE WORLD DRESSING
Top of the World
Disney's Contemporary Resort

Yield: 2½ cups

½ cup onion, finely chopped
1 tablespoon anchovy paste
2 teaspoons garlic, finely chopped
3 eggs
1¼ cups vegetable oil, divided
2 tablespoons cider vinegar, divided

⅛ teaspoon mustard
1 teaspoon salt
⅛ teaspoon white pepper
3 tablespoons water
½ teaspoon lemon juice
¼ teaspoon Worcestershire sauce

In a small bowl, combine onion, anchovy paste, and garlic. Set aside.

Place eggs in a medium bowl over hot, not boiling, water and stir gently until warm. Remove from heat and beat with an electric mixer for 5 minutes. Stir in onion mixture and gradually add half of oil and half of vinegar. Blend well and add mustard, salt, pepper and remaining oil.

In a separate bowl, combine remaining vinegar, water, lemon juice and Worcestershire sauce. Blend into dressing slowly and mix until smooth and creamy. Refrigerate.

Serve chilled.

NOTES

EGGS AND CHEESE

EGGS & CHEESE

BROWNED ROAST BEEF HASH
Walt Disney's Personal Recipe

Yield: 1 serving

1 medium onion, finely
  chopped
2 tablespoons butter
1 cup prime rib meat,
  cooked, finely chopped

1 medium potato, peeled,
  finely chopped
1 cup strong beef stock or
  broth
1 egg, poached or fried

Preheat oven to 350 degrees.

Sauté onion in butter until tender, not browned. Combine onion, beef and potato. Spoon into a buttered 1-quart baking dish and bake for 1 hour.

Remove from oven and shape into an oval patty. Place in a hot buttered skillet. Sauté until lightly browned on both sides. Top with a poached or fried egg.

Serve hot.

PUFFED FRENCH TOAST
The Crystal Palace
Main Street, U.S.A.   *MAGIC KINGDOM Park*

Yield: 6 servings

2 whole eggs
2½ tablespoons sugar
½ teaspoon salt
½ teaspoon vanilla extract
2 cups milk
1 cup flour
2½ teaspoons baking
  powder

12 slices Texas-style bread
  (or any bread of choice),
  cut in half diagonally
Cinnamon sugar topping
Maple syrup or fresh fruit
  topping

Mix eggs, sugar, salt, vanilla, and milk until well blended. Slowly add flour and baking powder and mix until smooth. Dip bread slices in batter, allowing any excess to drip off. Fry in a hot skillet with 1 inch of oil until golden brown on both sides. Drain on absorbent paper towels. While toast is still warm, roll in cinnamon sugar topping.

Serve immediately with maple syrup or fresh fruit topping.

Cinnamon Sugar Topping

4 teaspoons cinnamon   ¾ cup granulated sugar

CORAL ISLE SCRAMBLE
Coral Isle Cafe
Disney's Polynesian Resort

Yield: 2 servings

4 slices tomato
8 strips bacon, cooked
2 biscuits, sliced in half
4 eggs, scrambled

4 ounces cheddar cheese
   sauce (or 4 slices of
   cheddar cheese)
1 scallion, finely diced

Grill both sliced biscuits and tomato slices until lightly browned. Place 2 biscuit halves on each plate. Top each biscuit half with a tomato slice, 2 pieces of cooked bacon, scrambled eggs, and either cheese sauce or sliced cheddar. Brown under a hot broiler and top with diced scallion.

COUNTRY FRITTATA
Grand Floridian Cafe
Disney's Grand Floridian Beach Resort

Yield: 1 serving

3 whole eggs
¼ cup ham, diced
2 tablespoons onion, diced
¼ cup potato, cooked, diced
¼ cup whole-kernel corn

2 tablespoons butter or
   margarine
1 slice Swiss cheese
3 strips ham
2 slices tomato
Parsley, fresh, chopped

In a medium-size mixing bowl, beat eggs and fold in ham, onion, potato, and corn.

Melt butter or margarine in a 10-inch non-stick skillet or omelette pan and add egg mixture. Mix egg mixture in pan until partially set. When frittata begins to hold together, place garnish over top and continue to cook until cheese melts and eggs are done. Remove from pan.

Serve immediately.

FETTUCCINE ALFREDO
L'Originale Alfredo di Roma Ristorante
Italy   EPCOT Center

Yield: 4 servings

1 pound fettuccine noodles,
   fresh
4 quarts boiling salted
   water
1 cup butter, softened
⅓ to ½ cup Parmesan
   cheese, freshly grated

Black pepper, freshly
   cracked
Additional Parmesan
   cheese, as desired

Drop fettuccine noodles in boiling salted water and cook until noodles float to top of pot (2 to 3 minutes). Drain immediately and return to pot. Top with lumps of softened butter and cheese. Toss lightly until noodles are well coated. Season with pepper and additional cheese, if desired.
Serve immediately.

MAC AND CHEESE
Sci-Fi Dine-In Theatre
Disney-MGM Studios Theme Park

Yield: 1 serving

⅛ cup margarine
⅛ cup flour
½ cup milk
½ pound orange American
   cheese
1 teaspoon yellow mustard

Salt
Pepper
3 cups rotini pasta (or
   shells)
¼ cup cheddar cheese,
   grated

In a small saucepan, melt margarine and add flour. Cook 5 to 7 minutes. Do not brown. Heat milk separately and whisk into the roux. Simmer approximately 10 minutes until mixture thickens. Add American cheese and yellow mustard. Blend well and season to taste with salt and pepper. Do not boil sauce once cheese has been added, or sauce may break.
Cook pasta according to package directions. Drain well and rinse under cold water. Drain well again and mix with sauce. Place in an oven-proof baking dish and sprinkle top with grated cheddar cheese. Broil until cheese melts and top is lightly browned.

EGGS BENEDICT WITH HOLLANDAISE SAUCE
Chef Mickey's Village Restaurant
Disney Village Marketplace

Yield: 4 servings

8 whole eggs
4 English muffins
8 pieces ham, sliced in
circles (or Canadian
bacon slices)

1 cup hollandaise sauce
(recipe follows)
8 black olives, sliced
2 cups breakfast potatoes

Bring one quart of water almost to a boil. Crack eggs and drop in water slowly.

Toast muffin halves and place on plates side by side. Grill ham circles and place on top of English muffin halves. Remove poached eggs after 2½ to 3 minutes, and place atop ham. Cover each egg with 1 ounce of hollandaise sauce. Top each egg with black olive slices.

Serve with breakfast potatoes.

Hollandaise Sauce
Yield: 1 cup

6 egg yolks
1 pound butter or
margarine
¾ teaspoon Worcestershire
sauce

¼ teaspoon Tabasco sauce
1 lemon, juiced
½ teaspoon salt

Whip egg yolks and lemon juice in a stainless steel mixing bowl. Place mixing bowl over simmering pan of water, double-boiler style, and whip eggs constantly until soft peaks form. Remove from heat. Whisk in butter slowly until well blended. Add Tabasco, Worcestershire, and salt.

Serve warm.

EGGS CORONADO
Concourse Grille
Disney's Contemporary Resort

Yield: 4 servings

1 cup cottage cheese
2 tablespoons horseradish
2 tablespoons sour cream
1 bunch scallions, fresh,
   sliced

8 large eggs
½ cup milk
Salt
Pepper

In a large bowl, mix cottage cheese, horseradish, sour cream, and sliced scallions. Set aside.

In a separate bowl, mix eggs, milk, salt, and pepper.

Make 4 medium-size omelettes in a hot sauté pan, adding equal amounts of cottage cheese mixture to each omelette. Fold each omelette in half to hold filling.

EGGS KAMEHAMEHA
Papeete Bay Verandah
Disney's Polynesian Resort

Yield: 2 servings

4 eggs
4 slices bread, fried in
   butter
½ cup Gruyère cheese,
   shredded

¼ cup dry white wine
4 tablespoons butter
Salt
Cayenne pepper

Preheat oven to 400 degrees.

Arrange fried bread in an oven-proof serving dish. Melt cheese in a saucepan with wine. Season with salt and cayenne pepper. Pour wine and cheese over fried bread.

Melt butter in frying pan and fry eggs. Place 1 egg on each slice of bread. Put dish in oven or under broiler for 2 minutes to glaze tops of eggs.

Serve at once.

NEW YORK FRITTATA
Grand Floridian Cafe
Disney's Grand Floridian Beach Resort

Yield: 1 serving

3 whole eggs
3½ ounces smoked salmon, diced
2 tablespoons chives, chopped
2 tablespoons onion, diced
2 tablespoons herb cheese

2 tablespoons scallion, chopped
Pinch parsley, fresh, chopped
2 tablespoons butter or margarine

In a medium-size mixing bowl, beat eggs and fold in all remaining ingredients.

Melt 2 tablespoons of butter or margarine in a 10-inch non-stick skillet or omelette pan and add egg mixture. Mix eggs in pan until partially set. When eggs begin to hold together, stop mixing and allow frittata to set. Continue cooking until eggs are done and bottom is lightly browned.

Remove from pan and serve immediately.

PLANO CROISSANT SANDWICH
Concourse Grille
Disney's Contemporary Resort

Yield: 4 servings

8 ounces ham, shaved very thin
10 ounces cheddar cheese, shredded
4 large croissants

8 large eggs
½ cup milk
Salt
Pepper

Slice croissants in half, sandwich style, and toast in oven until slightly brown. Keep warm until ready to use.

Mix eggs, milk, salt, and pepper in a mixing bowl. Divide into 4 equal parts. In a medium sauté pan, prepare 4 cheese omelettes with egg mixture, including 2 ounces of ham and 2½ ounces of shredded cheddar cheese in the middle when folded over.

Put each omelette between halves of a croissant to make sandwich.

POLY BREAKFAST PIZZA SOUFFLÉ
Papeete Bay Verandah
Disney's Polynesian Resort

Yield: 6 servings

20 thin slices bread
2½ cups milk
1½ pounds mozzarella
  cheese, sliced
2½ cups tomato sauce
  (recipe follows)
1 tablespoon oregano, fresh,
  finely chopped

6 eggs
4 to 5 tablespoons
  Parmesan cheese, grated
3 tablespoons butter, cut in
  small pieces

Soak bread slices in milk for 15 minutes, then drain off any excess liquid. Line bottom of a buttered 2½- to 3-quart casserole dish with bread slices. Top slices with a layer of tomato sauce, sprinkle with a bit of oregano and add a layer of cheese. Continue making layers, finishing by covering last layer of bread with just tomato sauce and oregano. Casserole should be nearly full.

Preheat oven to 350 degrees.

Beat eggs with Parmesan cheese and pour over casserole. Pierce through layers in three or four places with a fork until mixture is completely absorbed by bread. Dot top of casserole with butter and bake for about 1 hour, or until top is browned and puffed.

Tomato Sauce

Yield: 2½ cups

6 medium tomatoes, ripe,
  chopped (about 3 cups)
¾ cup onion, chopped
1 tablespoon olive oil
1 clove garlic
1 tablespoon parsley,
  chopped

1 teaspoon dried basil
1 teaspoon marjoram
1 teaspoon thyme
1 tablespoon sugar
Salt
Pepper

In a large sauté pan, sauté onions in olive oil until tender but not brown. Add all other ingredients and simmer for 30 minutes, or until tomatoes have been reduced to a pulp. Press mixture through a sieve with a wooden spoon and reduce sauce further if necessary. Add salt and pepper to taste.

SCOTCH EGGS
Rose & Crown Pub & Dining Room
United Kingdom   EPCOT Center

Yield: 8 servings

1 pound sausage meat, half
  beef, half pork
1 cup parsley, chopped
½ teaspoon sage, rubbed
½ teaspoon thyme, ground
8 eggs, hard-boiled, peeled
¾ cup flour

½ teaspoon salt
Pepper, freshly ground
2 eggs, beaten lightly
1 cup bread crumbs, dry
Oil for frying
Mustard mayonnaise sauce
  (recipe follows)

Mix sausage with parsley, sage, and thyme. Shape into 8 flat patties and wrap around the hard-boiled eggs, covering each egg completely. Dredge sausage-wrapped egg in flour which has been seasoned with salt and pepper. Roll sausage egg in beaten egg and then in bread crumbs, coating completely. Deep-fry in hot oil until golden brown on all sides (about 5 minutes). The sausage should be cooked and brown.

Serve hot or cold with mustard mayonnaise sauce.

Mustard Mayonnaise Sauce

Yield: 2¼ cups

2 cups mayonnaise
¼ cup white chablis
2 teaspoons dry mustard
1½ teaspoons old English-
  style mustard
Salt

½ teaspoon Worcestershire
  sauce
⅛ teaspoon cayenne pepper
1 tablespoon lemon juice,
  fresh

Mix all ingredients gently into mayonnaise, stirring lightly to blend. Chill.

SPANISH OMELETTE
Concourse Grille
Disney's Contemporary Resort

Yield: 4 servings

12 large eggs
4 tablespoons milk
¼ cup onions, diced
½ cup green bell pepper, diced
½ cup mushrooms, sliced
1 clove garlic, chopped
1 12-ounce can tomatoes, whole, diced with juice
¾ teaspoon oregano
Salt
Pepper
1 teaspoon cornstarch
⅓ cup half-and-half or light cream
8 ounces cheddar or American cheese, grated
1 teaspoon cornstarch
¼ cup scallions, sliced
Non-stick vegetable spray

In a non-stick skillet, sauté onions, peppers, mushrooms, and garlic until tender (about 5 minutes). Add tomatoes with juice and simmer another 5 minutes. Dissolve 1 teaspoon of cornstarch in 1 teaspoon of water and add to vegetable mixture. Cook 2 to 3 minutes, or until sauce thickens. Remove from heat and set aside.

In a small saucepan, heat half-and-half and slowly add grated cheese. Simmer 2 minutes and add second teaspoon of cornstarch dissolved in 1 teaspoon of water. Allow cheese sauce to thicken and remove from heat.

In a non-stick omelette pan, spray pan with vegetable spray and quickly scramble 3 eggs mixed with 1 tablespoon of milk, forming into omelette. Repeat to form 4 separate omelettes.

Assemble as follows: On warm dinner plates, divide cheese sauce evenly. Place one omelette on each plate on top of cheese sauce and top with an equal amount of tomato sauce. All ingredients should be kept warm before preparation of plates.

Garnish with sliced scallions.

ALL IN ONE
Chef Mickey's Village Restaurant
Disney Village Marketplace

Yield: 1 serving

1 large egg, fried　　　　　**1 large buttermilk biscuit**
1 sausage patty, cooked

Cut biscuit in half, sandwich style. Set on a serving plate. Place cooked sausage patty on bottom half of biscuit and fried egg on top of sausage. Top with top half of biscuit.

ST. AUGUSTINE PIZZA
The Land Grille Room
The Land　　*EPCOT Center*

Yield: 1 10-inch pizza

6 ounces pizza dough,　　　　**3 ounces beef tenderloin**
**　frozen**　　　　　　　　　　**4 asparagus tips**
⅓ cup Monterey Jack　　　　**¼ cup mushrooms, thinly**
**　cheese with tarragon**　　　　**　sliced**
**　leaves**　　　　　　　　　　**Non-stick vegetable spray**
3 tablespoons plum tomato
**　sauce**

Allow pizza dough to thaw in refrigerator overnight. Let rise for 2 hours at room temperature before rolling into a 10-inch circle.

Slice beef tenderloin into 3 medallions. Quickly sear and brown in a hot skillet sprayed with vegetable spray. Remove and set aside.

Steam asparagus tips until al dente. Set asparagus aside, also.

Preheat oven to 400 degrees.

Top entire circle of dough with grated Monterey Jack cheese. Add plum tomato sauce on top of cheese in center of pizza only. Arrange tenderloin medallions around sauce on outside of dough on cheese. Fill in remaining spaces of cheese around tenderloin with mushrooms and asparagus tips.

Bake for 18 to 25 minutes. Cheese and sauce should be hot and beef medium rare. Serve immediately.

VEGETABLE FRITTATA
Grand Floridian Cafe
Disney's Grand Floridian Beach Resort

Yield: 1 serving

3 whole eggs
¼ cup tomato, diced
¼ cup zucchini, diced
¼ cup mushrooms, diced
2 tablespoons onion, diced
2 tablespoons chives,
   chopped

2 tablespoons frozen
   chopped spinach, thawed,
   drained
2 tablespoons butter
2 tablespoons Parmesan
   cheese, grated
2 slices tomato
2 thin slices zucchini

In a medium-size mixing bowl, beat eggs and fold in tomatoes, zucchini, mushrooms, onion, chives, and spinach.

Melt 2 tablespoons of butter or margarine in a 10-inch non-stick skillet or omelette pan and add egg mixture. Mix egg mixture in pan until partially set. When frittata begins to hold together, sprinkle with Parmesan cheese and top with sliced tomato and zucchini. Continue cooking until eggs are done and garnish is warm.

Remove from pan and serve immediately.

SEAFOOD

SEAFOOD

BAKED GROUPER WITH HERB BUTTER
Concourse Grille
Disney's Contemporary Resort

Yield: 4 servings

4 6-ounce grouper fillets
8 ounces herb butter
(recipe follows)

Salt
Pepper

Prepare herb butter.
Preheat oven to 325 degrees.
Lightly grease a baking sheet with about 1 ounce of herb butter. Wash grouper fillets with cold water and pat dry with a paper towel. Place fillets on prepared baking sheet. Lightly season each fillet with salt and pepper, then evenly brush top of each with about 1 ounce herb butter.
Bake fillets for 20 to 25 minutes, or until flesh is firm to touch. Remove from oven.
Just before serving, top each fillet with an additional ounce of herb butter and serve immediately. Butter should melt by the time fish is ready to be eaten.

Herb Butter

Yield: 8 ounces

6 ounces butter
1 teaspoon thyme, fresh,
  chopped
1 teaspoon rosemary, fresh,
  chopped
½ teaspoon tarragon, fresh,
  chopped
½ teaspoon oregano, fresh,
  chopped
½ teaspoon sage, fresh,
  chopped

½ teaspoon chervil, fresh,
  chopped
1 teaspoon parsley, fresh,
  chopped
¼ teaspoon lemon juice,
  fresh
1 teaspoon Dijon® Mustard
1 teaspoon Worcestershire
  sauce
½ teaspoon Tabasco sauce

Allow butter to soften at room temperature for 1 hour.
Blend all ingredients with butter until thoroughly mixed. Roll and shape butter mixture in a piece of waxed paper, forming a 1-inch tube.
Refrigerate 1 hour until firm.

BAKED STUFFED SHRIMP IMPERIAL
Fisherman's Deck
Disney Village Marketplace

Yield: 4 servings

16 jumbo shrimp (10-15 count)
2 tablespoons butter, clarified

¼ cup white wine
1 lemon, juiced
1½ pounds imperial stuffing (recipe follows)

Prepare imperial stuffing.

Preheat oven to 350 degrees.

Peel and clean shrimp. Split shrimp along bottom so that shrimp rests flat on pan and tails curl over stuffing. Stuff each shrimp with about 1½ ounces of stuffing. Lay shrimp on a buttered pan or casserole and sprinkle with lemon juice and white wine.

Bake for 15 to 20 minutes, or until tails curl and stuffing is lightly browned.

Serve immediately.

Imperial Stuffing
Yield: 1½ pounds

1 pound crab lump meat, fresh
1 cup imperial mayonnaise (recipe follows)
¼ cup bread crumbs, fresh

¼ teaspoon salt
¼ cup red bell pepper, finely diced
4 tablespoons chives, finely chopped

Prepare imperial mayonnaise.

Pick through crab meat carefully to remove any bits of shell or cartilage. Mix all ingredients until thoroughly blended.

Imperial Mayonnaise
Yield: 1 cup

1 cup mayonnaise
⅛ teaspoon Tabasco sauce
½ teaspoon lemon juice

⅛ teaspoon Worcestershire sauce
⅛ teaspoon Old Bay Seasoning

Mix all ingredients until thoroughly blended.

BOUILLABAISSE
Shipyard Inn
Disneyland Hotel

Yield: 4 servings

½ **pound sea bass fillet**
½ **pound shark fillet**
2 8-ounce lobster tails
20 medium shrimp (21-25
count)
16 mussels, in the shell
8 clams, in the shell
4 cloves garlic, chopped
1 cup onion, chopped
1 cup leek, chopped
1 stalk fennel, chopped
2 cups tomatoes, fresh,
chopped

¼ **cup tomato paste**
8 cups fish stock or bouillon
¼ **cup olive oil**
4 bay leaves
Pinch saffron
Pinch thyme
Pinch rosemary
Pinch parsley
Pinch pepper
Garlic croutons

Cube fish and lobster tails into ½-inch cubes. Peel and clean shrimp and scrub mussels and clams and set aside.

In a heavy-bottom pot, heat olive oil and quickly sauté cubed fish and lobster tails for 2 to 3 minutes. Add shrimp and continue cooking for another 3 to 5 minutes. Remove from pot and set aside.

In the same pot, add more oil if necessary and sauté garlic, onion, leek, and fennel until tender. Add chopped tomato and tomato paste and mix well. Add cooked seafood back into pot with shellfish and remaining ingredients. Bring mixture to a simmer and cook for 15 to 20 minutes. Do not boil. When clams and mussels have opened, remove from stove and carefully remove seafood to 4 individual serving bowls. Divide fish and sauce evenly.

Serve with garlic croutons.

BLACKENED SNAPPER WITH ROASTED GARLIC TARTAR SAUCE
Narcoossee's
Disney's Grand Floridian Beach Resort

Yield: 4 8-ounce servings

2 pounds red snapper, cut in 4 8-ounce pieces	Cajun blackening spice (recipe follows)
4 ounces butter	Roasted garlic tartar sauce (recipe follows)

Prepare Cajun blackening spice.
Prepare roasted garlic tartar sauce.
Preheat oven to 350 degrees.
Dredge snapper in Cajun spice, coating both sides well. Place in a well heated sauté pan with melted butter. (A black cast-iron skillet is preferred.) Cook over high heat until both sides are nicely browned.

Remove fish to a lightly buttered baking dish and bake until done (8 to 10 minutes).

Serve on a warmed dinner plate with roasted garlic tartar sauce.

Cajun Blackening Spice

2 tablespoons paprika	1 teaspoon black pepper
2 tablespoons salt	2 tablespoons thyme
2 tablespoons onion powder	2 tablespoons oregano
2 tablespoons garlic powder	2 tablespoons celery seed
1 teaspoon cayenne pepper	2 tablespoons basil
1 teaspoon white pepper	

Blend all ingredients well.

Roasted Garlic Tartar Sauce

6 ounces garlic cloves (about ½ cup)	1 tablespoon green bell pepper, diced
1½ cups mayonnaise	1 tablespoon whole-grain mustard
¼ cup sweet pickle relish	
1 tablespoon onion, diced	2 tablespoons white wine
1 tablespoon red bell pepper, diced	⅛ teaspoon salt
	⅛ teaspoon pepper

Peel garlic cloves and roast in a hot oven, under a hot broiler or in a frying pan until lightly browned and tender. Cool completely and mince to a fine mash. Combine with the remaining ingredients and refrigerate until ready to use.

BROILED SALMON WITH FINE HERB SAUCE
Concourse Grille
Disney's Contemporary Resort

Yield: 4 servings

4 6-ounce salmon fillets
¼ cup olive oil

8 ounces fine herb sauce

Prepare fine herb sauce.

Brush salmon fillets with olive oil and charbroil or barbecue on a low flame until flesh is firm and pink (8 to 10 minutes).

Serve on warmed dinner plates with about 2 ounces of warm fine herb sauce under each piece of salmon. Garnish with additional fresh herbs and lemon, if desired.

Fine Herb Sauce   Yield: 8 ounces

1 ounce red bell pepper,
** roasted (about ½ cup)**
⅓ cup olive oil
2 tablespoons basil, fresh,
** chopped**

2 teaspoons thyme, fresh,
** chopped**
2 teaspoons rosemary,
** fresh, chopped**
1 teaspoon salt
Pinch white pepper

Blend all ingredients in a food processor or blender for about 30 seconds. Do not puree. Blend only long enough to incorporate ingredients.

Serve warm.

CORAL REEF LINGUINE
Coral Reef Restaurant
The Living Seas   *EPCOT Center*

Yield: 6 servings

1½ pounds linguine, fresh
1 pound small shrimp,
    peeled and cleaned
1 pound bay scallops
½ cup olive oil, divided
1 teaspoon garlic, fresh,
    finely chopped
1 teaspoon basil, fresh,
    finely chopped

1 cup fennel fern, chopped
2 teaspoons shallots, diced
3 cups oven-dried tomatoes
    (recipe follows)
Salt
Pepper
1 cup Parmesan cheese,
    grated

Cook linguine in boiling salted water until al dente. Drain and rinse under cold running water. Set aside.

Marinate shrimp and scallops in ¼ cup oil, chopped garlic and fresh basil for about 10 minutes.

In a large skillet, heat remaining ¼ cup oil and sauté fennel fern and shallots until tender. Add marinated seafood and cook until shrimp turn pink and scallops are firm. Add cooked pasta and oven-dried tomatoes and toss until pasta is hot. Season with salt and pepper and divide evenly among 6 dinner plates.

Top each serving with grated Parmesan cheese and serve immediately.

Note: Fresh or canned plum tomatoes may be substituted for oven-dried tomatoes.

Oven-Dried Tomatoes
Yield: 3 cups

3 pounds Italian plum
    tomatoes
1 cup olive oil

½ cup basil, fresh, chopped
1 cup Parmesan cheese

Preheat oven to 200 degrees.

Slice tomatoes into ⅜-inch slices. Toss tomatoes in a bowl with olive oil, basil and cheese. Place a baking rack on a sheet pan and arrange tomatoes in a single layer on rack. Bake tomatoes for 2 to 3 hours.

Remove rack from oven and cool tomatoes for 1 hour. Store in an air-tight container.

CAPE COD PASTA WITH SCALLOPS
Liberty Tree Tavern
Liberty Square   *MAGIC KINGDOM Park*

Yield: 1 serving

5 ounces sea scallops
⅛ teaspoon Cajun
  seasoning
1 tablespoon butter
¼ cup red bell pepper, cut
  in ¼-inch pieces
¼ cup summer squash, cut
  in ¼-inch pieces
¼ cup zucchini, cut in
  ¼-inch pieces
¼ cup mushrooms, cut in
  quarters
⅛ cup plum tomatoes,
  peeled, seeded, diced

1 tablespoon scallions,
  chopped
1 clove garlic, chopped
⅛ teaspoon white pepper
Pinch salt
1 teaspoon Worcestershire
  sauce
2 tablespoons Parmesan
  cheese
6 ounces spinach linguine,
  cooked, cooled

In a heavy skillet, melt butter. Wash scallops and pat dry on paper towels. Sprinkle with Cajun seasoning and quickly sauté in butter until firm to touch (about 4 minutes). Add vegetables and sauté another 5 minutes. Season with salt, white pepper, Worcestershire sauce, and Parmesan cheese and toss lightly. Stir in cooked spinach linguine and heat only long enough to warm entire mixture.

Serve on a warmed dinner plate with additional Parmesan cheese, if desired.

Note: Vegetables will remain crispy and can be sautéed separately ahead of time if a softer vegetable is desired.

CRAB CAKE BATCH
Disney-MGM Studios Theme Park

Yield: 6 servings

2 teaspoons butter
½ cup celery, finely diced
¼ cup Spanish onion, finely diced
¼ cup scallions, finely diced
¼ cup mushrooms, finely diced
½ teaspoon garlic, finely diced
1½ teaspoons Dijon® Mustard
2 teaspoons parsley, chopped
1 teaspoon lemon juice
1½ teaspoons Worcestershire sauce

2 tablespoons Chablis
½ teaspoon dill, fresh, chopped
½ teaspoon Hungarian paprika
¼ teaspoon cayenne pepper
Pinch salt
Pinch pepper
2 large egg yolks
¾ cup bread crumbs
1 cup blue crab lump meat, drained
Oil for frying
Marinara sauce (recipe follows)
Lemon wedges

In a large skillet, melt butter and sauté celery, onions, mushrooms, and garlic until tender. Remove from heat and stir in mustard, parsley, lemon juice, Worcestershire sauce, Chablis, and spices. Blend well. Lightly beat egg yolks and add to vegetable mixture with bread crumbs. Mix well and fold in crab meat. Refrigerate for 30 minutes.

Prepare marinara sauce.

Form crab mixture into small patties and pan-fry in a small amount of oil until lightly browned on both sides and hot all the way through.

Serve hot with marinara sauce and garnish with fresh lemon.

Marinara Sauce
Yield: 2½ cups

1 tablespoon olive oil
1 teaspoon garlic, minced
⅓ cup green bell pepper, diced
⅓ cup celery, diced
⅓ cup onion, diced
¼ teaspoon oregano, dry
¼ teaspoon thyme, dry

¼ teaspoon basil, dry
¼ teaspoon black pepper
3 cups tomatoes, canned, diced, with juice
1 teaspoon granulated sugar
1 whole bay leaf

(continued on next page)

CRAB CAKE BATCH
(continued from previous page)

In a medium-size saucepan, heat olive oil. Add garlic, green pepper, celery, onion, and spices. Sauté about 5 minutes, until vegetables become transparent. Remove from heat and transfer to a food processor with a steel blade. Add tomatoes and sugar and puree until smooth. Place mixture back in saucepan and bring to a boil. Add bay leaf and simmer 15 to 20 minutes. Adjust the seasoning and remove bay leaf.

CREVETTES À LA PROVENÇALE
Club 33
New Orleans Square   *DISNEYLAND Park*

Yield: 4 servings

16 large shrimp, peeled, cut in half
¼ cup butter
¼ teaspoon seasoning salt
1 tablespoon shallots, finely diced

1 clove garlic, finely diced
¼ teaspoon thyme, dried
½ cup dry Sauternes wine
2 whole ripe tomatoes, peeled, diced
Hot cooked rice or noodles

Rinse and dry shrimp. Heat butter in a large skillet and sauté shrimp until tails curl and flesh begins to turn pink (1 to 2 minutes). Season with salt. Add shallots, garlic and thyme. Sauté another 1 to 2 minutes and add wine and tomatoes. Cook shrimp at a slow simmer for 3 to 4 minutes until sauce thickens and shrimp is fully cooked.

Serve over noodles or rice.

CRAB MEAT RAVIOLI
Tangaroa Terrace
Disney's Polynesian Resort

Yield: 6 servings

Filling

1 pound crab meat	⅔ cup white sauce, cooled
1 tablespoon butter	(recipe follows)
¼ cup shallots, minced	1 teaspoon thyme
½ cup mushrooms, minced	Salt
½ cup cracker crumbs	Pepper

Prepare dough.

Prepare white sauce.

In a small sauté pan, melt butter and sauté shallots until tender (about 5 minutes). Add mushrooms and crab meat and cook an additional 2 to 3 minutes. Remove from heat and allow to cool.

When cool, add cracker crumbs, white sauce, thyme, salt and pepper to taste. Mix well and refrigerate for 1 hour.

Dough

½ to ⅔ cup flour	1 tablespoon water
1 whole egg, beaten	1 teaspoon oil

Prepare dough by combining all ingredients. Knead for approximately 5 minutes until well blended and smooth. Wrap in plastic wrap and allow dough to rest at room temperature for 1 hour.

White Sauce

Yield: 3 cups

2 cups heavy cream	2 whole eggs
½ cup Romano cheese,	Salt
grated	Pepper
4 ounces butter, softened	

(continued on next page)

CRAB MEAT RAVIOLI
(continued from previous page)

In a 1-quart saucepan, add heavy cream and bring to a boil. Reduce cream by one third and fold in grated cheese. Quickly whisk in butter and egg, being careful not to scramble egg. Season to taste with salt and pepper. Allow sauce to cool.

To prepare ravioli, divide dough into 2 equal pieces. Roll each piece into a very thin rectangle.

Form filling into ½-inch balls. Place balls on bottom layer of dough, about 1½ inches apart, forming straight rows. Brush in between the rows with beaten egg and lay top layer of dough over filling. Press between rows with fingers to seal each piece of filling. Cut with a sharp knife into squares.

Drop individual ravioli into boiling salted water and cook for 5 minutes. Drain well.

Serve with remainder of white sauce, reheated.

CHAR-GRILLED SHRIMP WITH COCONUT BUTTER
Papeete Bay Verandah
Disney's Polynesian Resort

Yield: 4 servings

24 jumbo shrimp
Marinade
¼ cup unsalted butter
3 tablespoons piña colada drink mix
2 tablespoons sweet shredded coconut

1 teaspoon dark rum (optional)
Salt
Pepper

Mix marinade ingredients together and marinate shrimp for at least 6 hours prior to cooking.

After marinating shrimp, soften butter and mix with drink mix, shredded coconut, and dark rum, if desired. Blend together well. Skewer shrimp to facilitate handling on grill. Cook over open flame or under a hot broiler 3 to 4 minutes on each side. After turning once, brush with butter mixture. Continue cooking until done. Season to taste with salt and white pepper, if necessary.

Serve with tropical fruits.

Marinade
½ cup piña colada drink mix
1 tablespoon olive oil

1 teaspoon garlic, finely chopped

DUNGENESS CRAB ENCHILADAS
Special Events
Disneyland Hotel

Yield: 4 servings

1 pound Dungeness crab (or any crab meat available)
2 tablespoons butter or margarine
1 clove garlic, crushed
¼ cup scallions, diced
1 cup mushrooms, sliced
2 tablespoons jalapeño peppers, diced
¼ cup black olives, sliced

2 tablespoons pimiento, diced
½ teaspoon salt
½ teaspoon pepper
8 5-inch corn tortillas
Tomato sauce (recipe follows)
1½ cups Jack cheese and cheddar cheese, mixed and grated

Prepare tomato sauce.

In a large skillet, melt butter and sauté garlic, scallions, mushrooms, and jalapeño peppers for 2 to 3 minutes. Add olives, pimiento, and crab and season with salt and pepper. Mix well and heat thoroughly. Remove from heat.

Preheat oven to 350 degrees.

Warm tortillas in a frying pan and lay out on a flat surface. Divide crab filling into 8 equal parts and fill each tortilla. Roll up and place, seam side down, in an oven-proof casserole dish in a single layer. Top with tomato sauce and grated cheese mix. Bake until cheese melts and filling is hot (about 15 minutes).

Serve hot.

Tomato Sauce for Enchiladas
Yield: about 12 ounces

1 16-ounce can tomatoes, diced
1 clove garlic, crushed
2 teaspoons white pepper

1 tablespoon jalapeño pepper, minced
1 tablespoon cornstarch mixed with 1 tablespoon water

Combine all ingredients and bring to a boil. Thicken with cornstarch and simmer for 5 minutes. Add more cornstarch mixed with water, if necessary.

FETTUCCINI WITH LOBSTER
Caffe Villa Verde
Disneyland Hotel

Yield: 4 servings

2 pounds fettuccini noodles, fresh if available
1¾ pounds lobster meat, fresh or frozen, cut in 1-inch cubes
2 tablespoons butter

1 cup button mushrooms, sliced
2 tablespoons garlic, minced
4 cups heavy cream
2 cups Parmesan cheese, freshly grated

Cook noodles in boiling salted water until al dente. Drain and submerge in cold water. Drain again and set aside.

In a 12-inch skillet, melt butter. Add garlic and sauté 1 to 2 minutes. Add mushrooms and lobster meat and sauté lobster until firm and white (about 3 minutes). (If using fully cooked lobster meat, add mushrooms first and sauté 1 to 2 minutes, then lobster meat just to heat through.) Once mushrooms are cooked and lobster is hot, add cream and bring to a slow boil. Whisk in cheese and season with salt and pepper to taste. Add fettuccini noodles and stir. Bring back to a simmer.

Serve immediately.

FILET DE FLETAN À L'ACADIENNE
(Halibut Steak Acadian Style)
Blue Bayou Restaurant
New Orleans Square   DISNEYLAND *Park*

Yield: 4 servings

4 6- to 7-ounce halibut steaks
Salt
Pepper
1 egg, beaten
¼ cup butter

½ cup small shrimp, cooked (4 ounces)
1 tablespoon capers
¼ cup lemon juice, fresh
Hot cooked rice
Lemon wedges

Season halibut steaks with salt and pepper to taste. Dip in beaten egg and sauté in a hot skillet with melted butter 2 to 3 minutes on each side. Remove to a serving plate and keep warm.

Add shrimp to pan with capers and lemon juice. Cook for 1 to 2 minutes, scraping pan and stirring well. Spoon sauce and shrimp over halibut steaks and garnish with lemon wedges.

Serve hot with rice.

FISH 'N' CHIPS
Rose & Crown Pub & Dining Room
United Kingdom   *EPCOT Center*

Yield: 6 servings

3 pounds white-flesh fish, boneless (cod, snapper, haddock, grouper)
1 cup lemon juice
1 tablespoon Worcestershire sauce
¼ teaspoon salt
¼ teaspoon white pepper
2 tablespoons vegetable seasoning
Batter (recipe follows)
Oil for frying
Chips (French fries), fresh or frozen, cooked
Malt vinegar

Cut fish into fingers about 2 ounces each and place in a glass or stainless steel pan. Mix lemon juice with Worcestershire sauce, salt, pepper, and vegetable seasoning. Pour over fish and marinate in refrigerator for 1 hour, turning every so often to coat fish.

Prepare batter.

Remove fish from marinade, drain, dip in batter and fry in hot oil for about 5 minutes, turning to brown both sides, if necessary. Remove from oil and drain on paper towels.

Serve with chips and malt vinegar.

Batter

¾ cup cornstarch
2⅔ cups flour
1 teaspoon salt
3 teaspoons sugar
⅛ teaspoon white pepper
1¾ cups water
2 egg yolks
⅓ cup flat beer
2 teaspoons baking powder

Mix cornstarch, flour, salt, sugar, and pepper.

In a separate bowl, beat water, egg yolks, and beer together with a whisk and slowly add dry ingredients. Continue to mix with whisk until mixture is smooth. Stir in baking powder. Makes enough batter to coat 3 pounds of fish.

GRILLED FISH DINNER
King Stefan's Banquet Hall
Fantasyland   MAGIC KINGDOM Park

Yield: 8 servings

8 10-ounce dolphin fillets,
   (or any fish of choice)
1 cup soybean oil
Dash Worcestershire sauce
Dash Tabasco sauce
Pinch oregano leaves

¼ teaspoon white pepper
Parsley potatoes (recipe
   follows)
Mixed vegetables (recipe
   follows)

In a medium-size mixing bowl, combine oil, Worcestershire sauce, Tabasco, oregano, and white pepper. Mix well and coat each fish fillet with oil mixture. Broil or grill until fish is fully cooked.

Serve with fresh lemon.

Parsley Potatoes
Yield: 8 servings

4 potatoes (½ pound)
⅛ cup parsley, fresh,
   chopped
2 chicken bouillon cubes

⅛ cup butter or margarine,
   melted
2 quarts water

Peel potatoes and cut into quarters. Place in a large pot with water and bouillon cubes. Bring to a boil and simmer until tender. Drain well and mix with fresh chopped parsley and butter.

Mixed Vegetables
Yield: 8 servings

1 tablespoon olive oil
1 teaspoon garlic, finely
   minced
¼ cup onion, cut in ½-inch
   dice
1 cup carrots, sliced
1 cup zucchini, sliced

1½ cups broccoli, tops only
1 cup rutabaga, cut in
   ½-inch cubes
½ cup red bell pepper, cut
   in ½-inch pieces
Salt
Pepper

In a small saucepan, simmer carrots and rutabaga in water until tender and drain well.

In a large skillet or wok, heat oil and add garlic, onion, and pepper. Quickly sauté until tender (3 to 5 minutes). Add broccoli, zucchini, carrots, and rutabaga and cook an additional 3 to 5 minutes until broccoli is tender but still a little crispy. Season with salt and pepper to taste.

Note: Vegetables should remain a little crispy, and may be lightly browned.

GRILLED GROUPER
Coral Reef Restaurant
The Living Seas   *EPCOT Center*

Yield: 6 servings

**6 6- to 8-ounce grouper
  fillets**
**2 lemons, juiced, rinds
  zested**
¼ cup olive oil
¼ cup white wine
1 teaspoon sugar

**½ teaspoon black pepper,
  freshly ground**
**Braised napa cabbage
  (recipe follows)**
**Tomato basil sauce (recipe
  follows)**
Lemon wedges for garnish

Combine zest and juice from 2 lemons, olive oil, white wine, sugar, and pepper and mix well. Place grouper fillets in a shallow pan, cover with marinade, and refrigerate for 1 hour.

Prepare tomato basil sauce.

Prepare braised cabbage.

Grill, broil, or barbecue the fillets until fully cooked (3 to 4 minutes on each side). Place on top of braised cabbage and serve with tomato basil sauce and fresh lemon.

Braised Napa Cabbage   Yield: 6 servings

3 slices bacon, minced
2 purple shallots, minced
1 teaspoon white vinegar
**8 cups napa cabbage,
  shredded**

Salt
Pepper
Sugar

Sauté bacon in a large hot skillet until crispy. Add shallots and continue cooking until transparent. Deglaze pan with white vinegar and add cabbage. Reduce heat and cook until just tender (about 15 minutes). Season with salt and pepper to taste and add sugar if cabbage is at all bitter.

Tomato Basil Sauce

1 teaspoon vegetable oil
2 shallots, diced
1 cup fish stock, or bouillon
Salt
White pepper

**2 teaspoons cornstarch
  (more, if necessary)**
2 teaspoons water
12 plum tomatoes, chopped
**2 tablespoons basil, fresh,
  chopped**

In a medium skillet, heat oil and sauté shallots until transparent. Add fish stock and bring to a boil. Add salt and pepper to taste. Dissolve cornstarch in water and add to fish stock. Simmer 3 to 5 minutes until thickened. Add an additional teaspoon of cornstarch mixed with water for a thicker sauce, if desired. Add tomatoes and basil. Simmer an additional 3 to 5 minutes and check seasonings.

GRILLED SHRIMP PLATTER
50's Prime Time Cafe
Disney-MGM Studios Theme Park

Yield: 1 serving

**4 large shrimp (U-12 count),
 peeled, cleaned
1 teaspoon mesquite
 seasoning
½ cup egg rotini pasta**

**1 corn tortilla
Avocado salsa (recipe
 follows)
Watercress for garnish**

Cook egg rotini pasta in boiling salted water. While pasta cooks, season shrimp with mesquite seasoning and char-broil or grill until shrimp is firm and cooked.

Serve grilled shrimp with cooked pasta, warm avocado salsa, and corn tortilla. Garnish with fresh watercress.

Note: This recipe increases easily.

Avocado Salsa

**½ cup green chili salsa
 sauce or picante salsa**

**¼ cup avocado, fresh, diced
¼ cup tomato juice**

Combine all ingredients in a small saucepan and simmer over medium heat for 5 minutes.

GULF SNAPPER
Garden Gallery
The Disney Inn

Yield: 4 servings

**1½ pounds red snapper,
 4 skinless fillets,
 6 ounces each
3 tablespoons milk
¾ cup flour
Pinch salt**

**Pinch pepper
3 tablespoons vegetable oil
4 slices lemon, peeled, diced
2 tablespoons rosemary
4 tablespoons white wine**

Sprinkle fish fillets with salt and pepper. Pour milk into a bowl and put flour on a plate. Dip fish in milk and then in flour. Shake off any excess flour and place in a heated skillet with vegetable oil. Cook 4 to 5 minutes, turning only once, until golden brown. Remove fish to a warm platter. Add lemon, rosemary, and white wine to skillet and bring to a simmer. Remove from heat immediately and pour over fish fillets.

LOBSTER NANTUCKET
Ariel's
Disney's Beach Club Resort

Yield: 1 serving

1 to 1½ pounds Maine
  lobster, fresh
1 tablespoon sweet butter
1 clove garlic, finely
  chopped
2 tablespoons shallots,
  finely chopped
2 tablespoons white wine

¼ cup button mushrooms,
  cut in quarters
¼ cup heavy whipping
  cream
1 scallion, sliced
Salt
Pepper

Place live lobster in a pot of boiling water and pre-cook for 4 minutes. Remove from pot and ice down to prevent any further cooking. Allow lobster to rest for 15 minutes.

After 15 minutes, remove claws and pull out meat. Cut tail meat out of shell, keeping lobster tail intact. Remove any further meat from lobster and dice into large chunks. Set aside.

In a large skillet, melt butter and sauté garlic and shallots for 3 minutes. Add white wine and simmer until reduced by half. Add mushrooms and sauté until lightly browned (4 to 5 minutes). Add heavy cream and bring to a boil. Add partially cooked lobster meat and reduce heat to a simmer. Cook approximately 5 more minutes, or until lobster meat is fully cooked and sauce is slightly thickened. Season to taste with salt and pepper.

Rinse lobster tail shell and place on a dinner plate.

Serve lobster over shell and garnish with sliced scallion.

MAHI MAHI
Tahitian Terrace
Adventureland   *DISNEYLAND Park*

Yield: 6 servings

1 cup cold water
1 egg
1 teaspoon salt
2 teaspoons vegetable oil
1 cup flour
⅛ teaspoon yellow food
  coloring

6 boneless mahi mahi or
  dolphin fillets
Oil for frying
Mahi mahi sauce (recipe
  follows)

Prepare mahi mahi sauce.

In a mixing bowl, combine water, egg, salt, and vegetable oil. Beat slowly to blend. Gradually add flour, beating to form a smooth batter. Add food coloring if desired.

Dip fish fillets into batter and fry in hot oil (350 degrees), until golden brown (5 to 6 minutes).

Remove and drain on absorbent towels. Serve with mahi mahi sauce.

Mahi Mahi Sauce
2 cups pineapple juice
1 cup sugar
2½ tablespoons cornstarch

¾ cup cider vinegar
½ cup tomato ketchup
½ cup pineapple tidbits

In a small saucepan, combine pineapple juice, sugar, and cornstarch. Add remaining ingredients and cook and stir until mixture comes to a boil and is thickened.

Serve hot.

MIXED BAG
Ariel's
Disney's Beach Club Resort

Yield: 1 serving

3 ounces fresh fish
2 jumbo shrimp, peeled,
    cleaned
2 large scallops
3 mussels, out of shells
2 clams, out of shells
2 button mushrooms
1 sprig basil, fresh

1 tablespoon shallots,
    chopped
1 clove garlic, minced
Pinch salt
Pinch pepper
1 tablespoon white wine
1 sheet parchment paper
Non-stick vegetable spray

Preheat oven to 375 degrees.

Place parchment paper on a cookie sheet coated with vegetable spray. Spray parchment paper also. Place all seafood in a mound in center of parchment paper on cookie sheet. Add remaining ingredients to seafood and season with salt and pepper.

Bring all four sides of parchment together and fold or tie closed. Place in oven on cookie sheet for 15 to 20 minutes, or until all seafood is cooked.

Open bag carefully, allowing the steam to escape slowly. Serve over rice or pasta.

PENNE MARCO POLO
Flagler's
Disney's Grand Floridian Beach Resort

Yield: 1 serving

½ pound penne pasta,
    cooked and drained
4 large shrimp, (U-10 count)
¼ cup broccoli florets
¼ cup shiitake mushrooms,
    sliced
¼ cup artichoke hearts,
    quartered

¼ cup heavy cream
Salt
Pepper
2 tablespoons white wine
1 tablespoon olive oil
2 tablespoons Parmesan
    cheese, freshly grated
½ teaspoon garlic, chopped

Peel and clean shrimp. Prepare all other ingredients and have ready. This dish cooks quickly and requires all of your attention at the stove once you start.

(continued on next page)

PENNE MARCO POLO
(continued from previous page)

In a medium-size sauté pan, heat olive oil. Add garlic and shrimp and sauté over medium heat until shrimp turns pink. Add white wine and simmer until almost all wine evaporates. Add broccoli, mushrooms, and artichoke hearts and sauté 2 to 3 minutes. Add heavy cream and season with salt and pepper if necessary. Add pasta and toss lightly.

Sprinkle with Parmesan cheese and serve immediately.

Note: This recipe increases easily.

RED SNAPPER IN LOBSTER SAUCE
Narcoossee's
Disney's Grand Floridian Beach Resort

Yield: 4 servings

4 pieces red snapper, about 7 ounces each
4 tablespoons olive oil

4 tablespoons flour
Lobster sauce (recipe follows)

Prepare lobster sauce.
Preheat oven to 350 degrees.
In a heavy-gauge skillet, heat olive oil. Dust snapper with flour and quickly sauté on both sides until lightly browned. Place in oven and cook an additional 8 to 10 minutes until fully cooked.

Serve on a warmed dinner plate with lobster sauce.

Lobster Sauce

4 ounces butter
2 cloves garlic, minced
4 tablespoons shallots, chopped
⅛ cup sweet vermouth
1 cup lobster stock or fish bouillon

1 cup tomato juice
¼ cup lobster meat, cooked, diced
Salt
Pepper

In a medium-size skillet, melt butter and add garlic and shallots. Sauté 3 to 4 minutes over medium heat. Add vermouth and simmer 1 minute. Add lobster stock and tomato juice and bring to a boil. Season with salt and pepper to taste and reduce heat. Simmer 10 to 12 minutes, or until sauce reduces by one half. Add diced lobster meat.

Serve hot on top of red snapper.

SAUTÉED TROUT WITH CASHEW CILANTRO BUTTER
Fisherman's Deck
Disney Village Marketplace

Yield: 4 servings

4 rainbow trout fillets, 8 to 10 ounces each
½ cup flour
½ cup clarified butter
½ cup cashew halves

4 sprigs cilantro, fresh, for garnish
Cilantro butter sauce (recipe follows)

Prepare cilantro butter sauce.

Add clarified butter to a fairly hot sauté pan. Lightly flour trout and place in hot sauté pan, flesh side down. Cook over moderately high heat until golden brown. Turn fillets over and finish cooking, approximately 3 minutes on each side. Remove fillets from pan and keep warm. Add cashew halves to sauté pan and sauté quickly until heated through (about 1 minute).

Serve each trout fillet topped with one quarter of cashews and cilantro butter sauce.

Cilantro Butter Sauce

1 tablespoon shallot or onion, minced
1 tablespoon cider vinegar
¼ bay leaf
½ cup white wine
⅔ cup heavy cream

½ pound unsalted butter, cut in small pieces
3 tablespoons cilantro leaves, chopped
Salt
Pepper

In a small stainless steel saucepan, add shallots, vinegar, bay leaf and wine. Simmer and reduce liquid until almost dry. Add cream and reduce by two thirds. Remove pan from heat and slowly whisk in pieces of butter, one at a time, until thoroughly blended. Add cilantro and salt and pepper, if necessary.

Serve immediately.

SCAMPI NEWPORT
Shipyard Inn
Disneyland Hotel

Yield: 4 servings

2 pounds shrimp (16-20 count)
¼ pound sweet butter
½ cup green bell pepper, thinly sliced
1 cup tomato, fresh, peeled, diced
2 cloves garlic, crushed

2 whole shallots, minced
2 dashes Worcestershire sauce
1 lemon, juiced
1 bunch chives, chopped
¼ cup white wine
2 tablespoons parsley, chopped

Prepare all ingredients before cooking and have on hand. Shrimp cooks quickly and will become tough if left too long.

Peel and clean shrimp. In a 12-inch sauté pan, melt butter and quickly sauté shrimp until tails curl and skin turns pink (3 or 4 minutes). Remove from pan and set aside. Add to same pan, peppers, tomatoes, garlic, and shallots. Sauté 3 to 5 minutes, or until tender. Season with Worcestershire sauce, lemon juice, chives, and wine. Add shrimp back into pan and simmer 2 minutes.

Sprinkle with chopped parsley and serve immediately.

SCAMPI WITH FRESH TOMATOES ITALIAN STYLE
Club 33
New Orleans Square   *DISNEYLAND Park*

Yield: 4 servings

1 pound shrimp, (16-20 count)
2 tablespoons butter
1 teaspoon garlic, crushed
1 tablespoon shallot, minced
3 tablespoons dry sherry
2 whole tomatoes, ripe, peeled, diced
½ teaspoon Worcestershire sauce

½ teaspoon Tabasco sauce
½ teaspoon steak sauce
¼ teaspoon white pepper
⅛ teaspoon oregano
⅛ teaspoon thyme
2 tablespoons parsley, fresh, chopped
Salt
Hot cooked rice

Peel, clean and rinse shrimp. Heat butter in a large skillet and sauté shrimp for 2 minutes, until flesh begins to turn pink. Add garlic and shallot and sauté an additional 1 minute. Add sherry, tomatoes, and seasonings. Cook for about 5 minutes, or until shrimp are fully cooked and sauce has thickened slightly. Add salt to taste.

Serve over rice.

SEAFOOD BROCHETTE
King Stefan's Banquet Hall
Fantasyland   *MAGIC KINGDOM Park*

Yield: 6 servings

24 large shrimp (22-26 count), fresh, peeled, cleaned
1½ pounds dolphin fillet, fresh, (or any fish of your choice) cut in ¾-inch cubes

24 large scallops (about 1 pound)
12 4-inch bamboo skewers
Kebab sauce (recipe follows)
Rice pilaf (recipe follows)

Prepare kebab sauce.
Prepare rice pilaf.
Soak bamboo skewers in cold water for 1 hour to prevent burning when cooked. Skewer seafood onto skewers, starting with a shrimp, then a piece of dolphin, scallop, dolphin, scallop, and finally a shrimp. Set up remaining skewers in same manner as first. Broil brochettes until fish is firm but not dry (6 to 8 minutes).

Remove seafood from skewers and serve on beds of rice pilaf with kebab sauce.

Rice Pilaf

¾ cup brown rice, uncooked
1 stalk celery, leaves removed, cut in ¼-inch slices
3 tablespoons soybean oil

1 chicken bouillon cube
⅓ cup mushrooms, sliced
1½ cups water
Salt
Pepper

Preheat oven to 350 degrees.
In a medium-size skillet, heat oil and sauté celery about 2 minutes. Add rice and cook an additional minute. Do not brown rice. Transfer to a 1 quart casserole dish and add bouillon cube, mushrooms, and water. Season with a dash of salt and pepper and cover with foil or casserole lid.
Bake for 45 minutes, or until all water has been absorbed and rice is tender.

(continued on next page)

SEAFOOD BROCHETTE
(continued from previous page)

Kebab Sauce

1½ cups plum tomatoes, fresh, peeled, seeded, diced
1 teaspoon olive oil
1 teaspoon basil, fresh, finely chopped
½ teaspoon parsley, fresh, finely chopped

½ teaspoon shallots, finely chopped
½ teaspoon garlic, finely chopped
4 teaspoons white wine
Salt
Pepper

In a simmering pan of hot water, submerge tomatoes for about 45 seconds. Remove from water and submerge in ice water. Let cool and peel with a sharp paring knife. Cut tomatoes in half and remove seeds. Cut into ¼-inch cubes and set aside.

In a small skillet, heat olive oil and lightly sauté basil, parsley, shallots, and garlic about 2 minutes. Add tomatoes and sauté an additional 2 minutes. Add white wine and simmer for 3 to 5 minutes. Season with salt and pepper to taste and serve with seafood brochettes.

SEAFOOD FETTUCCINE
Garden Gallery
The Disney Inn

Yield: 4 servings

1 pound fettuccine pasta
4 tablespoons olive oil
½ cup heavy cream
½ cup parmesan cheese, finely grated

8 mussels, fresh or frozen, cleaned
12 shrimp, peeled, deveined
12 scallops
Pinch pepper, freshly ground

Combine 5 quarts of water and 1 tablespoon olive oil in a 6-quart sauce pot. Bring to a rolling boil, then add fettuccine. When water returns to a boil, cook for approximately 10 minutes. Remove from stove and drain in a large colander. Return to pot and toss with 1 tablespoon of olive oil.

Sauté shrimp, scallops, and mussels in a large skillet with 2 tablespoons of olive oil. Cook 3 to 5 minutes, or until shrimp turns pink and scallops are firm to touch. Add cream, cheese, and fettuccine. Reduce to a creamy texture.

Remove from heat and arrange on serving plates. Top with pepper, if desired.

SEAFOOD PASTA
Disney-MGM Studios Theme Park

Yield: 4 servings

½ pound spinach linguini
½ pound tomato linguini
½ pound egg linguini
4 cups heavy cream
¼ cup butter or margarine
½ cup onion, minced
1 cup small shrimp, peeled,
   cleaned

1 cup bay scallops (or sea
   scallops), cut in ½-inch
   cubes
6 ounces feta cheese
Salt
Pepper, freshly ground
2 tablespoons parsley,
   chopped

In a large pot of boiling salted water, cook linguini until al dente. Drain well and rinse under cold water. Set aside.

In a small saucepan, heat cream and simmer until reduced by half. Cool and set aside.

In a large skillet or sauté pan, melt butter or margarine and sauté onion until tender. Add shrimp and scallops and continue cooking for 5 to 8 minutes. When shrimp is pink and scallops are firm to touch, crumble cheese over seafood and add reduced cream. Bring to a simmer and add linguine. Season with salt and pepper and sprinkle with parsley. Toss lightly.

Serve immediately. Accompany with garlic bread.

SHRIMP PASTA
Papeete Bay Verandah
Disney's Polynesian Resort

Yield: 1 serving

8 large shrimp (15 count),
   peeled, cleaned
1½ teaspoons olive oil
¼ teaspoon oregano
1 clove garlic, chopped
¾ cup heavy cream
¾ cup Parmesan cheese
7 ounces linguine noodles,
   cooked

1 egg yolk, beaten
Salt
Pepper
1 teaspoon parsley, chopped
1 wedge lemon
Parsley, chopped, for
   garnish

Marinate shrimp in oil, oregano and garlic for 30 minutes.

(continued on next page)

SHRIMP PASTA
(continued from previous page)

Remove shrimp from marinade and sauté in a skillet over medium heat just until tails curl and flesh turns pink. Season lightly with salt and pepper. Add cream, cheese, and linguine. Simmer about 3 minutes, stirring constantly. When shrimp is fully cooked, whisk in egg yolk and parsley.

Remove from heat immediately and serve. Garnish with additional chopped parsley and lemon wedge.

SEAFOOD PRIMAVERA
Fisherman's Deck
Disney Village Marketplace

Yield: 4 servings

12 ounces spinach linguini	½ cup snow peas, trimmed
12 ounces egg linguini	¼ cup parsley, chopped
¼ cup olive oil, divided	2 tablespoons tarragon, fresh, chopped
¼ cup butter, clarified	
3 tablespoon garlic, chopped	1 teaspoon thyme, dried
	¼ cup chives, fresh
1½ cups bay scallops	¼ cup lemon juice, fresh
1½ cups swordfish, cut in ½-inch cubes	½ cup white wine
	Salt
8 jumbo shrimp, peeled, cleaned	Pepper
	Parsley, chopped, for garnish
½ cup carrots, julienne	
½ cup zucchini, julienne	Lemon slices for garnish

Cook pasta in boiling salted water and drain well. Rinse in cold water and toss lightly with olive oil to keep from sticking together. Set aside.

In a large skillet or saucepan, combine remaining oil and butter. Add garlic and sauté until tender (about 5 minutes). Do not brown. Add scallops, swordfish cubes, shrimp, carrots, zucchini, and snow peas and sauté until fish is firm and white and vegetables are tender (7 or 8 minutes). Add remaining ingredients and simmer for 3 to 5 minutes. Season with salt and pepper to taste.

Quickly reheat pasta in boiling water and drain well. Divide among 4 serving bowls and spoon seafood over pasta.

Garnish with additional chopped parsley and lemon and serve immediately.

Note: Any firm white-flesh fish may be substituted in this recipe.

SEARED SWORDFISH WITH THAI CURRY SAUCE
Coral Reef Restaurant
The Living Seas   *EPCOT Center*

Yield: 4 servings

8 2½- to 3-ounce pieces
  swordfish
3 tablespoons lemon grass,
  minced
2 tablespoons grape seed
  oil
1 tablespoon garlic, minced
1 tablespoon shallots,
  minced
½ tablespoon ginger, fresh,
  minced
Pinch cayenne pepper
1½ cups lobster butter
  sauce (recipe follows)

½ ounce Thai curry paste
¼ cup tomato conçasse
¼ cup basil, chopped
½ cup shiitake mushrooms
1 cup peppers, red, green,
  yellow, julienne
¼ cup lentils, cooked until
  tender
2 tablespoons sesame oil
Salt
Pepper
Pickled ginger

In a small bowl, combine lemon grass, grape seed oil, garlic, shallots, ginger, and cayenne pepper. Coat swordfish and refrigerate for 30 minutes.

Prepare lobster butter sauce.

In a small saucepan combine lobster butter sauce, Thai curry paste, tomato conçasse, and basil. Warm on low heat. Set aside until ready to serve.

Sauté mushrooms, peppers, and lentils in sesame oil until tender (about 5 minutes). Keep warm until ready to serve.

In a hot skillet, sear swordfish for about 3 minutes on each side, turning only once.

When sauce is hot, mushrooms and peppers tender, and fish cooked, divide mushrooms and peppers evenly between 4 dinner plates. Place 2 pieces of swordfish on each plate and serve with sauce. Garnish with pickled ginger if desired.

Note: lemon grass, Thai curry paste, pickled ginger and grape seed oil are all available at oriental markets.

(continued on next page)

SEARED SWORDFISH WITH THAI CURRY SAUCE
(continued from previous page)

Lobster Butter Sauce   Yield: 1½ cups

¾ cup white wine
2 tablespoons white vinegar
1 tablespoon shallots,
    minced
½ cup heavy cream

10 ounces unsalted butter,
    softened
1 ounce lobster paste
Salt
Pepper

In a heavy saucepan, combine white wine, white vinegar, and shallots. Reduce over low heat until only ¼ cup remains. Stir in heavy cream and reduce over low heat until only ⅓ cup remains. Slowly add butter and whisk continually. Strain sauce and add lobster paste. Blend well and serve.

SHELLFISH STEW
Ariel's
Disney's Beach Club Resort

Yield: 4 servings

8 cups fish stock or bouillon
1 tablespoon butter
2 cups tomatoes, cut in
    ½-inch cubes
12 leaves basil, fresh,
    coarsely chopped
1 pinch thyme, fresh,
    coarsely chopped
1 pinch dill, fresh, coarsely
    chopped

1 cup onion, diced
1 cup celery, diced
1 tablespoon garlic, minced
½ teaspoon salt
½ teaspoon pepper
2 strands saffron
12 mussels in shell, fresh
8 clams in shell, fresh
8 oysters in shell, fresh

In a 4-quart soup pot, melt butter and add all above ingredients except fish stock and shellfish. Sauté for 8 to 10 minutes. Add fish stock and bring to a boil. Reduce heat and simmer for 15 minutes.

Meanwhile, steam shellfish for 6 to 8 minutes, or until all shells open. Discard any that do not open.

Portion mussels, clams, and oysters evenly among 4 large serving bowls and spoon hot fish stock over shellfish. Serve immediately.

SHOGUN DINNER
Mitsukoshi Restaurant
Japan   *EPCOT Center*

Yield: 4 servings

A shogun dinner is composed of several parts. To make it easier to prepare, make ginger sauce and mustard sauce first. They can be prepared several days in advance and refrigerated until ready to serve. Shell and clean shrimp, cut steak and chicken in serving-size pieces, and arrange on a plate ready to cook. Have vegetables cleaned and ready to cook also.

Ginger Sauce
Yield: 2½ cups

1½ tablespoons ginger root, fresh, coarsely cut
2 tablespoons onion, coarsely cut
2 tablespoons water
1 ¼-inch slice lemon
1 cup Japanese soy sauce
½ cup rice wine vinegar
¼ cup vegetable oil
4 sprigs parsley

Soak fresh ginger root in water for a few minutes to easily remove skin. Put all ingredients in a blender or food processor with a steel blade and blend until smooth. Store in the refrigerator up to a week.

Mustard Sauce
Yield: 1 cup

2½ tablespoons sesame seeds
1 tablespoon onion, coarsely cut
½ cup soy sauce
1 tablespoon dry mustard
1 ounce vegetable oil
⅔ cup water

Preheat oven to 400 degrees.
Spread sesame seeds on a flat baking dish and bake until lightly toasted (about 10 minutes). Combine with remaining ingredients in a blender and blend until well mixed.

Appetizer
16 medium shrimp, (21-26 count), raw, in shell
2 tablespoons butter
Salt
Pepper
Dash soy sauce
½ teaspoon lemon juice
Ginger sauce

Wash, peel, clean, rinse and dry shrimp. Heat butter in a skillet or wok and quickly sauté shrimp until fully cooked. Season with salt, pepper, soy sauce, and lemon juice.
Serve with ginger sauce as an appetizer.

(continued on next page)

SHOGUN DINNER
(continued from previous page)

Main Dish

4 tablespoons butter
1 cup onions, sliced
1 cup zucchini, sliced
1 cup mushroom buttons
¼ cup sesame seeds,
    roasted
1 pound chicken breast
    meat, boneless, cut in
    ½-inch cubes

1 pound strip sirloin steak,
    cut in ½-inch cubes
Salt
Pepper
Dash soy sauce
Mustard sauce (recipe
    above)

In a large skillet or wok, melt butter and quickly sauté vegetables until tender. Season with salt, pepper, and soy sauce. Add roasted sesame seeds and remove vegetables from wok. Set aside and keep warm.

Add cubed chicken to wok and quickly sauté until tender. Season with same ingredients as vegetables. Remove and repeat with sirloin steak. When steak is cooked as desired, remove to a serving plate with vegetables and chicken arranged across plate.

Serve with mustard sauce.

SHRIMP FAJITAS
Special Events
Disneyland Hotel

Yield: 6 to 8 servings

1 pound shrimp, peeled,
  cleaned, cut into long
  thin strips
½ cup onion, sliced
⅓ cup olive oil
1 cup green bell pepper, cut
  in long julienne strips
1 cup red bell pepper, cut in
  long julienne strips
1 tablespoon cumin, ground
1 teaspoon chili powder
1 teaspoon garlic powder

1 teaspoon oregano, ground
1 teaspoon salt
½ cup lime juice, sweetened
1 tablespoon cornstarch
8 12-inch flour tortillas
Sour cream
Cheddar cheese, grated
Lettuce, shredded
Black olives, sliced
Tomatoes, fresh diced
Green chili salsa

Sauté onions in oil until tender. Add shrimp, peppers, and spices and cook until shrimp are pink and peppers are slightly wilted. Add lime juice and mix in. Push shrimp mixture to one side in pan and allow juices to run to the other side. Soften cornstarch in water and add to juices to thicken and glaze shrimp.

Warm tortillas and add a spoonful of shrimp filling to each. Garnish with sour cream, cheese, lettuce, olives, tomatoes, and salsa.

SHRIMP SCAMPI
Concourse Grille
Disney's Contemporary Resort

Yield: 4 servings

1 pound shrimp, raw (21-25 count)
2 tablespoons butter
2 teaspoons garlic, chopped
3 tablespoons shallots, chopped
¼ cup Sauternes wine

¼ teaspoon lemon juice
¼ teaspoon Worcestershire sauce
1/16 teaspoon cayenne pepper
Hot cooked rice
Fish sauce (recipe follows)

Prepare fish sauce.

Peel, clean, rinse, and dry shrimp. Heat butter in a large skillet and sauté garlic and shallots with shrimp until tails curl and flesh turns pink. Add Sauternes, lemon juice, Worcestershire sauce, and cayenne pepper. Add fish sauce and bring to a simmer.

Remove from heat and serve over rice.

Fish Sauce
Yield: 1 cup

1 teaspoon dry sherry
4 teaspoons Sauternes wine, divided
3 tablespoons onion, chopped
½ teaspoon garlic, granulated
3 tablespoons butter or margarine
2 tablespoons flour

¼ teaspoon paprika
⅛ teaspoon white pepper
⅛ teaspoon dry mustard
⅛ teaspoon ginger, ground
1 cup water
1 fish bouillon cube
1 tablespoon half-and-half
¼ teaspoon lemon juice
Salt

Heat sherry, 3 teaspoons of Sauternes, onion, and garlic in a saucepan until wine is evaporated. Add butter or margarine and let melt. Stir in flour, paprika, pepper, mustard, and ginger. Cook and stir for 10 minutes over low heat. Slowly stir in water, using a whisk to blend. Add fish bouillon cube and cook long enough to dissolve. Add half-and-half, remaining teaspoon of Sauternes, and lemon juice. Taste and add salt if necessary. Cook over low heat 10 minutes, stirring occasionally.

SNAPPER
Liberty Tree Tavern
Liberty Square   MAGIC KINGDOM *Park*

Yield: 1 serving

8 ounces red snapper, skinless and boneless (or any white fish of your choice)
1 tablespoon lemon juice, fresh (about ½ lemon)
½ cup Worcestershire sauce
¼ cup flour

1 egg, beaten
2 tablespoons butter or margarine
2 tablespoons lemon butter (recipe follows)
Salt
Pepper

Prepare lemon butter.

Combine lemon juice, Worcestershire sauce and a dash of salt and pepper. Coat both sides of fish fillet and allow to marinate for 1 hour.

Preheat oven to 350 degrees.

In an oven-proof skillet or frying pan, melt butter on medium heat. When pan is fairly hot and butter melted, remove fish from marinade, dust with flour, and dip in beaten egg. Immediately place in hot frying pan and brown on both sides. When fish is brown, place entire skillet in oven for 10 to 15 minutes or until fish is done.

Remove from oven and put 2 tablespoons of lemon butter over fish. Serve with fresh vegetables.

Lemon Butter

¼ cup butter, softened
1 tablespoon white wine

1 tablespoon lemon juice, fresh

In a small bowl, combine all ingredients and mix well. Roll in a piece of waxed paper, log style, and refrigerate.

STIR FRY SHRIMP AND SCALLOPS
WITH GINGER SAUCE
Papeete Bay Verandah
Disney's Polynesian Resort

Yield: 3 servings

¾ pound bay shrimp, peeled, cleaned
¾ pound bay scallops
½ cup pea pods
¼ cup carrots, sliced
½ cup baby corn, canned in brine, rinsed
¼ cup red bell pepper, sliced
2 leaves bok choy

⅛ cup water chestnuts
⅛ cup straw mushrooms
¼ cup bamboo shoots
1 tablespoon sesame oil
½ cup oyster sauce
2 cups ginger sauce (recipe follows)
Salt
Pepper

Cook pea pods, carrots, baby corn, red pepper and bok choy in boiling water for 8 to 10 minutes. Drain well and set aside.

Prepare ginger sauce.

In a large cast-iron skillet or wok, heat sesame oil and quickly sauté seafood until shrimp turn pink and scallops are firm. Add cooked vegetables and continue to cook for an additional 2 to 3 minutes. Add water chestnuts, mushrooms, bamboo shoots, oyster sauce, and ginger sauce and heat through. Season to taste with salt and pepper.

Serve immediately.

Ginger Sauce   Yield: 2 cups

1½ cups chicken stock
½ teaspoon ginger powder
¼ cup white wine

2 cloves garlic, minced
4 teaspoons cornstarch
¼ cup water

Dissolve cornstarch in water and set aside.

In a medium-size saucepan, add stock, ginger powder, wine, and garlic. Bring to a boil and add cornstarch. Simmer for 10 minutes, stirring constantly until thickened.

TUNA STEAK WITH BLACK BEAN SAUCE
Papeete Bay Verandah
Disney's Polynesian Resort

Yield: 1 serving

1 7-ounce tuna steak	Black bean sauce (recipe follows)

Prepare black bean sauce.

Grill or sauté tuna steak until lightly browned and flesh is firm to touch.

Serve with black bean sauce on side.

Black Bean Sauce

1 tablespoon vegetable oil	1 tablespoon cornstarch
1 tablespoon ginger root, fresh, chopped	2 tablespoons water
	1 tablespoon sesame oil
1 clove garlic, chopped	2 tablespoons soy sauce
2 tablespoons black beans, canned	3 tablespoons scallions, diced
¼ cup sherry	
½ cup chicken stock or broth	

Heat vegetable oil in a large saucepan or wok. Mix ginger root, garlic, and black beans and quickly sauté in vegetable oil 2 to 3 minutes. Add sherry and cook 30 seconds. Add chicken stock and bring to a boil. Dissolve cornstarch in water and add to chicken stock. Simmer 5 minutes to thicken. Add sesame oil and soy sauce and blend until smooth. Add scallions.

Serve immediately.

VONGOLE RIPIENI PUCCINI
(Baked Clams)
L'Originale Alfredo di Roma Ristorante
Italy   *EPCOT Center*

Yield: 4 servings

12 clams, scrubbed, cleaned
1 teaspoon garlic, chopped
3 teaspoons olive oil, divided
3 teaspoons bread crumbs, dry
1 teaspoon parsley, chopped
4 teaspoons crab meat, chopped

½ teaspoon oregano, dried
Dash cayenne pepper
Salt
2 tablespoons dry white wine
Lemon wedges

Steam clams in a small amount of water just long enough to open shells. With a small sharp knife, cut clam shells apart at hinges and remove clams. Drain well and set shells aside.

Place clams in a food processor with a steel blade and chop 5 to 10 seconds. Do not puree. Set aside.

Preheat oven to 350 degrees.

In a small skillet, heat 1 teaspoon of olive oil and sauté garlic until lightly browned. Remove from heat and add bread crumbs, chopped parsley, crab meat, oregano, pepper, and salt. Blend well.

Place clam shells on a baking sheet and divide chopped clams among shells. Sprinkle bread crumb mixture over clams and drizzle with remaining olive oil. Bake for 12 to 15 minutes until bread crumbs are lightly browned and clams are hot. Remove from oven and sprinkle with white wine.

Serve immediately with lemon wedges.

NOTES

POULTRY

BREAST OF CHICKEN CITRON
Club 33
New Orleans Square *DISNEYLAND Park*

Yield: 4 servings

4 large chicken breasts,
boneless (about
8 ounces each)
¼ cup flour
⅛ teaspoon salt
⅛ teaspoon pepper
½ cup butter
1 tablespoon sherry

1 tablespoon white wine
3 tablespoons orange juice
1 teaspoon orange rind,
grated
2 teaspoons lemon juice
1 cup half-and-half
12 lemon slices, very thin
Parmesan cheese, grated

Preheat oven to 400 degrees.

Combine flour, salt, and pepper in a small bowl. Dust chicken with seasoned flour and place in a buttered casserole dish in a single layer. Dot chicken with butter and place in oven for 25 minutes. Reduce the temperature to 325 degrees.

Combine sherry, white wine, orange juice, orange rind, and lemon juice and pour over chicken and cook for an additional 25 minutes, covered. Remove casserole from oven and pour half-and-half around chicken. Let hot casserole cool slightly with half-and-half.

On a broiler-proof oven pan, arrange thinly sliced lemon slices and sprinkle with grated Parmesan cheese. Broil until lightly browned.

Remove chicken from casserole and arrange on a serving platter. Stir sauce with a fork and pour over chicken. Garnish with broiled lemon slices.

BRIDGETOWN CHICKEN FAJITAS
Bridgetown Broiler
Disney's Caribbean Beach Resort

Yield: 8 tortillas

2 pounds chicken breast meat, boneless
½ cup soy sauce
1 large green bell pepper, julienne
2 large onions, julienne
1 tablespoon soybean oil
1 head iceberg lettuce, shredded

1 cup guacamole
1¼ cups mild cheddar cheese, grated
1 cup salsa
1 cup sour cream
8 large flour tortillas
Marinade (recipe follows)

Prepare marinade.

Rinse chicken breasts in cold water and remove any excess fat. Cut into ¼-inch strips and add to marinade. Refrigerate overnight.

Heat a large skillet with soybean oil and quickly sauté green pepper and onions until tender and lightly browned. Remove from skillet and keep warm. Drain chicken and add to hot skillet. Sauté for 5 to 7 minutes, or until fully cooked. Remove from pan and keep warm with onions and peppers.

Warm flour tortillas on a cookie sheet in a 250-degree oven for approximately 5 minutes. Do not let tortillas dry out.

When ready to serve, place warm tortillas, cooked chicken, and onion and pepper mixture on the table family-style with shredded iceberg lettuce, guacamole, cheddar cheese, salsa, and sour cream. Fill tortillas as desired.

Marinade

½ cup water
2 tablespoons soybean oil
¼ cup scallions, chopped

1 bunch cilantro, chopped
2 limes
1 clove garlic, crushed

In a 2-quart bowl, combine soy sauce, water, soybean oil, chopped scallions, chopped cilantro, juice from 2 limes, and crushed garlic. Blend well and set aside.

CHICKEN AND LEEK PIE
Rose & Crown Pub & Dining Room
United Kingdom   EPCOT Center

Yield: 4 to 6 servings

2 tablespoons butter
⅓ cup onion, diced
½ cup celery, cut on bias
1 cup leeks, whites only,
    cleaned, diced
1 pound chicken breast,
    boneless, cubed
2 tablespoons flour
1½ cups chicken stock or
    broth

¼ cup parsley, chopped
2 teaspoons salt
¼ teaspoon pepper
¼ teaspoon thyme
Pastry dough for a single-
    crust pie
1 egg, beaten
¼ cup heavy cream

Melt butter in a large skillet. Add onion, celery, and leeks and sauté until tender (10 to 15 minutes on medium heat). Add cubed chicken meat and continue cooking until chicken is tender. Sprinkle with flour and stir well. Add stock, parsley, salt, pepper, and thyme. Bring to a boil and cook for 3 to 5 minutes. Remove from heat and let cool slightly.

Preheat oven to 400 degrees.

Place mixture in a 2-quart casserole dish at least 2 inches deep. Roll out pie dough to ⅛ inch thick and place on casserole dish. Trim edges and use any excess dough to decorate top of pie. Cut a 1-inch hole in center of pie and brush crust with beaten egg. Bake for 20 to 30 minutes, or until crust is golden brown and filling is hot.

Heat heavy cream to lukewarm and pour through 1-inch hole in top of pie. Allow pie to rest for 10 minutes before serving.

CHICKEN BREAST FLORENTINE
Grand Floridian Cafe
Disney's Grand Floridian Beach Resort

Yield: 2 servings

2 5-ounce chicken breasts,
  boneless
1 teaspoon olive oil
½ teaspoon shallots, minced
½ teaspoon garlic, minced
½ cup white wine
¼ cup heavy cream
2 tablespoons Parmesan
  cheese, grated

½ cup spinach, fresh, cut
  in strips
Salt
Pepper
4 ounces angel hair pasta,
  cooked
Marinade (recipe follows)

Prepare marinade. Marinate chicken breasts for 24 hours.
Preheat oven to 350 degrees.
Remove chicken from marinade and pat dry with paper towels. Quickly sauté chicken in olive oil in a hot skillet until lightly browned on both sides. Remove from pan and finish cooking in oven until fully cooked (45 to 50 minutes).
Meanwhile, add to skillet shallots, garlic, white wine, cream, Parmesan cheese, spinach, and salt and pepper to taste and simmer 3 to 5 minutes until well blended and spinach is limp.
Serve sauce hot over chicken with angel hair pasta.

Marinade
½ cup olive oil
½ teaspoon garlic, chopped

½ teaspoon oregano
1 teaspoon rosemary

Blend ingredients and use them to thoroughly coat chicken.

CHICKEN AND MEATBALL STEW
Le Cellier Restaurant
Canada   *EPCOT Center*

Yield: 4 to 6 servings

⅓ cup flour
1 teaspoon salt
¼ teaspoon white pepper
2 pounds chicken thighs
    (about 6)
¼ cup vegetable oil
4½ cups chicken stock or
    broth
2 tablespoons butter

1 cup onions, chopped
1 clove garlic, chopped
1 cup carrots, sliced
2 medium potatoes, peeled,
    cubed
1 whole clove
1 bay leaf
Meatballs (recipe follows)

Combine flour, salt, and white pepper in a small bowl. Dredge chicken thighs in flour and brown well on both sides in a large hot skillet or dutch oven in hot vegetable oil. Sprinkle any leftover flour on chicken while browning to help thicken stew. Add chicken stock and bring to a boil. Reduce heat and simmer chicken, covered, approximately 30 minutes, or until tender. Remove chicken from broth and set aside. Reserve broth.

In another skillet, heat butter and sauté onion until tender. Add garlic and cook another 2 minutes. Add remaining ingredients and cook until tender. Add reserved broth and simmer 10 to 15 minutes. Meanwhile, make meatballs.

To serve, return chicken thighs to broth and add meatballs. Heat stew to a simmer.

Serve immediately.

Meatballs

1 pound pork, ground
1 pound veal, ground
1 teaspoon salt
½ teaspoon chives, freeze-
    dried
⅛ teaspoon vegetable
    seasoning

½ teaspoon white pepper
⅛ teaspoon thyme, ground
⅛ teaspoon coriander,
    ground
½ cup half-and-half
⅔ cup bread crumbs, dry
¼ cup water (or as needed)

Preheat oven to 375 degrees.

Mix ground pork and veal with seasonings, blending well. Add half-and-half and bread crumbs and blend well. Gradually add water until a medium-firm texture is achieved. Shape into 20 to 25 meatballs and place on a greased baking sheet. Bake until meatballs are lightly browned and fully cooked (30 minutes).

CHICKEN MEDITERRANEAN
Chef Mickey's Village Restaurant
Disney Village Marketplace

Yield: 4 servings

2½ cups chicken, boneless,
  dark meat
1½ cups chicken, boneless,
  white meat
6 teaspoons flour
4 teaspoons olive oil

2 cups tomato sauce
½ cup water, as needed
1½ cups rice, cooked
4 sliced black olives
4 sliced green olives,
  pimiento-stuffed

Cube chicken meat into 1-inch cubes and dust with flour. Heat olive oil in a skillet and sauté chicken until almost done (4 to 5 minutes). Chicken should be lightly browned and juicy. Add tomato sauce and simmer about 5 minutes, until chicken is fully cooked. Add water only if sauce has become too thick.

Serve chicken over cooked rice and garnish with sliced black and green olives.

CHICKEN PICCATA
Club 33
New Orleans Square   *DISNEYLAND Park*

Yield: 6 servings

4 whole chicken breasts,
  skinned, boned, halved
½ cup flour
Salt
Pepper
½ teaspoon paprika
¼ cup butter, clarified
1 tablespoon olive oil

4 tablespoons Madeira wine
  or water
3 tablespoons lemon juice,
  fresh
6 slices lemon
3 tablespoons capers
¼ cup parsley, chopped
Hot cooked fettucini

Place chicken breasts between 2 sheets of wax paper and pound with a wooden mallet until thin (about ¼ inch). Combine flour, salt, pepper and paprika in a bag. Add chicken and coat well. Shake off any excess. Heat butter and olive oil in a large skillet and add chicken breasts, a few at a time, and sauté until lightly browned on both sides. Remove and continue until all chicken has been sautéed. Drain on absorbent paper and keep warm.

Drain off all but 2 tablespoons of butter and oil from skillet. Deglaze pan with wine or water, scraping pan. Add lemon juice and return chicken to skillet. Layer lemon slices over chicken and add capers and chopped parsley. Heat briefly and serve over fettucini.

CHICKEN FLORENTINE
Tony's Town Square Restaurant
Main Street, U.S.A.   *MAGIC KINGDOM Park*

Yield: 4 servings

4 6-ounce chicken breasts, boneless
Chicken marinade (recipe follows)
3 cups Florentine sauce (recipe follows)

4 slices provolone cheese
1 pound fettucine, cooked (optional)

Prepare chicken marinade.
Marinate chicken breasts for 1 hour in marinade.
Prepare Florentine sauce.
Remove chicken from marinade and pat dry. Broil or grill chicken until fully cooked (7 to 8 minutes on each side). Place cooked chicken over hot cooked fettucine, if desired, and top with Florentine sauce and provolone cheese. Lightly broil cheese just to melt.
Serve immediately.

Chicken Marinade
Yield: 1½ cups

¾ cup olive oil
¾ cup vegetable oil
1 tablespoon garlic, chopped
1 teaspoon vegetable seasoning

1 teaspoon Cajun seasoning
1 teaspoon basil, dried
½ teaspoon thyme, dried

Mix all ingredients and refrigerate.

Florentine Sauce
Yield: 3 cups

4 tablespoons butter or margarine, divided
2 tablespoons flour
2 tablespoons onion, finely diced
1½ teaspoons garlic, finely chopped
1 12-ounce package frozen chopped spinach, thawed, drained

2½ cups half-and-half
½ teaspoon Worcestershire sauce
½ teaspoon vegetable seasoning
3 tablespoons Romano cheese, grated
Salt
Pepper

In a medium-size skillet, melt 2 tablespoons butter or margarine and add flour to make a roux. Cook for about 5 minutes until well blended. Remove to a small bowl and set aside.
Melt remaining 2 tablespoons of butter or margarine and sauté onion and garlic until tender. Add spinach and half-and-half and bring to a simmer. Do not boil. Add roux made earlier and whisk until sauce thickens. Add remaining ingredients and season with salt and pepper to taste.

161

CHICKEN POT PIE
50's Prime Time Cafe
Disney-MGM Studios Theme Park

Yield: 2 to 4 servings

**2 cups chicken tenderloins,
uncooked**
1 cup broccoli, tops only
½ cup carrots, cubed
½ cup celery, cubed
¼ cup leeks, diced
3 tablespoons butter
3 tablespoons flour

3 cups milk or half-and-half
**1 cup Parmesan cheese,
grated**
2 chicken bouillon cubes
**Pastry dough for a single-
crust pie**
1 egg, beaten

In boiling salted water, simmer chicken tenderloins, broccoli, carrots, celery, and leeks until chicken is fully cooked and vegetables are tender but still firm (about 15 minutes). Drain well and set aside.

In a medium-size skillet, melt butter and add flour. Cook for 5 minutes and add milk or half-and-half. Bring to a boil and simmer until thickened (about 10 minutes). Dissolve chicken bouillon cubes in ¼ cup warm water and add to sauce. Blend in grated Parmesan cheese and remove from heat. Add cooked chicken and vegetables and mix well.

Preheat oven to 400 degrees.

Pour mixture into a deep-dish pie plate and cover with pie dough. Seal edges well and brush top with beaten egg. Bake until crust is golden brown and filling is hot (45 to 50 minutes).

CHICKEN ROBIN
King Stefan's Banquet Hall
Fantasyland　　*MAGIC KINGDOM Park*

Yield: 6 servings

6 8-ounce chicken breasts, boneless
Salt
Pepper

Mustard sauce (recipe follows)
Vegetable pasta (recipe follows)

Trim chicken breasts of any excess fat and lightly season both sides with salt and pepper. Broil on both sides until fully cooked but not dried out.

Serve on a warmed dinner plate with mustard sauce and vegetable pasta.

Mustard Sauce

1 cup brown sauce
1 teaspoon olive oil
1 tablespoon onion, finely chopped

1 teaspoon tarragon, fresh, finely chopped
3 tablespoons mustard, whole-grain
¼ cup heavy whipping cream

In a heavy saucepan, heat olive oil and sauté onions for 1 minute. Add brown sauce, tarragon, and mustard. Bring to a boil and mix thoroughly. Reduce heat and simmer for 4 minutes. Reduce heat and stir in heavy cream. Simmer 2 to 3 minutes.

Serve warm.

Vegetable Pasta

Yield: 6 servings

1 pound bow-tie pasta (or pasta of your choice)
2 ounces vegetable oil
1 cup red bell pepper, cut in ½-inch dice
1½ cups rutabaga, cut in ½-inch cubes
2 cups broccoli florets, stems removed

1 cup summer squash, cut in half moons
1½ cups carrots, cut in ¼-inch slices
2 tablespoons Parmesan cheese, grated
Salt
Pepper

In a large pot, boil pasta with 1 ounce of vegetable oil until al dente. Drain and rinse pasta and set aside.

Blanch all vegetables in boiling water until almost fully cooked. Cook carrots and rutabaga separately, since they will take longer to cook. Drain all vegetables and allow to steam dry in a colander.

In a large skillet, heat 1 ounce of oil. Add vegetables and quickly sauté until heated through. Add cooked pasta and season with Parmesan cheese, salt and pepper to taste. Toss lightly.

Serve hot.

CHICKEN SARASOTA
Concourse Grille
Disney's Contemporary Resort

Yield: 4 servings

4 5-ounce chicken breasts,
  boneless, skinned
11 ounces chicken marinade
  (recipe follows)
4 slices sugar-cured ham,
  about 4 ounces

4 slices mozzarella cheese,
  about 4 ounces
1 cup hickory barbecue
  sauce (recipe follows)

Marinate chicken breasts in chicken marinade for 24 hours.

Remove chicken from marinade and grill on a charcoal grill until cooked (about 5 minutes on each side). Brush with hickory barbecue sauce while cooking. After chicken breasts are cooked, but before removing them from grill, place a slice of ham and cheese on top of each piece of chicken. Continue cooking just long enough to warm ham and melt cheese.

Serve immediately.

Chicken Marinade

Yield: 11 ounces

½ cup soy bean oil
¾ cup white wine
½ cup onion, diced
1 teaspoon celery salt
½ teaspoon black pepper
1 teaspoon garlic powder
½ teaspoon thyme, fresh
  sprigs

1 teaspoon rosemary, fresh
  sprigs
½ teaspoon tarragon, fresh
  sprigs
1 teaspoon salt

Combine all ingredients and blend well.

Hickory Barbecue Sauce

Yield: 1 cup

½ cup chili sauce
⅛ teaspoon black pepper
⅛ teaspoon salt
½ tablespoon onion,
  dehydrated
1 tablespoon honey

½ tablespoon mesquite
  seasoning
½ cup barbecue sauce,
  hickory-flavored if
  available

Combine all ingredients and blend well.

CHICKEN WITH LOBSTER
Special Events
Disney's Yacht and Beach Club Resorts

Yield: 8 servings

4 chicken breasts, boneless, split
1½ teaspoons salt, divided
¼ teaspoon pepper, divided
½ cup butter
2 tablespoons sherry
½ pound mushrooms, fresh, sliced
2 tablespoons flour

1½ cups chicken broth
1 tablespoon tomato paste
1 bay leaf
2 tablespoons chives, chopped
1½ cups tomatoes, ripe, chopped
½ pound lobster meat, ½-inch cubes

Preheat oven to 350 degrees.

Lightly season chicken breasts with 1 teaspoon of salt and ⅛ teaspoon of pepper. Melt butter in a skillet and sauté chicken breasts about 5 minutes until lightly browned on both sides. Spoon sherry over chicken. Remove chicken and place in an oven-proof dish and cover with foil. Bake for 30 minutes, or until tender.

While chicken cooks in oven, add sliced mushrooms to skillet with drippings and sauté approximately 5 minutes. Blend in flour and cook another 3 to 5 minutes. Slowly add chicken broth, stirring constantly while sauce thickens. Add tomato paste, bay leaf, chives, and remaining salt and pepper and simmer 15 minutes.

Five minutes before chicken is finished, add lobster meat and diced tomatoes to sauce and heat through.

Remove chicken from oven and place on a serving platter. Top with hot sauce and serve at once.

CHOW YUK STIR FRY (TURKEY)
Tahitian Terrace
Adventureland   DISNEYLAND Park

Yield: 4 servings

2 tablespoons vegetable oil
6 ounces turkey breast
  meat, sliced
1 teaspoon salt
½ cup onion, sliced
1½ cups celery, thinly sliced
½ cup mushrooms, fresh,
  sliced
¼ cup bamboo shoots,
  sliced

¼ cup water chestnuts,
  sliced
1 cup chicken broth
¼ cup Chinese pea pods,
  cut in half
1 tablespoon cornstarch
2 tablespoons water
Hot cooked rice or noodles

Heat oil in a large skillet or wok. Add turkey and salt and stir-fry until turkey is lightly browned. Add onion, celery, mushrooms, bamboo shoots, and water chestnuts. Stir-fry until tender but still a little crispy. Add broth and pea pods and simmer 2 to 3 minutes. Mix cornstarch with water and add to skillet. Bring mixture to a full boil, stirring constantly. When mixture has boiled for 1 minute, remove.

Serve over rice or noodles.

Note: Sliced veal, chicken, pork, or beef may be substituted for turkey.

CLEAR CHICKEN POT PIE
The Land Grille Room
The Land   EPCOT Center

Yield: 2 servings

1 cup chicken breast, skinless, diced (¼-inch cubes)

2 tablespoons celery, diced (¼-inch cubes)

2 tablespoons carrot, diced (¼-inch cubes)

2 tablespoons mushrooms, diced (¼-inch cubes)

2 tablespoons leek, diced (¼-inch cubes)

2½ cups chicken consommé, canned

1 6"x6" sheet puff pastry, thawed overnight in refrigerator

Pinch tarragon

Pinch basil

Cook chicken breast meat, celery, carrot, mushrooms, and leeks in boiling water until chicken is cooked and vegetables are tender but still firm. Drain and set chicken and vegetables aside until ready to use.

Roll out puff pastry on a floured board to a thickness of ⅛ inch. Sprinkle with tarragon and basil and fold over once. Roll again and cut into circles large enough to cover individual over-proof serving dishes.

Preheat oven to 375 degrees.

Divide chicken and vegetables between 2 individual serving dishes and cover with consommé. Place a piece of puff pastry over top of each pie and crimp edges to seal. Bake for 25 to 30 minutes until crust is golden brown and filling is hot.

Remove from oven and serve immediately.

COCONUT AND ALMOND CHICKEN
With Pommery Mustard Sauce
Disney Village Resort Club
Disney Village Resort

Yield: 4 servings

4 5-ounce chicken breasts, boneless, skinless	¼ cup blanched almonds, sliced
½ cup flour	Salt
2 eggs, lightly beaten	Pepper
½ cup bread crumbs, fresh, unseasoned	Oil for frying
⅓ cup coconut, shredded	Pommery mustard sauce (recipe follows)

Prepare breading mixture by combining bread crumbs, coconut, and almonds in a small bowl. Place beaten egg in a bowl and flour on a plate.

Preheat oven to 350 degrees.

Rinse chicken breasts under cold running water and pat dry with paper towels. Lightly season chicken with salt and pepper. First coat chicken in flour, shaking off any excess, then dip in freshly beaten egg. Coat thoroughly with the bread crumb/coconut mixture and place in a hot frying pan with oil. Pan-fry chicken until golden brown on both sides. Finish cooking in oven for 8 to 10 minutes, if necessary. Drain on absorbent paper.

Serve immediately with Pommery mustard sauce.

Pommery Mustard Sauce

2 tablespoons butter or margarine	2 tablespoons heavy cream
2 tablespoons flour	4 teaspoons mustard, whole-grain
1½ cups chicken stock, fresh or canned	Salt
	Pepper

In a medium-size saucepan, melt butter. Add flour and cook 5 minutes to make a roux. Do not brown. Whisk in chicken stock and boil 10 minutes, stirring occasionally until sauce thickens. Whisk in cream and simmer an additional 5 minutes. Strain sauce and stir in mustard. Season with salt and pepper, if necessary.

DUCKLING WITH ORANGES
Club 33
New Orleans Square   *DISNEYLAND Park*

Yield: 2 servings

1 3- to 3½-pound duck
Salt
White pepper
4 cups brown gravy
½ cup orange juice, fresh
  if available
½ lemon, juiced

Orange peel from 3
  oranges, grated
1 tablespoon sugar
¼ teaspoon vinegar
6 whole oranges, peeled
  and segmented
Orange peel from 1 orange,
  cut in thin julienne strips

Preheat oven to 350 degrees.

Wash and remove giblets from duck. Prick skin with a fork and rub both inside and out with salt and white pepper. Place duck on a wire rack in a heavy roasting pan and roast duck for 1½ hours.

While duck is roasting, in a heavy saucepan, melt sugar and cook until lightly browned and caramelized. Add vinegar slowly while sugar is still hot. Should sugar thicken, reheat before adding to sauce.

After 1½ hours, remove duck from oven (don't turn oven off) and pour off any grease from roasting pan, as well as any that has accumulated inside duck. Remove rack and place duck directly in roasting pan. Add brown gravy and return duck to oven for 30 minutes.

Remove duck from oven and place on a serving platter. Keep warm while preparing sauce.

Skim off any fat from brown gravy and place gravy in a small saucepan. Add orange juice, lemon juice, grated orange peel, caramelized sugar, orange segments, and orange peel strips. Bring to a boil and pour some of gravy over duck. Serve remaining sauce on the side.

Note: For Oriental Duck, baste duck with a mixture of ¼ cup each brown sugar, white wine, and soy sauce and 2 tablespoons grated fresh ginger after fat has been poured off and roast for 15 minutes longer.

FREEDOM FIGHTER CHICKEN
Liberty Tree Tavern
Liberty Square   *MAGIC KINGDOM Park*

Yield: 2 servings

2 8-ounce chicken breasts
3 tablespoons butter or
   margarine
4 artichoke hearts
4 mushroom buttons
8 pea pods
¼ cup red bell pepper, cut
   in ¼-inch dice
4 small onions, pearl,
   peeled and steamed till
   tender
1 clove garlic, crushed

⅛ teaspoon thyme
⅛ teaspoon basil
⅛ teaspoon Cajun
   seasoning
1 tablespoon white wine
   Worcestershire sauce
¼ cup white wine
½ cup heavy cream
Salt
Pepper
2 cups spinach, fresh,
   firmly packed

Remove any fat from chicken breasts and cut each breast into 6 equal-sized strips. Wash and cut the vegetables and pat dry.

In a large skillet, melt butter or margarine and sauté chicken strips for 3 to 5 minutes. Add artichoke hearts, mushrooms, pea pods, diced pepper, steamed pearl onions, and garlic and continue to cook for an additional 5 minutes. Season and add remaining ingredients, except spinach. Reduce heat and simmer for 5 minutes.

In a quart of boiling water, add spinach and cook for 1 minute until leaves wilt. Drain well and divide spinach between 2 dinner plates. Arrange in a circle around rim of plate. Spoon half chicken mixture in center of each plate.

Serve immediately.

FETTUCINE DERBY
Disney-MGM Studios Theme Park

Yield: 4 servings

1½ pounds chicken tenders (or chicken breast meat, cut in strips)
¼ cup butter
1 cup red bell pepper, cut in ¼-inch julienne strips
1 cup green bell pepper, cut in ¼-inch julienne strips
2 cups heavy whipping cream
¾ cup Parmesan cheese, freshly grated
4 cups linguine, cooked (8 ounces before cooking)
Salt
Black pepper, freshly ground

Rinse chicken under cold running water and pat dry with paper towels. Cut peppers and prepare remaining ingredients.

Melt butter in a large skillet. Add chicken tenders or strips and sauté lightly until about half done. Add peppers and continue cooking until chicken is fully cooked and peppers are tender but not mushy. Add heavy cream and bring to a boil. Simmer for a minute or two and add pasta, then fold in grated cheese. Season to taste with salt and pepper.

Serve immediately.

CHICKEN ENCHILADAS
Special Events
Disneyland Hotel

Yield: 4 servings

12 corn tortillas
10 ounces red chili sauce
1 whole chicken, cooked, meat removed from bones
¾ cup onion, chopped
3 cups Monterey Jack cheese, shredded
1 cup lettuce, shredded
½ cup tomato, diced

In a small sauté pan, cook onion until tender in a small amount of vegetable oil. Shred chicken meat and combine with cooked onion. Set aside.

Preheat oven to 350 degrees.

Quickly fry corn tortillas in hot vegetable oil for approximately 15 seconds. Tortillas should remain soft. Dip each tortilla in red chili sauce and fill with chicken and onion mixture. Divide chicken evenly among 12 tortillas. Place in a baking dish or casserole, seam side down, and repeat procedure until all tortillas have been fried and stuffed. Pour any remaining red chili sauce over stuffed tortillas and top casserole with shredded Monterey Jack cheese. Bake for 25 to 30 minutes, or until cheese melts and turns golden brown.

Remove casserole from oven and serve immediately with shredded lettuce and diced tomato on the side.

LAND HO
(Cornish Game Hen)
Yacht Club Galley
Disney's Yacht Club Resort

Yield: 4 servings

4 Cornish game hens,
  fresh or frozen (thawed
  if frozen)

1 cup tomato basil sauce
  (recipe follows)
4 lemon halves

Remove any giblets from hens and discard. Thoroughly rinse cavities of hens under cold running water and drain well. With a sharp knife, remove backbone from each hen and discard. Flatten hens with palm of your hand and squeeze half a lemon over each hen. Cover with plastic wrap and refrigerate for 1 hour.

Prepare tomato basil sauce.

To cook game hens, char-broil, barbecue, or roast until wings easily pull apart from bodies (about 30 minutes).

Serve immediately with hot tomato basil sauce.

Tomato Basil Sauce   Yield: 1 quart

2 cans tomatoes, crushed
  (about 20 ounces)
1 cup onion, diced
2 teaspoons garlic, crushed
2 tablespoons butter
2 cups chicken broth

1 teaspoon basil
1 teaspoon sugar
1 tablespoon white wine
Salt
Pepper

In a large pan, sauté onion and garlic in butter until tender. Add remaining ingredients except basil. Simmer over low heat 25 to 30 minutes. Add basil and season with salt and pepper, if necessary.

PAELLA VALENCIANA
Special Events
Disneyland Hotel

Yield: 4 servings

1 8-ounce chicken breast, cut in cubes
¼ cup olive oil
4 ounces lobster meat, cubed
8 ounces octopus, cleaned, sliced
4 medium shrimp, cleaned
2 cloves garlic, crushed
½ cup green bell pepper, chopped
½ cup Spanish onion, chopped
1 cup tomato, diced
⅔ cup white wine
5 cups chicken stock or broth
1 pound rice, long-cooking
½ cup peas, frozen

4 artichoke hearts, canned, quartered
4 ounces Spanish sausage, cooked
8 small black mussels, scrubbed, cleaned
4 fresh clams
4 ounces butter, melted
¼ cup red pimiento
4 sprigs parsley
Salt
Pepper
Paprika
Saffron
Cayenne pepper
Tarragon
Thyme
Rosemary
Basil

Preheat oven to 350 degrees.

In a large heavy-bottom oven-proof pot, heat olive oil. Season cubed chicken with salt, pepper, and paprika and sauté until golden brown. Add lobster, shrimp, garlic, green pepper, onion, and tomato. Continue cooking another 3 to 4 minutes. Add white wine, chicken stock, and the listed spices to taste, as desired. Bring mixture to a boil and add rice. Continue cooking on high heat for 3 minutes. Add green peas and artichoke quarters. Cover pot and place in oven for 30 minutes.

Uncover pot after 30 minutes and stir gently. Add additional chicken stock if necessary to moisten.

Arrange the Spanish sausage, mussels and clams over partially cooked rice mixture. Add melted butter and cover pot. Place back in oven for approximately 15 minutes. Shellfish will steam open and rice will finish cooking.

Remove from oven and garnish with red pimiento and sprigs of parsley.

Serve piping hot in original cooking pot.

POLYNESIAN LUAU CHICKEN
Luau Cove
Disney's Polynesian Resort

Yield: 4 servings

1 whole chicken (2-3 pounds)
1 tablespoon black pepper, ground
1½ tablespoons garlic powder
1½ tablespoons garlic salt
3 tablespoons fennel, ground
1 tablespoon poultry seasoning
3 tablespoons rosemary, ground
1 tablespoon curry powder
2 tablespoons onion powder
1 tablespoon Chinese five-spice powder
2 cups sugar
1 cup chicken base

Wash whole chicken in fresh running water. Pat dry and cut into 8 pieces (2 breasts, 2 legs, 2 wings, 2 thighs).

Combine all seasoning ingredients in a large mixing bowl. Sprinkle on chicken evenly and allow to marinate at least 3 hours, or overnight, if possible.

Preheat oven to 375 degrees.

Place seasoned chicken on a wire rack in a roasting pan. Bake for 20 minutes. Turn down oven to 250 degrees and continue to bake for another 30 to 40 minutes. Chicken will be crispy and golden brown.

ROASTED DUCK WITH ORANGE SAUCE
Top of the World
Disney's Contemporary Resort

Yield: 4 servings

**2 domestic ducklings
(3-pound average)
2 medium onions, peeled,
quartered**

**4 stalks celery, cut in
½-inch dice
Duck seasoning (recipe
follows)
Orange sauce (recipe follows)**

Preheat oven to 375 degrees.

Thoroughly wash ducklings, removing giblets, and pat dry. Rub entire ducks with duck seasoning, inside and out, and stuff cavities with onion and celery. Prick skin of ducks with a fork to allow any fat to escape. Place ducks on a wire baking rack in a large roasting pan. Rub any remaining seasoning over ducks and roast for 1½ to 2 hours.

Test ducks with a fork, and when juices run clear from thigh, ducks are done. Remove from oven and allow ducks to cool for 10 minutes before carving.

Serve with orange sauce.

Duck Seasoning

**1 tablespoon paprika
1 tablespoon white pepper
2 tablespoons onion powder
1 tablespoon thyme
1 tablespoon sage, rubbed
2 teaspoons celery seed**

**2 teaspoons anise
2 teaspoons fennel, ground
2 tablespoons spike
seasoning
1 tablespoon rosemary**

Combine all ingredients well.

Note: Spike seasoning may be found in oriental markets.

Orange Sauce

**2 tablespoons sugar
2 tablespoons vinegar
2 cups brown sauce
2 tablespoons orange juice
concentrate**

**1 teaspoon lemon juice
1 tablespoon cornstarch
4 tablespoons brandy-based
liqueur**

In a heavy saucepan, combine sugar and vinegar and simmer until light brown and slightly caramelized. Add brown sauce, orange juice concentrate, and lemon juice and mix well. Dissolve cornstarch in liqueur and add to sauce. Stir well and simmer until thickened. Simmer 1 to 2 minutes.

Serve with roasted duck. Accompany with wild rice, if desired.

SAUTÉED CHICKEN IN PUFF PASTRY
Special Events
Disney's Yacht and Beach Club Resorts

Yield: 8 servings

4 tablespoons butter
1 tablespoon flour
1¼ cups chicken broth
2 tablespoons sherry
3 cups brown gravy
Salt
Pepper

3 cups chicken meat (about
5 breasts), cut in ½-inch
cubes
8 puff pastry shells, baked,
kept warm
Scallions, chopped, for
garnish

Melt butter in a heavy saucepan. Sauté chicken breasts 3 to 5 minutes on each side, until done. Cook on low heat to prevent browning. Remove chicken and set aside. Add flour and cook 3 to 5 minutes to form a roux. Add chicken broth slowly and stir constantly to prevent lumping. Simmer until thickened. Stir in sherry and brown gravy and season to taste with salt and pepper. Add diced, cooked chicken meat and heat through.

Divide chicken evenly among 8 pastry shells and serve immediately. Garnish with chopped scallions.

Note: cubed turkey meat may be substituted for chicken.

SPIT ROASTED CHICKEN
The Crystal Palace
Main Street, U.S.A.   *MAGIC KINGDOM Park*

Yield: 2 servings

1 2½- to 3-pound roasting
chicken
½ teaspoon salt
2 sprigs rosemary, fresh (or
½ teaspoon dried)

1 sprig thyme, fresh
(or ¼ teaspoon dried)

Preheat oven to 350 degrees.

Open chicken cavity. Remove giblets and neck. Cut off wing-tips and discard. Wash chicken thoroughly inside and out under cold running water. Drain well and pat dry. Rub cavity with salt; stuff with fresh herbs and truss with butcher's twine. Roast for 1 hour, or until done. Baste chicken occasionally with its own natural juices.

Using a sharp knife, split chicken in half before serving.

STUFFED CHICKEN BREAST
Disney-MGM Studios Theme Park

Yield: 6 servings

6 8- to 10-ounce chicken breasts, boneless
Shrimp mousse (recipe follows)

Champagne sauce (recipe follows)

Wash chicken breasts and pat dry. Make a small incision in side of each breast and insert a knife just enough to form a small pocket. Refrigerate and prepare shrimp mousse.

Preheat oven to 350 degrees.

Place shrimp mousse in a pastry bag. Insert tip in each chicken breast pocket and fill with approximately 2 ounces of filling. Use a toothpick to secure opening, if necessary. Lightly flour chicken breasts and sauté in melted butter until lightly browned on both sides. Place chicken in an oven-proof baking dish and bake for 25 minutes. Chicken should be firm to touch and nicely browned.

Serve with champagne sauce.

Shrimp Mousse

1 pound shrimp, raw, peeled, cleaned
2 egg whites
1 cup heavy whipping cream
2 teaspoons parsley, finely chopped

1 teaspoon dill, fresh, finely chopped
1 teaspoon imitation truffles, chopped fine
Salt
White pepper

Thaw, shell, and clean shrimp. Separate eggs and place egg whites in a food processor with a steel blade. Add raw, cleaned shrimp and blend until shrimp is smooth. Add salt and pepper to taste and slowly blend in heavy cream. When mixture thickens, be careful not to over-mix, or cream will curdle. Add remaining ingredients and blend just enough to incorporate.

Champagne Sauce

Yield: 2¼ cups

¼ cup butter
¼ cup flour
2½ cups chicken stock or bouillon
¼ cup champagne

Salt
Pepper
½ cup heavy whipping cream

In a 3-quart saucepan, melt butter and add flour. Cook 5 to 7 minutes, forming a roux. Do not brown. Heat chicken stock and add to roux. Stir well to blend and continue cooking approximately 10 minutes. Add champagne and heavy cream and season with salt and pepper to taste. Simmer for an additional minute and strain through a fine sieve.

TRI-COLOR ANGEL HAIR PASTA
with Chicken Tenders and Pesto Sauce
Caffe Villa Verde
Disneyland Hotel

Yield: 4 servings

4 cups heavy cream
Pesto sauce (recipe follows)
2 pounds tricolor angel
 hair pasta, fresh if
 available (spinach,
 tomato, and egg)
2 tablespoons butter or
 olive oil

1 tablespoon garlic,
 chopped
1 tablespoon shallots,
 chopped
1 pound chicken tenders

Add heavy cream to a 2-quart saucepan. Bring to a slow boil over medium heat. Using a whisk, add 1 cup of pesto sauce, mixing well. Remove from heat and set aside.

Cook pasta in boiling water. When al dente, drain and rinse with cold water. Set aside.

In a large skillet, add butter or olive oil and heat over medium-high heat. Add garlic and shallots and sauté for about 1 minute. Add chicken tenders and sauté until firm and lightly browned (4 to 5 minutes). Add pesto and cream mixture and bring to a simmer. Cook an additional 2 to 3 minutes, until chicken is fully cooked. Add pasta and continue cooking only long enough to heat through.

Serve hot.

Pesto Sauce
1 pound basil leaves, fresh
¼ cup pine nuts
¼ cup Parmesan cheese,
 freshly grated

¼ cup garlic, chopped
¼ cup olive oil

In a food processor with a steel blade, combine all ingredients. Blend until a stiff puree has been made. Set aside.

TURKEY BURGERS
50's Prime Time Cafe
Disney-MGM Studios Theme Park

Yield: 4 servings

2 pounds turkey meat,
  ground
2 tablespoons vegetable
  seasoning
2 eggs, beaten
4 rolls, whole-wheat or deli

4 lettuce leaves
4 tomato slices
4 onion slices
Pickle slices
Cranberry chutney (or
  cranberry sauce)

Season ground turkey with vegetable seasoning and mix well with beaten eggs. Form into 4 8-ounce patties and grill or broil for 4 to 5 minutes on each side.

When burgers are fully cooked, serve immediately on toasted rolls with fresh leaf lettuce, sliced tomato, onion, pickles and cranberry chutney.

TURKEY CHILI
Mazie's Pantry
Disneyland Hotel

Yield: 10 to 12 servings

4 pounds turkey meat,
  ground
1½ cups onion, diced
2 tablespoons vegetable oil
2 tablespoons chili powder
1 tablespoon cumin, ground
1 teaspoon salt
1 teaspoon pepper

2 28-ounce cans tomatoes,
  diced
2 16-ounce cans red kidney
  beans, drained
2 10-ounce cans green
  beans, French-cut,
  drained

In an 8-quart sauce pot, heat oil and sauté onion until tender (about 10 minutes). Add ground turkey and sauté 8 to 10 minutes, breaking up any large chunks. Add seasoning and mix well. Add remaining ingredients and bring to a boil. Reduce heat and simmer for 50 to 60 minutes. Remove from heat and adjust seasoning.

TURKEY PICCATA
Tony's Town Square Restaurant
Main Street, U.S.A.   *MAGIC KINGDOM Park*

Yield: 4 servings

1½ pounds turkey breast
cutlets, 8 pieces (about
3 ounces each)
Flour mixture (recipe
follows)
12 ounces mushroom
buttons, sliced (about
1 cup)

½ cup lemon juice, fresh
¾ cup Chablis wine
1½ cups hot water
2 chicken bouillon cubes
¾ cup butter or margarine
1 pound fettucine, cooked
(optional)

Lightly pound turkey breast cutlets between 2 pieces of waxed paper to a thickness of about ¼ inch. Dust with flour mixture and sauté in a hot skillet with melted butter, about 3 minutes on each side. Remove from pan and set aside.

Add sliced mushrooms to pan and sauté 2 to 3 minutes. Carefully add water and bouillon cubes to hot frying pan, being careful not to spatter fat. Add lemon juice and wine and bring mixture to a boil. Reduce heat and simmer about 15 minutes. Reduce liquid by half the amount first added to the pan. Return turkey cutlets to sauce and simmer about 5 minutes, or until the turkey is fully cooked and tender.

Note: Turkey piccata is best served on fettucine noodles with sauce.

Flour Mixture

½ cup flour
⅛ teaspoon white pepper
¼ teaspoon salt

1 teaspoon vegetable
seasoning

Sift all ingredients together.

TURKEY WING PIE
Yacht Club Galley
Disney's Yacht Club Resort

Yield: 4 servings

1½ cups carrots, diced
1½ cups potatoes, cut in
  ½-inch cubes
1 cup onions, diced
1 tablespoon butter
2 cups turkey meat, cooked,
  diced
1 tablespoon white wine
3 12-ounce jars turkey
  gravy

Salt
Pepper
4 turkey wings, cooked
Butter
4 pieces puff pastry, cut to
  fit tops of individual
  12-ounce oven-proof
  crocks
1 egg, lightly beaten

In a small saucepan, combine carrots and potatoes with cold water and bring to a boil. Simmer until tender and remove from heat. Drain well and set aside.

In a large skillet, melt butter and sauté onion until tender. Add turkey meat, vegetables, white wine, and gravy. Bring to a boil and simmer for 5 minutes. Season with salt and pepper and remove from heat.

Preheat oven to 375 degrees.

Lightly butter 4 individual oven-proof crocks and place a cooked turkey wing in each. Evenly divide turkey and vegetable mixture among crocks and cover each with a piece of puff pastry. Allow part of each turkey wing to stick through pastry. Brush with beaten egg and bake for 20 to 30 minutes, or until crust is golden brown.

MEATS

MEATS

BEEF FILET WITH FRESH GROUND PEPPER
Chefs de France
France   EPCOT Center

Yield: 6 servings

6 8-ounce beef fillets
1 tablespoon butter
1 tablespoon olive oil
3 tablespoons pepper,
  freshly ground
Salt

6 tablespoons brandy
¾ cup dry red wine
1 shallot, chopped
1½ cups veal or beef stock
  or broth
1 tablespoon butter

Trim any excess fat from fillets if necessary. Heat butter and olive oil in a skillet. Dip steaks in pepper and season with salt. Pan-fry in hot butter and oil until cooked as desired, turning to evenly brown both sides. Add brandy and flambé. Remove steaks from skillet to a serving platter and keep warm.

Add wine and shallots to skillet and sauté 5 minutes. Add stock and butter and cook approximately 2 minutes longer. Sauce should thicken slightly.

Serve sauce with steak.

BEEF SATE WITH PEANUT SAUCE
Special Events
Disneyland Hotel

Yield: 4 to 6 servings

2 pounds beef tenderloin
32 bamboo skewers
½ cup peanut butter
¼ cup coconut cream

⅓ cup chutney
1⅛ cups water
Dash soy sauce

Soak bamboo skewers in cold water for 1 hour to prevent burning when cooked.

Cut tenderloin into 1-ounce strips about 5 inches long. Thread meat onto skewers and refrigerate until ready to cook.

In a small saucepan, combine peanut butter, coconut cream, chutney, water, and soy sauce. Bring to a boil and reduce heat to a simmer. Stir well and remove from heat when well blended.

Broil or grill meat, as desired, and serve with hot peanut sauce.

BEEF STEW WITH BISCUIT
Chef Mickey's Village Restaurant
Disney Village Marketplace

Yield: 4 servings

2 pounds stew meat, cubed
4 tablespoons oil
4 tablespoons flour
½ cup onions, cut in ½-inch
 pieces
½ cup carrots, halved
 lengthwise and cut
 on bias
½ cup celery, cut on bias
3 tablespoons tomato paste
4 beef bouillon cubes

2 cups water
3 cups brown gravy
1 teaspoon paprika
1 bay leaf
1 teaspoon garlic,
 granulated
Salt
Pepper
1 cup peas, cooked
Baking powder biscuits
 (recipe follows)

In a heavy-gauge stew pot, add 4 tablespoons of oil and place on high heat. Dust stew meat with flour and quickly sear, a few pieces at a time, until all meat has been lightly browned. Add onions, carrots, celery, and water to pot with stew meat and simmer 15 minutes. Add remaining ingredients, except peas. Mix well and simmer on low heat until meat is tender and vegetables are cooked. Remove bay leaf and adjust seasoning, if necessary.

Just before serving, add cooked peas and serve stew over baking powder biscuits.

Baking Powder Biscuits

2 cups flour, sifted
1 tablespoon sugar
4 teaspoons baking powder
½ teaspoon salt

½ cup shortening
1 egg, beaten
⅔ cup milk

Preheat oven to 425 degrees.

Sift together flour, sugar, baking powder, and salt into a bowl. Cut in shortening with a pastry cutter or two knives. Combine milk and eggs and mix into flour mixture with a fork, just enough to moisten flour. Turn dough onto a lightly floured surface and knead gently. Roll dough to a ¾-inch thickness. Cut with a 2-inch figured cutter and place on an ungreased baking tray.

Bake approximately 12 minutes, or until golden brown.

BRAISED SHORT RIBS
Plaza Inn
Main Street, U.S.A.   *DISNEYLAND Park*

Yield: 4 servings

4 pounds beef short ribs
Salt
Pepper, freshly ground
1 cup celery, diced
1 cup carrots, diced
1 cup onions, diced
1 clove garlic, finely
  chopped

5 tablespoons flour
1 cup tomato puree
1 bay leaf
¼ teaspoon thyme
2 cups dry red wine
4 cups chicken or
  beef stock

Preheat oven to 350 degrees.

Trim any excess fat from ribs, if necessary. Evenly season both sides with salt and pepper. Place ribs in deep roasting pan and roast for 1 hour.

After 1 hour, add celery, carrot, and onions to roasting pan and sprinkle with flour. Roast an additional 30 minutes. Add puree, bay leaf, thyme, red wine, and stock. Mix all ingredients in roasting pan and bake 1 to 1½ hours longer, or until the meat is tender.

Remove meat and strain gravy. Spoon off any excess fat and serve gravy with ribs.

BRIDGETOWN BEEF FAJITAS
Bridgetown Broiler
Disney's Caribbean Beach Resort

Yield: 8 servings

2 pounds beef skirt steak
Marinade (recipe follows)
1 large green bell pepper, julienne
2 large onions, julienne
1 tablespoon soybean oil
1 head iceberg lettuce, shredded

1 cup guacamole
1¼ cups mild cheddar cheese, grated
1 cup salsa
1 cup sour cream
8 large flour tortillas

Trim skirt steak of any excess fat and cut into ¼-inch strips. Add steak to marinade and refrigerate overnight.

Heat a large skillet with soybean oil and quickly sauté green pepper and onion until tender and lightly browned. Remove from skillet and keep warm.

Drain skirt steak and add to hot skillet. Sauté for 5 to 7 minutes, or until cooked as desired. Remove from pan and keep warm with onions and peppers.

Warm flour tortillas on a cookie sheet in a 250-degree oven for approximately 5 minutes. Do not let tortillas dry out.

When ready to serve, place warm tortillas, cooked steak, onions, and peppers on table, family style, with shredded iceberg lettuce, guacamole, cheddar sheese, salsa, and sour cream. Fill tortillas as desired.

Marinade

½ cup soy sauce
½ cup water
2 tablespoons soybean oil
¼ cup scallions, chopped

1 bunch cilantro, chopped
2 limes
1 clove garlic, crushed

In a 2-quart bowl combine soy sauce, water, soybean oil, chopped scallions, chopped cilantro, the juice from 2 limes and crushed garlic. Blend well and set aside.

CHILI AND BEANS
Concourse Grille
Disney's Contemporary Resort

Yield: 1 gallon

2 pounds ground beef
2¼ cups Spanish onion,
**   coarsely chopped**
½ teaspoon garlic,
**   granulated**
2 teaspoons chili powder
**   (more, if desired)**
¼ teaspoon cumin, ground

1 tablespoon Spanish
**   paprika**
2 cups tomato ketchup
3 cups tomato puree
3½ cups pinto or kidney
**   beans, cooked, drained**
1 cup bread crumbs, dry

Sauté beef and onions in a 1½-gallon sauce pot until meat is lightly browned. Add all spices, ketchup, puree, and beef stock. Mix well and bring to a boil. Reduce heat to simmer and cook covered, stirring occasionally, for 1 hour. Add drained beans and bring back to a boil. Add bread crumbs and remove from heat. Add salt and pepper to taste and stir well.

Note: This recipe can be cut in half if a smaller amount is desired.

COTTAGE PIE
Rose & Crown Pub & Dining Room
United Kingdom   EPCOT Center

Yield: 4 servings

¼ cup butter
1 cup onion, diced
1½ pounds lean
**   beef, ground**
Salt

Pepper
¼ teaspoon savory, ground
1 cup brown gravy
2 cups potatoes, mashed
Additional butter

Heat ¼ cup butter in a 9-inch skillet. Add onion and cook until lightly browned, stirring. Add beef, salt, pepper, and savory and continue cooking 5 minutes longer. Stir in gravy and heat until bubbling. Spoon into a buttered 8-cup flat casserole dish. Top meat mixture with mashed potatoes. Dot with pieces of butter.

Bake at 400 degrees for 30 minutes, or until potatoes are lightly browned.

FETTUCINE AND MEATBALLS
Tony's Town Square Restaurant
Main Street, U.S.A.   *MAGIC KINGDOM Park*

Yield: 6 servings

1½ pounds fettucini, fresh
or dried
Tony's house sauce (recipe
follows)

26 Tony's Italian meatballs
(recipe follows)

Prepare Tony's house sauce and Tony's meatballs.

Meanwhile, cook 1½ pounds of either fresh or dried fettucini according to package directions. Drain and serve fettucini with Tony's house sauce topped with Tony's Italian meatballs.

Tony's House Sauce

1 celery stalk, diced (⅔ cup)
1 small onion, diced
(1½ cups)
1½ teaspoons garlic,
chopped
⅛ cup extra-virgin olive oil
12 ounces tomato paste
10¾ ounces tomato puree
2 28-ounce cans tomatoes,
whole, cut in half with
juice
½ teaspoon salt

¼ teaspoon black pepper,
freshly ground
½ teaspoon sweet basil,
dried
½ teaspoon oregano
1½ bay leaves
¼ cup sugar
Dash thyme, dried
Dash chili powder
Dash rosemary, dried
Dash Spanish paprika

In a large pot, sauté celery, onion, and garlic in olive oil. Add all other ingredients. Remember to use juice from both cans of tomatoes. Simmer for 1½ hours. Taste and correct seasoning, if necessary.

Note: Fresh herbs may be used instead of dried herbs. When using fresh herbs, use half the amount and taste for additional seasoning. Add more, if necessary. Flavors of fresh herbs are much more intense than those of dried herbs; use very carefully.

(continued on next page)

FETTUCINE AND MEATBALLS
(continued from previous page)

Tony's Italian Meatballs

1½ pounds ground beef
½ pound Italian sausage,
  bulk
¼ cup onions, minced
½ cup bread crumbs
¾ cup water
1 teaspoon salt
½ teaspoon black pepper,
  ground

Yield: approximately 26 meatballs,
  depending on size

2 teaspoons oregano
1½ teaspoons garlic,
  granulated
2 teaspoons parsley flakes,
  dried
1 egg
¼ cup Parmesan cheese,
  grated
½ teaspoon caraway seeds
2 teaspoons basil leaves

Preheat oven to 350 degrees.
Combine ingredients and mix thoroughly. Refrigerate for 4 hours before making into meatballs.
Prepare meatballs about the size of golf balls and place on a cookie sheet side by side. Cook in oven for 15 to 20 minutes, or until firm to touch.

TONY'S MEATBALL SUB SANDWICH
Tony's Town Square Restaurant
Main Street, U.S.A.   MAGIC KINGDOM Park

Yield: 6 servings

6 sub rolls (or hoagie rolls)
18 meatballs (recipe above)
2 cups spaghetti sauce, any
  variety

6 1-ounce slices mozzarella
  cheese

Preheat oven to 350 degrees.
In a 4-quart saucepan, heat sauce. Place meatballs in sauce and cook for 5 minutes. Slice sub rolls lengthwise and put 3 meatballs in each roll with an equal amount of sauce. Top meatballs with a slice of cheese and bake on a cookie sheet for 5 minutes, or until roll is warm and cheese has melted.
Serve immediately.

FILETTO PIZZAIOLO
Flagler's
Disney's Grand Floridian Beach Resort

Yield: 4 servings

4 8-ounce beef tenderloin
  steaks
2 tablespoons olive oil
¼ cup red wine

½ cup marinara sauce
Pinch oregano
Pinch basil
1 teaspoon garlic, chopped

Cut each steak into 3 equal parts, forming 3 medallions per steak. Sauté quickly in a hot skillet with olive oil to desired degree of doneness. Remove medallions from skillet and keep warm.

Deglaze pan with red wine and add remaining ingredients. Simmer 3 to 4 minutes. Divide sauce among 4 serving plates and place 3 tenderloin medallions on top of sauce on each plate.

Serve immediately

FRESH PORK SAUSAGE
Crockett's Tavern
Disney's Fort Wilderness Resort and Campground

Yield: 18 2-inch patties

2 pounds pork butt
½ pound pork trimmings
1 tablespoon salt
1 teaspoon black pepper
1 tablespoon rubbed sage

½ teaspoon ginger
1 teaspoon nutmeg
1½ teaspoons thyme
½ teaspoon cayenne pepper
½ ice water

Grind pork butt and trimmings through a ³⁄₁₆-inch grinder plate and place in a mixing bowl. A food processor with a steel blade will also chop meat fine enough for sausage, but the final product will be a little more tough.

Add all spices and blend by hand or with a mixer until well incorporated. Add ice water and mix to consistency of meatloaf. Form meat into 2-inch patties and sauté in a hot skillet until fully cooked. Keep all unused raw meat refrigerated and well covered to prevent spoiling.

Serve with your favorite breakfast foods.

GRILLED PORK CHOPS
Disney-MGM Studios Theme Park

Yield: 6 servings

12 center-cut pork chops, ½
   inch thick (2 per person)
2 cups hot pepper relish
2 cups hollandaise sauce
   (recipe follows)

Salt
Pepper

Season pork chops on both sides with salt and pepper. Charcoal-broil or barbecue until fully cooked.

Top each chop with 2 tablespoons hot pepper relish and 2 tablespoons hollandaise sauce and serve immediately.

Hollandaise Sauce   Yield 2 cups

1¾ cups butter, clarified,
   (from 2 pounds of whole
   butter)
6 egg yolks
2 teaspoons water
1 tablespoon lemon juice,
   fresh

¼ teaspoon Worcestershire
   sauce
Salt
Cayenne pepper

Melt butter in a double boiler or microwave. Do not allow butter to boil and do not stir while melting. Once melted, let butter stand 30 minutes while milk solids settle to bottom and foam rises to top. To clarify butter, skim top and discard foam. Carefully remove yellow oil, leaving white milk solids on bottom of pan. Reserve only yellow oil part of butter. Keep warm but not hot.

Place egg yolks in a stainless steel bowl with water and lemon juice. Place bowl over a pan of hot, not boiling, water and whisk egg yolks until pale yellow and foamy. Remove eggs from heat any time they appear too hot, or they may scramble. Slowly add clarified butter to eggs, in a steady stream, whipping after each addition. Return eggs to hot water while whipping to help incorporate and thicken sauce. Add butter slowly, or sauce could separate. Add more warm water to sauce if it becomes too thick. The final result should be like runny mayonnaise. When all butter has been incorporated, add Worcestershire sauce and season with salt and cayenne pepper.

Serve immediately.

HEARTY CHILI
Yacht Club Galley
Disney's Yacht Club Resort

Yield: 8 servings

2½ pounds top round beef, cut in 1-inch cubes
2 cups onion, chopped
1½ cups red, yellow, and green bell peppers, cut in ½-inch dice
2 tablespoons garlic, minced

5 cups beef stock or broth
4 teaspoons chili powder
2 teaspoons cumin
2 cups kidney beans, rinsed, drained
2 tablespoons vegetable oil
Salt
Pepper

Heat oil over high heat. Add top round and sauté for 4 to 5 minutes, or until all meat is browned. Add onions, peppers, and garlic and cook an additional 5 minutes. Add beef stock and simmer until meat is tender (about 1 hour). When meat is tender, add chili powder, cumin, and beans. Season with salt and pepper, if necessary.

Note: For a slightly thicker chili, add 2 tablespoons tomato paste when meat is tender. Simmer 5 minutes and add spices.

JAMBALAYA
(Pork)
French Market Restaurant
New Orleans Square DISNEYLAND *Park*

Yield: 6 to 8 servings

1 pound boneless pork, fresh, diced into ½-inch cubes
3 tablespoons vegetable oil
¼ teaspoon black pepper, freshly ground
¼ teaspoon thyme, dried
¼ teaspoon garlic powder
1 16-ounce can tomatoes, crushed
4 cups water
1¼ cups rice, uncooked
2 chicken bouillon cubes
1½ cups onion, diced
1 cup celery, diced
1 cup green bell pepper, diced
¾ cup zucchini, diced
1 teaspoon yellow chili pepper
¼ cup scallions, chopped
1 tablespoon parsley, chopped
1 cup ham, diced
1 cup Polish sausage, cooked, diced
1 cup Italian sausage, cooked, diced
1 cup okra, frozen, cut
1½ cups small shrimp, cooked

In a large saucepan, sauté pork in oil over medium heat for 15 minutes, stirring occasionally. Add pepper, thyme, garlic powder, and tomatoes. Cover and cook for 15 minutes. Add water, rice, bouillon cubes, onions, celery, green pepper, zucchini, chili peppers, scallions, and parsley. Bring to a boil. Stir to blend ingredients, cover and simmer for 10 to 15 minutes. Stir once or twice and add remaining meat ingredients. Cook for another 10 minutes and add okra and shrimp.

Heat well and serve hot.

LAMB SHANKS
50's Prime Time Cafe
Disney-MGM Studios Theme Park

Yield: 4 servings

4 large lamb shanks
1 cup vegetable oil
Salt
Pepper
1 clove garlic, chopped
½ cup carrots, roughly
  chopped
½ cup onion, roughly
  chopped

½ cup celery, roughly
  chopped
1 small tomato, roughly
  chopped
¼ cup brandy
1 tablespoon rosemary
3 cups brown sauce (recipe
  follows)

Prepare brown sauce.

In a large skillet or cast-iron pan, heat oil. Lightly season both sides of lamb shanks with salt and pepper and sauté in hot oil until well browned on both sides. Remove from oil and set aside. Remove all but about 3 tablespoons of oil from pan and add garlic, carrots, onion, celery, and tomato. Sauté approximately 5 minutes and add brandy. Reduce liquid by half and add brown sauce. Bring to a boil and simmer 3 to 5 minutes.

Preheat oven to 375 degrees.

Place lamb shanks in a roasting pan and add hot sauce. Cover with foil and bake for 1½ to 2 hours, or until meat pulls away from bone easily.

Remove from oven and serve hot with brown sauce.

Brown Sauce

Yield: 3 cups

3 cups water
2 teaspoons beef base or
  bouillon (follow label
  directions for 3 cups of
  water)

3 tablespoons butter
3 tablespoons flour

In a 1-quart saucepan, melt butter and add flour. Cook for approximately 10 minutes. Stir constantly and brown lightly. Dissolve beef base in water and add to saucepan with roux. Cook approximately 15 minutes, until sauce is thickened and smooth.

LO MEIN CHILI
Coral Isle Cafe
Disney's Polynesian Resort

Yield: 2 servings

½ pound ground beef
¼ cup onions, diced
1 tablespoon garlic powder
2 teaspoons salt
1 teaspoon cayenne pepper
Dash Tabasco sauce
2 teaspoons chili powder
2 teaspoons cumin

1 cup tomatoes, diced
1 tablespoon tomato paste
¼ cup water
2 cups lo mein noodles, cooked
¼ cup scallions, sliced
¼ cup cheddar cheese, shredded

Brown ground beef in a 10-inch skillet (about 10 minutes). Drain any excess fat. Add diced onions and spices. Sauté 3 to 5 minutes. Slowly add diced tomatoes, tomato paste, and water. Reduce heat and simmer for 8 to 10 minutes, stirring constantly. Remove from heat.

To serve, place 1 cup of cooked lo mein noodles in a bowl. Top with half the chili and garnish top with sliced scallions and grated cheese.

MEATLOAF
Chef Mickey's Village Restaurant
Disney Village Marketplace

Yield: 6 servings

2 pounds ground beef
1 pound ground pork
1½ cups onion, diced
⅛ teaspoon garlic, granulated
2 cups bread crumbs, fresh
⅔ cup cold water

⅛ teaspoon thyme
¼ cup parsley, chopped
1 whole egg
1 teaspoon Worcestershire sauce
⅛ teaspoon salt

Soak bread crumbs in cold water and set aside. Sauté diced onion until tender. Set aside and allow to cool.

Preheat oven to 350 degrees.

In a large bowl, combine ground beef, ground pork, onions, granulated garlic, and bread crumbs mixed with water. Mix well and add remaining ingredients. Mix well and mold into loaves. Form in either loaf pans or in a meat pan with sides high enough to hold juices.

Bake for 45 minutes to 1 hour.

MESQUITE GRILLED PORTERHOUSE
Yachtman's Steakhouse
Disney's Yacht Club Resort

Yield: 4 servings

4 20-ounce porterhouse
  steaks
2 cups Yachtman's
  Steakhouse steak sauce
  (recipe follows)

Barbecue grill with
  mesquite charcoal

Light grill and allow coals to burn to a rich red glow (about 20 minutes). When ready, grill steaks to your desired specifications. Serve with steak sauce.

Yachtman's Steakhouse Steak Sauce   Yield: 2 cups

4 to 6 ounces butter
2 tablespoons shallots,
  diced
1 sprig thyme, fresh
⅓ cup brown gravy
2 tablespoons tomato paste
½ cup prepared steak sauce

1 tablespoon distilled
  vinegar
1 tablespoon mesquite
  seasoning
⅔ cup water
Salt
Pepper

Lightly sauté shallots and thyme in 1 ounce of butter. Add remaining butter and remaining ingredients. Simmer for 10 to 15 minutes and add salt and pepper to taste.

Serve with your favorite grilled steak.

MUFFULETTA
Tony's Town Square Restaurant
Main Street, U.S.A.   *MAGIC KINGDOM Park*

Yield: 2 servings

1 6-inch loaf muffuletta
  bread
3 thin slices mortadella,
  (about ½ ounce each)
3 thin slices Genoa salami
  (about ½ ounce each)
3 thin slices smoked ham
  (about ½ ounce each)

1 slice mozzarella cheese
1 slice provolone cheese
¼ cup green olives, stuffed,
  sliced, drained
2 teaspoons extra-virgin
  olive oil

Preheat oven to 350 degrees.

Cut bread in half, sandwich style. Brush each half with olive oil. On bottom slice of bread, layer mortadella, salami, ham, mozzarella, provolone, and sliced olives. Cover with top half of bread. Place in oven for 8 to 10 minutes, or until cheese melts and entire sandwich is hot. Remove from oven and cut into squares.

Serve warm.

Note: If muffuletta bread is not available, one large round or oval loaf of Italian, rye, or sourdough, approximately 8 to 10 inches in diameter, may be sustituted. If a larger loaf of bread is used, double the filling ingredients.

NEW ENGLAND STYLE BOILED DINNER
The Land Grille Room
The Land   *EPCOT Center*

Yield: 5 servings

2 pounds beef brisket,
  boiled and trimmed
5 baby bok choy
2 medium parsnips
15 baby carrots

5 small red skin potatoes
1 quart beef consommé
  (recipe follows)
1 small bunch basil, fresh
Horseradish, freshly grated

In a 4-quart pot with a lid, place beef brisket with enough water to cover meat. Bring water to a boil and reduce heat to a gentle simmer. Cook for 1½ to 2 hours, or until meat is tender when pierced with a fork. Remove beef from pan and allow to cool. Trim any excess fat and set aside.

Cut baby bok choy in half. Peel and dice parsnips. Clean carrots. Wash and slice potatoes into ¼-inch slices. Peel and grate horseradish.

In a large saucepan with 2 cups of beef consommé, add parsnips, carrots, and potatoes. Simmer until tender but still firm. Add baby bok choy and continue to cook for another 5 minutes. Remove from heat and keep warm.

In a shallow sauté pan, add remaining beef consommé and warm brisket. When ready to serve, slice brisket.

Serve in shallow serving bowls with an assortment of vegetables, potatoes and sliced brisket. Garnish with fresh basil and freshly grated horseradish.

Notes: Prepared horseradish may be substituted if fresh is not available.
Regular bok choy may be substituted for baby bok choy.
If parsnips are not available, substitute another root vegetable like turnips.

Consommé   Yield: 1 quart

1½ quarts beef stock or
  broth, cold
¼ cup carrots

¼ cup celery
¼ cup onions
¼ cup egg whites

Combine vegetables in a food processor with a steel blade and blend until finely chopped. Place chopped vegetables in a soup pot and add egg whites. Mix well. Add cold stock and stir everything together well. Bring mixture to a simmer, do not boil, and allow to cook for 45 to 50 minutes. Strain consommé through a fine cheesecloth after 45 to 50 minutes and refrigerate any unused portion.

MUSHROOM WRAPPED TENDERLOIN OF BEEF
The Land Grille Room
The Land   EPCOT Center

Yield: 8 servings

28 ounces beef tenderloin
4 ounces beef tenderloin
  trimmings
4 cups white mushrooms,
  chopped
3 cups shiitake mushrooms,
  chopped
8 tablespoons basil, fresh,
  chopped
4 tablespoons thyme, fresh,
  chopped
4 tablespoons butter or
  margarine

2 egg whites
¼ teaspoon salt
1 teaspoon garlic powder
1 teaspoon onion powder
2 large bags spinach (or
  enough good leaves to
  wrap the tenderloin
  strips)
4 tablespoons parsley, fresh,
  chopped
4 tablespoons pepper,
  freshly cracked

Trim beef tenderloin. Cut in half lengthwise, then cut each half in half again lengthwise, forming 4 cigar-shaped strips. Refrigerate.

Steam chopped mushrooms in a steamer for 4 to 6 minutes. Remove and pat dry. Place steamed mushrooms, tenderloin trimmings, basil, thyme, and margarine in a food processor with a steel blade and process until smooth. Add egg whites, salt, garlic, and onion powder and continue blending until well incorporated. Refrigerate 1 hour.

Place cold mushroom mixture between 2 sheets of cellophane. Roll cellophane with a rolling pin until an even sheet of mushroom mixture, about ¼ inch thick, is formed between the 2 sheets. Refrigerate.

Remove stems from spinach and tightly wrap each strip of tenderloin with spinach leaves. Place refrigerated mushroom mixture on a flat surface and remove top layer of cellophane. Place wrapped tenderloin pieces on mushroom sheet and, using edge of cellophane, roll mushroom mixture around tenderloin. Carefully remove mushroom-wrapped tenderloin and roll in a mixture of chopped parsley and freshly cracked pepper.

Return wrapped meat to cellophane and roll up tightly. Tie ends of cellophane and tie several spots in center of beef with butcher twine. Refrigerate for 1 hour to firm up roll.

Place tenderloin wrapped in cellophane in a pot of boiling water. Remove from heat immediately and allow water temperature to cool to 145 degrees. This should take approximately 45 minutes. Remove tenderloin from water and untie string. Do not remove cellophane. Slice tenderloin through cellophane and remove only after sliced.

Serve immediately.

ORANGE BEEF
Papeete Bay Verandah
Disney's Polynesian Resort

Yield: 2 servings

8 ounces flank steak
1 egg, beaten
1 tablespoon cornstarch
1 tablespoon flour
1 cup oil
2 scallions, chopped
2 tablespoons soy sauce

½ cup orange juice
1 tablespoon sugar
¼ cup water
2 chili peppers, dry
   (optional)
Orange slices

Slice flank steak into ½-inch strips. Combine cornstarch and flour. Dip steak first in cornstarch and flour mixture, then in beaten egg. Allow to stand for five minutes while oil heats in a heavy skillet. Brown a few pieces of meat at a time until all meat has been cooked. Set aside and keep warm.

In another clean skillet or wok, sauté scallions (and chili peppers, if used) in a small amount of oil for about 2 minutes. Combine soy sauce, orange juice, sugar and water and slowly pour into skillet. Cook 2 to 3 minutes, or until mixture thickens. Pour over warm beef and garnish with orange slices.

OSSO BUCCO (Veal)
Club 33
New Orleans Square　　*DISNEYLAND Park*

Yield: 4 to 6 servings

½ cup flour
1 teaspoon seasoning salt
¼ teaspoon white pepper
2 veal shanks, (about 3
   pounds), cut into 1½-inch
   pieces
¼ cup vegetable oil
1 clove garlic, finely
   chopped
2 tablespoons onion, finely
   chopped

1 quart brown veal stock or
   beef broth
½ cup dry white wine
2 tablespoons tomato puree
½ teaspoon thyme
½ teaspoon lemon peel,
   grated
2 tablespoons parsley,
   chopped
Hot cooked rice

Mix together flour, salt, and pepper. Dredge veal shank pieces in flour mixture and brown on all sides in a hot skillet with oil. Remove to a covered casserole dish and keep warm.

(continued on next page)

OSSO BUCCO
(continued from previous page)

Preheat oven to 350 degrees.

In the same oil, sauté garlic and onion until lightly browned. Stir in remaining seasoned flour and cook for 2 to 3 minutes. Gradually add stock, wine, and tomato puree, stirring until mixture boils. Remove from heat and add thyme, lemon peel, and chopped parsley. Pour sauce over veal shanks in the casserole dish.

Cover and bake for 1 hour, or until veal is very tender.

Serve with hot rice.

STEAK TARTARE
Yachtman's Steakhouse
Disney's Yacht Club Resort

Yield: 4 servings

10 ounces beef tenderloin, finely chopped

2 tablespoons capers, finely chopped

1 tablespoon anchovies, finely chopped

2 egg yolks, raw

1 teaspoon Worcestershire sauce

2 tablespoons Dijon® Mustard

Tabasco sauce

Salt

Pepper

Capers, chopped

Red onion, finely chopped

Egg white and yolk, cooked, finely chopped

Chop tenderloin very fine with a knife. Add finely chopped anchovies, capers, egg yolks, Worcestershire sauce, and mustard. Season with Tabasco, salt, and pepper to taste.

Serve well chilled with toast points and garnish with additional chopped capers, finely chopped red onion, finely chopped cooked egg whites and finely chopped cooked egg yolks.

ROAST PRIME RIB
King Stefan's Banquet Hall
Fantasyland   *MAGIC KINGDOM Park*

Yield: 10 to 12 servings

1 10-pound prime rib roast, trimmed, tied, with or without bones

2 tablespoons black pepper, crushed
2 tablespoons kosher salt

Preheat oven to 325 degrees.

Mix salt and pepper together and rub evenly over roast. Place prime rib in a roasting pan and cook approximately 2 hours and 45 minutes.

Note: A good rule of thumb to remember for rare roast beef is to start with meat at room temperature and cook for 20 minutes per pound.

Internal Meat Temperature Guide:
Rare to Medium Rare . . . . .125-130 degrees
Medium. . . . . .135 degrees
Medium Well . . . . .145 degrees
Well. . . . . .145 degrees and above

Note: Roasted meats have what is called "carryover cooking." Roasts will continue to cook after they are removed from the oven, raising the internal temperature as much as 5 to 10 degrees. Keep this in mind when cooking roasts, and always allow meat to rest 15 to 20 minutes before carving.

SCALOPPINE DI VITELLO AL LIMONE
(Veal Piccata)
L'Originale Alfredo di Roma Ristorante
Italy   EPCOT Center

Yield: 4 servings

**1 pound veal steak, thinly
  sliced, pounded flat**
**⅓ cup flour, (seasoned with
  salt and pepper to taste)**
2 tablespoons olive oil
2 tablespoons lemon juice

2 tablespoons white wine
¼ cup butter
**2 tablespoons parsley, finely
  chopped**
½ lemon, sliced

Heat olive oil in a large skillet until very hot. Coat veal with seasoned flour and shake off any excess. Sauté veal in hot olive oil until lightly browned on both sides (3 to 5 minutes total). Remove veal from pan and place on a warm serving platter.

Deglaze pan with wine and lemon juice, scraping any browned pieces from the pan. Add butter and parsley and continue cooking only long enough to melt butter. Return veal to skillet and turn once to coat with sauce.

Return veal to serving platter and serve immediately with sliced lemon.

SIRLOIN STEAK WITH HERB SAUCE
Liberty Tree Tavern
Liberty Square   MAGIC KINGDOM Park

Yield: 6 servings

**6 12-ounce sirloin steaks (or
  steak of your choice),
  broiled or grilled, as
  desired**
**2 12-ounce cans brown
  gravy**
2 beef bouillon cubes
¼ cup Dijon® Mustard
1 clove garlic, chopped

**¼ teaspoon black pepper,
  freshly ground**
**1 tablespoon
  Worcestershire sauce**
**1 tablespoon butter or
  margarine**
10 large mushrooms, sliced
¼ cup brandy

In a 4-quart saucepan, mix brown gravy, beef bouillon cubes, Dijon mustard, garlic, pepper, and Worcestershire sauce. Simmer for 10 to 15 minutes, stirring occasionally to prevent sticking. In a small skillet, melt butter and sauté sliced mushrooms. Add brandy and flambé quickly. Add mushrooms to sauce and mix well.

Serve sauce over broiled or grilled steak with a baked potato and fresh vegetables.

STEAK AND KIDNEY PIE
Rose & Crown Pub & Dining Room
United Kingdom   EPCOT Center

Yield: 4 to 6 servings

1½ pounds sirloin or top round steak, lean, boneless
1 pound veal kidneys
5 tablespoons vegetable oil
2 teaspoons salt
1 teaspoon white pepper
¼ teaspoon thyme
¼ cup flour
3 cups dry red wine
1 cup mushrooms, quartered
½ cup onion, coarsely chopped
¼ cup Madeira wine
1 tablespoon parsley, chopped
½ recipe standard pie crust
1 egg yolk
1 tablespoon milk

Cut steak into 1-inch cubes. Peel off any membrane around kidneys and remove any fat. Cut into 1-inch cubes.

Heat oil in a large skillet. Add steak and kidneys and cook quickly until seared on all sides. Reduce heat and season with salt, pepper, and thyme. Add flour and toss lightly to coat all meat. Cook a few minutes longer. Add red wine and stir from bottom of skillet to deglaze pan. Simmer 10 minutes to thicken sauce.

In a separate pan, sauté mushrooms and onions in 1 tablespoon of oil. Add Madeira and parsley. Simmer for 10 minutes. Add mushroom mixture to meat mixture and blend well.

Preheat oven to 350 degrees.

Spoon meat mixture into a buttered 2-quart casserole. Roll pie dough to fit, cover casserole dish, and crimp edges. Cut 2 vent holes in top of crust and brush with beaten egg yolk and milk.

Bake for 45 to 50 minutes, or until crust is golden brown and meat is tender.

STEAK SANDWICH
Yachtman's Steakhouse
Disney's Yacht Club Resort

Yield: 4 servings

4 6-ounce strip sirloin
  steaks
6 ounces flour
2 tablespoons red pepper
  flakes

4 6-inch sub rolls
1 pound onion, thinly sliced
  circles
2 cups milk

Combine flour and pepper. Mix well. Soak thinly sliced onion circles in milk about 15 minutes. Drain and dust with flour and pepper mixture. Deep-fry in hot oil until golden brown and crisp.

Broil steaks as desired and place in sub rolls. Top with fried onions.

ROAST BEEF SANDWICH
50's Prime Time Cafe
Disney-MGM Studios Theme Park

Yield: 1 serving

3 slices rye bread, toasted
¼ pound roast beef, rare,
  thinly sliced
2 slices Muenster cheese
3 slices bacon, cooked
½ cup iceberg lettuce,
  shredded

¼ cup Thousand Island
  dressing
Tomato, sliced
Onion, sliced
Dill pickle spears

Preheat oven to 400 degrees.

Divide roast beef in half and place on a cookie sheet. Top each portion of beef with a slice of cheese and bake until cheese melts and roast beef is warm. Remove from oven and assemble sandwich as follows;

Spread all 3 slices of bread evenly with dressing. On 1 slice of bread add a portion of roast beef. Top with lettuce and another slice of bread with dressing. Add another portion of roast beef, lettuce, bacon, and finally third piece of toast with dressing. Secure with toothpicks and cut in half.

Serve with sliced tomato, sliced onion and pickle spears.

STIR FRIED BEEF WITH BROCCOLI
AND SNOW PEAS
Papeete Bay Verandah
Disney's Polynesian Resort

Yield: 2 servings

8 ounces beef tenderloin or
   flank steak
1 whole egg
3 tablespoons cornstarch,
   divided
1 tablespoon soy sauce
2 tablespoons white wine

10 snow peas
½ cup white onion, chopped
1½ cups broccoli, tops only,
   cut in small pieces
1 tablespoon sugar
½ cup cooking oil, divided

Slice beef tenderloin or flank steak into ½-inch strips. Combine egg, ½ teaspoon of cornstarch, and 1 tablespoon of oil and combine with the beef. Marinate for 15 to 20 minutes.

Cut broccoli into small pieces and blanch in boiling water with snow peas. Drain well and set aside. Keep warm.

In a large skillet or wok, add remaining oil and quickly sauté onion for about 1 minute. Add sliced beef and continue cooking until beef is medium to well done. Combine white wine, soy sauce, sugar, remaining cornstarch, and water and add no more than ½ cup of soy sauce mixture to beef. Cook an additional minute and remove from heat.

Arrange broccoli and snow peas around edge of a serving plate and pour cooked beef in middle of plate. Serve immediately.

STIR FRY BEEF AND BROCCOLI
Concourse Grille
Disney's Contemporary Resort

Yield: 4 servings

1 pound beef sirloin tips,
  sliced against grain into
  ½-inch slices
2 cups broccoli pieces,
  tops only
1 cup button mushrooms

2 tablespoons sesame oil
12 ounces oriental sauce,
  hot
1 tablespoon sesame seeds,
  toasted

Prepare oriental sauce

In a large cast-iron skillet or wok, heat sesame oil until a light smoking appears from oil. Add sliced beef and quickly sauté until browned on all sides and no red meat remains. Add broccoli pieces and button mushrooms and continue sautéing until vegetables are hot. Add hot oriental sauce and bring to a simmer. Remove from heat immediately and sprinkle with toasted sesame seeds.

Serve immediately.

Oriental Sauce
Yield: 2½ cups (20 ounces)

⅓ cup soy sauce
2 cups water
2 teaspoons brown sugar
2 tablespoons honey
1 teaspoon ginger, fresh,
  chopped

⅛ teaspoon white pepper
1 chicken bouillon cube
3 tablespoons cornstarch,
  dissolved in 1 tablespoon
  water

Mix all ingredients together in a small saucepan, except cornstarch and second water. Bring to a simmer on low heat. Whisk cornstarch into simmering sauce. Continue simmering until sauce thickens, plus an additional 2 to 3 minutes. Set aside until ready to use.

THE COACHMAN
King Stefan's Banquet Hall
Fantasyland   *MAGIC KINGDOM Park*

Yield: 6 servings

¾ pound prime rib or roast beef, sliced
¾ pound turkey, cooked or smoked, sliced
¾ pound ham, sliced
¾ pound Swiss cheese, thinly sliced
12 slices cheese bread (or any bread of choice)

1 head green leaf lettuce
3 medium tomatoes, washed and sliced
Thousand Island dressing, as needed
Marinated vegetables (recipe follows)

Order meats thinly cut into ½-ounce slices. Clean leaf lettuce and pat dry with paper towels.

For each sandwich, assemble as follows: On one slice of bread, spread Thousand Island dressing. Place 2 slices of prime rib or roast beef, 2 slices of turkey, 3 slices of ham, and 1 or 2 slices of cheese. Fold meats individually and top sandwich with an additional slice of bread spread with Thousand Island dressing. Secure sandwich with frill picks and cut in half on an angle.

Serve with a leaf of lettuce and sliced tomatoes on side. Can also be accompanied with Marinated Vegetables, if desired.

Marinated Vegetables   Yield: 6 servings

1 cup cauliflower, cut in 1-inch cubes
1 cup carrots, sliced
1 cup broccoli florets
½ cup red bell pepper, cut in thin strips

½ cup green bell pepper, cut in thin strips
1 10-ounce can kidney beans, drained and rinsed
2 cups light Italian dressing

Blanch cauliflower, carrots, and broccoli in boiling salted water until almost done. Drain and allow to steam dry in a colander. Cool slightly and mix with remaining ingredients. Refrigerate for at least 2 hours.

Mix well and serve on a bed of lettuce.

TOURNEDOS OF BEEF WITH CABERNET RAISIN SAUCE
Disney Village Resort Club
Disney Village Resort

Yield: 4 Servings

8 4-ounce beef tenderloin
  steaks
2 tablespoons butter
Salt

Pepper
Cabernet raisin sauce
  (recipe follows)

Prepare Cabernet raisin sauce.

Melt butter in a skillet large enough to hold steaks. Season each side of steaks with a pinch of salt and pepper and sauté steaks to desired degree of doneness, browning on both sides.

Serve 2 steaks per person on a warm dinner plate with Cabernet raisin sauce.

Cabernet Raisin Sauce

⅓ cup raisins, golden or
  regular
½ cup Cabernet Sauvignon
  wine
2 tablespoons butter
1 teaspoon sugar
1 tablespoon shallots, finely
  chopped

1 sprig thyme, fresh (or
  ¼ teaspoon dried thyme)
1 cup brown sauce, fresh or
  canned
1 teaspoon parsley, finely
  chopped

Two hours before making sauce, soak raisins in Cabernet Sauvignon.

Drain raisins and reserve wine. Add raisins to a small saucepan with 1 tablespoon of butter, sugar, shallots, and thyme. Sauté lightly over low heat for 1 minute. Do not brown. Add red wine and reduce by two thirds. Add brown sauce and bring back to a boil. Simmer 3 to 5 minutes. Reduce slightly. Remove from heat and stir in remaining tablespoon of butter.

If using canned brown stock, sauce may become too thick. If this happens, add a teaspoon of water at a time to achieve consistency desired.

Just before serving, bring back to a boil and stir in chopped parsley.

TOURTIERE
Le Cellier Restaurant
Canada   EPCOT Center

Yield: 1 9-inch pie

2 tablespoons vegetable oil
⅔ cup onion, finely diced
⅔ cup carrot, finely diced
⅔ cup celery, finely diced
¼ teaspoon garlic, minced
1 pound lean pork, ground
⅛ teaspoon cloves, ground

½ teaspoon sage, ground
1 teaspoon salt
¼ teaspoon white pepper
⅔ cup potatoes, finely diced
¼ cup chicken stock or
   broth
Pastry for 2-crust 9-inch pie

Preheat oven to 400 degrees.

Heat oil in a large skillet over medium heat. Sauté onion until transparent. Add carrot, celery, and garlic and cook 3 to 4 minutes longer. Turn heat to high and add ground pork. Cook and stir until pork is lightly browned. Reduce heat and stir in seasonings, potatoes, and chicken stock. Cook for 5 minutes, or until potatoes are tender. Remove from heat and cool completely.

When filling is cooled, line a deep 9-inch pie plate with pastry. Add filling and top with remaining pastry. Seal edges and decorate top of crust with any remaining pastry. Cut 2 vent holes in top of crust and bake for 30 to 40 minutes, or until the crust is golden brown.

Serve hot.

VEAL CALVADOS
Club 33
New Orleans Square   DISNEYLAND Park

Yield: 4 servings

4 4-ounce veal cutlets
   (boneless chicken breasts
   may be substituted)
1 teaspoon seasoning salt
2 tablespoons shallots,
   finely chopped

¼ cup butter or margarine
2 tablespoons brandy
2 cups dairy sour cream
½ cup heavy cream
Hot cooked rice or noodles

Place veal (or boneless chicken breasts) between 2 sheets of wax paper and pound with a mallet until thin, about ¼ inch. Sprinkle with seasoning salt and quickly sauté in hot butter until lightly browned (about 2 minutes on each side). Splash with brandy, remove from pan and keep warm. Add sour cream and heavy cream to pan and cook and stir until reduced by about one third and sauce is creamy.

Serve sauce with cutlets over rice or noodles.

VEAL MARSALA
Garden Gallery
The Disney Inn

Yield: 4 servings

4 5-ounce veal cutlets
½ cup flour
2 tablespoons butter,
  unsalted
2 cups mushrooms, sliced
1 tablespoon olive oil

½ cup Marsala wine
1 tablespoon parsley, fresh,
  chopped
Salt
Pepper

Lay veal between 2 pieces of waxed paper and flatten each cutlet with a mallet until thin (about ⅛ inch thick). Dredge lightly in flour. Shake off any excess.

Melt butter in a skillet, add mushrooms and sauté over medium heat until nicely browned (about 5 minutes). Remove mushrooms and set aside.

Add olive oil to skillet and heat until very hot. Sauté veal quickly over high heat (about 1 minute on each side). Remove to a platter and keep warm.

Add Marsala to skillet and simmer until it has reduced slightly (about 2 minutes). Add reserved mushrooms, and salt and pepper to taste. Add chopped parsley and pour over warm veal.

VEAL MEATLOAF
50's Prime Time Cafe
Disney-MGM Studios Theme Park

Yield: 4 servings

1 pound veal, ground
Pinch thyme, fresh or dried
Pinch rosemary, fresh or
 dried
½ teaspoon black pepper
1 teaspoon salt
1 egg
¼ cup bread crumbs, fresh

¼ cup red bell peppers,
 finely diced
¼ cup green bell peppers,
 finely diced
¼ cup mushroom buttons,
 fresh, thinly sliced
Mushroom gravy (recipe
 follows)

Preheat oven to 350 degrees.

In a large mixing bowl, add ground veal. Season with thyme, rosemary, salt, and pepper. If using fresh herbs, chop well before adding. Mix in remaining ingredients and blend until well incorporated. Place mixture in a standard loaf pan lined with waxed paper and sprayed with non-stick spray. Bake approximately 25 minutes, or until internal temperature reaches 160 degrees.

Prepare mushroom gravy.

Remove from oven and remove meatloaf from pan. Discard waxed paper and any excess grease.

Serve with mushroom gravy.

Mushroom Gravy   Yield: 1 cup

1 tablespoon butter
2 tablespoons Spanish
 onion, diced
2 teaspoons garlic, finely
 diced
2 tablespoons shallots,
 finely diced

⅔ cup brown gravy
1 cup button mushrooms,
 sliced
⅓ cup heavy cream
Black pepper

Heat butter in a small saucepan. Add onion, garlic, shallots, and mushrooms. Sauté until onions are tender (about 5 minutes). Add brown gravy and simmer 5 more minutes.

In a separate pan, reduce heavy cream by half and add to gravy. Season with black pepper, as needed.

WALT DISNEY'S OWN CHILI AND BEANS
Walt Disney's Personal Recipe

Yield: 6 to 8 servings

2 pounds pink (pinto)
   beans, dry
2 medium onions, sliced
¼ cup vegetable oil
2 cloves garlic, diced
1 cup celery, chopped
2 pounds lean beef, ground
1 teaspoon Chili Powder
   (more if desired)

1 teaspoon paprika
1 teaspoon thyme, dried
3 cups (about 28 ounces)
   tomatoes, solid-pack,
   canned
Salt
Pepper

Note: Optional ingredients for a more spicy chili: ⅛ teaspoon each coriander, turmeric, chili seeds, fennel, cloves, cinnamon, dry ginger, or 1 small Mexican chili pepper.

Wash and sort beans and soak overnight in cold water.

Next morning, drain beans and place in a 2-quart saucepan. Add fresh water to cover 2 inches over beans. Add sliced onions and simmer in a covered pot until tender (about 2 hours).

Meanwhile, heat oil in a large sauce pot and sauté garlic until lightly browned. Add celery and beef and cook until lightly browned also. Add chili powder, paprika, and thyme. Break up tomatoes with a spoon and mix with meat mixture. Cover and simmer for 1 hour.

When beans are tender, combine with meat, stirring gently. Add salt and pepper to taste and additional spices, as desired, and continue cooking an additonal 30 minutes.

VEGETABLES

VEGETABLES

ASSORTED FRESH VEGETABLES
Liberty Tree Tavern
Liberty Square   MAGIC KINGDOM *Park*

Yield: 4 servings

3 medium-size zucchini
   (about ½ pound)
3 medium-size summer
   squash (about ½ pound)
1 medium-size carrot

1 small onion
½ teaspoon garlic, minced
Salt
Pepper
2 tablespoons margarine or
   butter

Wash and trim zucchini and summer squash, removing ends. Cut in ¼-inch thick, round slices. Peel onion and cut in half, then in ¼-inch strips. Peel and trim carrot. Slice in ¼-inch round pieces.

In a heavy skillet or frying pan, add margarine. Add carrots and onions and sauté on medium heat for 4 to 5 minutes. Add summer squash, zucchini, garlic, salt, and pepper to taste and continue to cook until vegetables are soft but not mushy. Season again, if necessary.

BRAISED NAPA CABBAGE
Coral Reef Restaurant
The Living Seas   EPCOT *Center*

Yield: 6 servings

3 slices bacon, minced
2 purple shallots, minced
1 teaspoon white vinegar
8 cups napa cabbage,
   shredded

Salt
Pepper
Sugar

Sauté minced bacon in a large hot skillet until crispy. Add shallots and continue cooking until transparent. Deglaze pan with white vinegar and add shredded cabbage. Reduce heat and cook until just tender (about 15 minutes). Season with salt and pepper to taste and add sugar if cabbage is at all bitter.

CARCIOFI RIPIENI (STUFFED ARTICHOKES)
L'Originale Alfredo di Roma Ristorante
Italy   EPCOT Center

Yield: 4 servings

4 large artichokes
4 tablespoons lemon juice
2 quarts water
3 tablespoons butter
3 tablespoons olive oil, divided
¼ cup onion, finely chopped
1 clove garlic, minced
½ cup mushrooms, fresh, finely diced
½ cup cauliflower, finely diced
½ cup asparagus, finely diced
2 tablespoons white bread crumbs
1 tablespoon parsley, chopped
Salt
Black pepper, freshly ground
⅓ cup white wine
Parsley sprigs for garnish
⅓ cup Parmesan cheese, grated

Cut off stalks and trim bases of artichokes so they stand upright. Pull off coarse outer leaves and cut off top of each artichoke about one third of the way from top (about 1 inch). Trim points of remaining leaves and remove hairy choke from center. In a large bowl, combine water and lemon juice and soak artichokes, cut side down, in water for 20 minutes.

Heat butter and 1 tablespoon of olive oil in a medium-size skillet. Add onion, garlic, mushrooms, cauliflower, and asparagus and cook until tender. Remove from heat and mix with bread crumbs and parsley. Season to taste with salt and pepper.

Drain artichokes well and fill center of each artichoke with vegetable mixture. Place artichokes in a large skillet with remaining olive oil and white wine. Cover tightly and cook over very low heat for 45 minutes to 1 hour. When base of the artichoke is tender when pierced with a knife, remove from pan. Garnish with parsley sprigs and sprinkle with Parmesan cheese.

Serve immediately.

CAULIFLOWER VICTORIA
Victoria and Albert's
Disney's Grand Floridian Beach Resort

Yield: 2 to 4 servings

1 small head cauliflower, whole
4 tablespoons English mustard
2 tablespoons Parmesan cheese, grated

2 tablespoons bread crumbs, seasoned
½ cup cheese sauce
1 leaf kale
1 cherry tomato

Boil cauliflower for 5 to 7 minutes. It should only be half-cooked at this point. Drop into ice water to keep from cooking any further. Drain cauliflower and pat dry.

Mix Parmesan cheese and bread crumbs together and set aside. Preheat oven to 350 degrees.

Coat top of cauliflower with English mustard. Sprinkle on cheese/bread crumb mixture and pat lightly. Bake for 15 minutes, or until golden brown. Remove from oven and place on a dinner plate.

Use kale and cherry tomato for garnish and serve with cheese sauce.

DERBY VEGETABLES
Disney-MGM Studios Theme Park

Yield: 6 servings

1 bunch broccoli, tops only
¾ cup carrots
1 large red bell pepper
2 cups small button mushrooms

½ bunch cilantro
4 ounces butter or margarine
Salt
Pepper

Cut broccoli into florets. Peel carrots and slice, first lengthwise, and then in ⅛-inch slices. Wash mushrooms and dice red pepper. Roughly chop cilantro and set aside.

Blanch broccoli and carrots in boiling salted water until about half-cooked. Drain well and allow to steam dry in a colander. Melt butter or margarine in a skillet and add vegetables and cilantro. Quickly sauté until almost tender.

Season with salt and pepper and serve immediately.

Note: Vegetables should remain a little crunchy for best flavor. Serve with additional butter or margarine, if desired.

EGGPLANT CRÊPES
Victoria and Albert's
Disney's Grand Floridian Beach Resort

Yield: 6 to 8 servings

2 medium-size eggplants
Salt
2 pounds mushrooms,
  sliced
2 tablespoons shallots,
  minced
1 tablespoon butter or
  margarine
1 cup provolone cheese,
  grated
1 cup Gruyère cheese,
  grated

¼ cup Parmesan cheese,
  grated
¼ cup tomatoes, sun-dried
1½ cups bread crumbs,
  seasoned
Pinch basil
Pinch oregano
Pinch garlic
3 cups marinara sauce
  (recipe follows)

Remove stem from eggplant and slice lengthwise into long slices, ¼ inch thick. Sprinkle both sides of sliced eggplant with salt and place between paper towels for 30 minutes. Rinse after 30 minutes under cold water and pat dry.

In a medium-size sauté pan, melt butter and sauté shallots and mushrooms until tender. Remove from heat and allow to cool slightly. Combine with remaining ingredients and seasoning and mix well.

Preheat oven to 350 degrees.

Remove 1 cup of mushroom filling and set aside. Divide remaining mushroom filling evenly among eggplant slices. Fill each slice and roll lengthwise. Place stuffed eggplant in an oven-proof casserole dish, seam side down. Sprinkle remaining cup of stuffing over top of stuffed eggplant and bake for 30 minutes.

Remove from oven and cool slightly before serving. Accompany with hot marinara sauce.

(continued on next page)

EGGPLANT CRÊPES
(continued from previous page)

Marinara Sauce

Yield: 3 cups

2½ tablespoons olive oil
1 cup onions, diced small
1 cup green bell pepper,
   diced small
6 tablespoons tomato paste
1 cup tomatoes, diced
½ teaspoon garlic, chopped

1½ teaspoons sugar
1¼ tablespoons beef base
   (or 4 bouillon cubes)
1 bay leaf
Pinch salt
Pinch pepper
Pinch oregano

Heat olive oil in a 3-quart sauce pot. Add onions and peppers and cook until tender. Add tomato paste and cook for 30 seconds. Add all other ingredients and let simmer 20 minutes.

Remove from heat and serve.

GREEN BEANS
Chef Mickey's Village Restaurant
Disney Village Marketplace

Yield: 6 servings

1 pound whole green beans,
   fresh
2 ounces olive oil
3 tomatoes
⅓ cup onion

⅓ cup bacon, cooked,
   crumbled
Salt
Pepper

In a large pot, boil green beans for 10 minutes. Drain into a colander and transfer to an ice bath to stop cooking process. Set aside. Dice tomatoes into ½-inch pieces. Cut onion in half and then into thin slices. In a medium-size sauté pan, heat olive oil and cook onion, tomato, and green beans for 3 to 4 minutes over medium heat. Add crumbled bacon and season with salt and pepper to taste.

MELANZANE ALLA PARMIGIANA
(Eggplant Parmigiana)
L'Originale Alfredo di Roma Ristorante
Italy   EPCOT Center

Yield: 4 to 6 servings

**3 small or 1 large eggplant
  (about 1½ pounds)**
Coarse salt
**1 pound tomatoes, very ripe
  (about 2 cups)**
5 or 6 leaves basil, fresh
1 tablespoon olive oil
Salt
**Black pepper, freshly
  ground**

Vegetable oil
**2 ounces Swiss cheese,
  grated (about ⅓ cup)**
**2 ounces mozzarella cheese,
  grated (about ⅓ cup)**
**½ cup Parmesan cheese,
  freshly grated**
2 tablespoons butter

Cut unpeeled eggplant into ⅓-inch slices, lengthwise. Sprinkle with coarse salt and let stand 30 minutes.

Meanwhile, puree tomatoes in a blender or food processor with a steel blade. Add tomato paste, basil, and olive oil and mix only to combine. Place tomato mixture in a saucepan and bring to a boil. Cover, reduce heat and simmer for 15 minutes. Season to taste with salt and pepper. Set aside.

Rinse eggplant with cold water and pat dry with paper towels. Heat about 1 inch of vegetable oil in a large skillet and pan-fry eggplant slices on both sides until lightly browned. Drain on paper towels while frying remaining eggplant.

Preheat oven to 375 degrees.

When eggplant is fried, put casserole together as follows: Mix Swiss and mozzarella cheeses together. Spoon a layer of sauce in the bottom of a flat buttered casserole dish. Add a layer of eggplant slices. Sprinkle with half of mixed cheese and half of grated Parmesan cheese. Spoon on half of remaining sauce; add remaining eggplant slices and add remaining cheese. Top with sauce and dot with butter.

Bake for 25 to 30 minutes.

MOM'S CHILI
50's Prime Time Cafe
Disney-MGM Studios Theme Park

Yield: 8 servings

3 tablespoons olive oil
¼ cup red bell pepper, diced
¼ cup green bell pepper, diced
¼ cup celery, diced
¼ cup onion, diced
¼ cup carrots, diced
1 tablespoon garlic, crushed
¼ cup mushroom buttons, sliced
½ cup corn, canned
1 cup tomatoes, canned, diced
¼ cup black olives, sliced
½ teaspoon chili powder
⅛ teaspoon cayenne pepper

¼ teaspoon thyme
¼ teaspoon oregano
¼ teaspoon black pepper
¼ teaspoon cumin
⅛ cup jalapeño peppers
¼ cup tomato paste
2 cups chicken stock or broth
2 tablespoons cornstarch
½ cup great northern beans, canned
½ cup pinto beans, canned
½ cup black beans, canned
½ cup kidney beans, canned
8 ounces angel hair pasta or thin spaghetti

In a 4-quart saucepan, heat olive oil and add fresh vegetables. Sauté until tender and add corn, tomatoes and black olives. Add spices and cook a minute or two longer. Add jalapeño peppers, tomato paste and chicken stock and bring to a boil. Add cornstarch mixed with 2 tablespoons water and cook an additional 5 minutes, until thickened. Add beans and simmer until heated through.

Cook pasta in a separate pot. When cooked, drain well and serve 1 ounce of pasta with 1 cup of chili in the same bowl.

SESAME GREEN BEANS AND ASPARAGUS
Papeete Bay Verandah
Disney's Polynesian Resort

Yield: 6 servings

¼ pound green beans, cut
   in half, or 2 inches long
¼ pound pencil asparagus,
   cut in 2-inch lengths
1 teaspoon sesame oil
1 tablespoon dry sherry

1 teaspoon soy sauce
2 tablespoons chicken stock
   or broth
1 tablespoon sesame seeds,
   toasted

In a heavy skillet or wok, heat sesame oil. Quickly sauté green beans and asparagus until skins wrinkle. Add sherry, soy sauce, and chicken stock and simmer until tender.

Toss with toasted sesame seeds and serve.

SPANISH RICE
Monorail Cafe
Disneyland Hotel

Yield: 6 servings

½ cup onion, diced
½ cup celery, diced
¼ cup butter, clarified
½ cup tomato, ripe, diced
1 bay leaf

½ teaspoon paprika
1 cup rice, uncooked
½ cup tomato juice
2 cups water

Sauté onion and celery in butter until tender. Add tomato, bay leaf, paprika, and rice and sauté 2 to 3 minutes. Do not brown rice. Add tomato juice and water and bring to a boil. Reduce heat and cover pan. Simmer for 20 to 25 minutes, or until rice is tender and water has been absorbed.

POLYNESIAN RATATOUILLE
Tangaroa Terrace
Disney's Polynesian Resort

Yield: 6 servings

1 cup eggplant, cut in ¼-inch cubes (hold in cold water and drain before use)
1 cup zucchini, cut in ¼-inch cubes
1 cup crookneck squash, cut in ¼-inch cubes
½ cup onion, cut in ¼-inch pieces

12 ounces tomatoes, canned, diced, in juice
1 tablespoon garlic, chopped
1 tablespoon ginger root, fresh, chopped
¼ cup soy sauce
¼ cup sugar
¼ cup white vinegar
2 tablespoons sesame seeds
2 tablespoons peanut oil

In a large sauté pan or wok, heat peanut oil. Add sesame seeds, diced vegetables, garlic, and ginger. Toss quickly in oil until vegetables begin to turn brown. Add tomatoes in juice, soy sauce, sugar, and vinegar. Cook approximately 6 to 8 minutes, or until vegetables become tender.

Serve immediately.

POTATO SOUFFLÉ
Victoria and Albert's
Disney's Grand Floridian Beach Resort

Yield: 4 servings

1 baking potato
2 eggs, separated
⅓ cup heavy cream
2 tablespoons butter
2 tablespoons flour

4 tablespoons chives, finely chopped
¼ teaspoon cream of tartar
Salt
Pepper

Peel and dice potato into 8 small pieces. Steam potato until soft.

In a food processor, add potato, cream, salt, pepper, and flour. Blend 4 to 5 minutes until light and well whipped. Add butter and egg yolks and blend well. Beat egg whites with cream of tartar until soft peaks form. Fold into potato mixture and add chives. Transfer potato mixture into a buttered soufflé dish.

Preheat oven and a water bath large enough to hold soufflé dish to 350 degrees.

Set potato soufflé in hot water bath and bake 20 to 30 minutes. Soufflé will rise and turn golden brown.

Serve immediately.

227

STIR FRY VEGETABLES
Papeete Bay Verandah
Disney's Polynesian Resort

Yield: 8 servings

1 cup bok choy, fresh, cut at an angle
½ cup carrots, fresh, peeled, cut at an angle
½ cup red bell pepper, julienne
1 cup broccoli florets
1 cup onion, julienne
½ cup baby corn, drained, not pickled
½ cup straw mushrooms, or quartered white mushrooms
½ cup bamboo shoots, sliced

1 tablespoon garlic, chopped
1 tablespoon ginger, fresh, chopped fine
1 cup chicken broth
½ tablespoon cornstarch

Seasoning:
1 teaspoon five-spice powder
1 tablespoon soy sauce
⅛ teaspoon salt
⅛ teaspoon white pepper

Properly measure and cut first 5 ingredients. Mix with next 3 ingredients and set aside. Mix cornstarch and chicken broth. Preparation is the key to cooking with a wok; be prepared to work quickly.

Heat wok on stove. Add 2 tablespoons of peanut oil and immediately add vegetable mixture, garlic and ginger. Stir quickly with a spoon or toss wok back and forth to mix vegetables. Season with five-spice powder, soy sauce, salt, and pepper. Cook vegetables until good and hot, yet still crisp. Add chicken broth mixed with cornstarch and stir quickly until liquid thickens. Taste and adjust seasoning, if necessary.

TEMPURA VEGETABLES
Papeete Bay Verandah
Disney's Polynesian Resort

Yield: 4 servings

1 cup broccoli florets
1 cup white mushrooms,
  fresh, cut in quarters
1 cup cauliflower florets
1 cup zucchini, cut in
  ¼-inch circles

3 cups vegetable oil for
  frying
1 cup cornstarch
1 cup flour

Tempura Batter
1 cup cornstarch
1 cup flour
½ cup ice water
2 whole eggs
¼ cup white vinegar

1 tablespoon baking
  powder
½ teaspoon baking soda
1 tablespoon oil
1 teaspoon salt

In a large mixing bowl with a wire whisk, combine cornstarch and flour. Slowly add ice water and blend until smooth. Whisk in remaining ingredients and whip smooth.

Heat oil in a deep pot to 375 degrees, using a thermometer.

Combine additional 1 cup of flour and 1 cup of cornstarch for dusting vegetables and mix well.

Dust vegetables to be cooked in cornstarch/flour mixture, then dip in tempura batter. Immediately place in hot oil and fry, a few pieces at a time, until golden brown. Repeat until all vegetables have been cooked.

TONY'S BREAKFAST POTATOES
Tony's Town Square Restaurant
Main Street, U.S.A.   MAGIC KINGDOM Park

Yield: 6 servings

2 pounds small red "new"
  potatoes
1 teaspoon salt
2 quarts water

2 tablespoons butter or
  margarine, melted
1½ teaspoons vegetable
  seasoning

Wash potatoes with skins on and cut into quarters. Larger potatoes should be cut into sixths. In a 4-quart saucepan, add water, salt, and potatoes. Bring to a boil and cook for approximately 10 minutes. Potatoes should still be firm. Drain potatoes into a colander and allow to steam dry for 5 minutes.

Preheat oven to 350 degrees.

Place potatoes back into saucepan with melted butter and vegetable seasoning. Toss gently until evenly coated. Transfer potatoes into a 13 x 9 x 2-inch pan and bake for 20 to 25 minutes, or until evenly browned and fork-tender.

VEGETABLE LASAGNA
Tony's Town Square Restaurant
Main Street, U.S.A.   *MAGIC KINGDOM Park*

Yield: 12 servings

4 cups Tony's house sauce (or your favorite spaghetti sauce)
½ pound spinach lasagna noodles, fresh
4½ cups ricotta cheese mix (recipe follows)
½ pound tomato lasagna noodles, fresh
6½ cups five-cheese blend (recipe follows)

12 ounces crookneck squash, round cut, sliced paper-thin
1 pound egg lasagna noodles, fresh
12 ounces zucchini, round cut, sliced paper-thin
6 ounces frozen spinach, thawed, drained

Preheat oven to 350 degrees.

Arrange the following ingredients in order given below in a 13 x 9 x 2-inch lasagna pan. Spread layers evenly and make sure to cover each layer completely.

1. 1½ cups sauce
2. ½ pound egg lasagna, raw
3. 1½ cups zucchini (4 ounces)
4. 1½ cups crookneck squash (4 ounces)
5. 2 cups five-cheese blend (8 ounces)
6. ½ cup spinach (3 ounces)
7. 1½ cups ricotta cheese mix
8. ½ pound spinach lasagna, raw
9. 1½ cups zucchini (4 ounces)
10. 1½ cups crookneck squash (4 ounces)
11. 2 cups five-cheese blend (8 ounces)
12. ½ cup spinach (3 ounces)
13. 1½ cups ricotta cheese mix
14. ½ pound tomato lasagna, raw
15. 1½ cups ricotta cheese mix
16. 1½ cups zucchini (4 ounces)
17. 1½ cups crookneck squash (4 ounces)
18. 2 cups five-cheese blend (8 ounces)
19. ½ pound egg lasagna, raw (8 ounces)
20. 1½ cups sauce
21. ½ cup five-cheese blend (4 ounces)

(continued on next page)

VEGETABLE LASAGNA
(continued from previous page)

Bake assembled lasagna for 1 hour.

Remove from oven and let stand 15 minutes before cutting. This will ensure that each portion of lasagna is firm enough to serve.

Note: If fresh lasagna noodles are unavailable, 1 pound of dried lasagna noodles may be substituted. These noodles must be prepared according to directions on box before assembling lasagna. Eight ounces, or ½ pound, of cooked lasagna noodles will be used per layer.

Ricotta Cheese Mix

1 pound ricotta cheese
1½ cups Tony's house sauce
(12 ounces) (or your
favorite spaghetti sauce)

¼ cup plus 1 tablespoon
Romano cheese, grated
4 eggs

Mix all ingredients thoroughly in a mixing bowl. Refrigerate until ready to use.

Five-Cheese Blend

½ pound imported
provolone cheese
½ pound mozzarella cheese
½ pound imported Gruyère
cheese

¼ pound imported
Parmesan cheese
¼ pound imported Romano
cheese

Grate all cheeses. Mix and toss until all cheeses are mixed evenly. Refrigerate. Store any leftover cheese mixture in an airtight container in freezer for future use.

WILD MUSHROOM RAGOÛT
Victoria and Albert's
Disney's Grand Floridian Beach Resort

Yield: 2 cups

3 pounds wild mushrooms, or a variety of other mushrooms to equal 3 pounds
2 tablespoons butter
1 clove garlic, crushed
2 whole shallots, minced
½ teaspoon rosemary, fresh
½ teaspoon thyme, fresh
½ cup veal stock or beef broth
4 tablespoons sherry
2 tablespoons heavy cream
Salt
Pepper
1 tablespoon cornstarch
2 tablespoons water

Clean and slice mushrooms. Set aside.

In a medium-size skillet, melt butter and sauté garlic and shallots for 2 to 3 minutes. Add mushrooms and continue cooking for 5 minutes. Stir constantly. Add seasoning, sherry, and stock and bring to a boil. Add heavy cream and reduce heat. Simmer for 5 minutes and season with salt and pepper to taste. Add cornstarch mixed with water and cook until mixture thickens (3 to 4 minutes). Remove from heat and serve.

DESSERTS

DESSERTS

APPLE WALNUT COBBLER
Concourse Grille
Disney's Contemporary Resort

Yield: 1 cobbler

½ pound pie dough

¼ cup shortening

Filling

4 large apples, fresh
1 cup light brown sugar,
   lightly packed
6 tablespoons butter
1 tablespoon lemon juice,
   fresh

1 teaspoon cinnamon
½ teaspoon allspice
1 teaspoon cloves
⅓ cup flour

Topping

½ cup light brown sugar,
   lightly packed
1 teaspoon cinnamon

3 tablespoons water
1½ cups walnuts, chopped
4 tablespoons butter

Lightly grease 4 individual soufflé dishes with shortening. Roll out pie dough to ⅛″ and cut dough to fit bottom of each soufflé dish. Place 1 piece of dough in bottom of each dish.

Preheat oven to 325 degrees.

Peel, core, and cut apples into thin slices and put in a small mixing bowl. Melt butter and mix with apples. Add remaining filling ingredients and mix together. Divide apple mixture evenly among 4 soufflé dishes. Top with another piece of pie dough and press lightly on dough to make sure filling is firm.

Bake for 35 to 40 minutes. Top crust should be lightly browned.

Combine all topping ingredients in a small saucepan and heat until sugar dissolves. Do not boil. When cobblers are done, remove from oven and spoon ¼ of topping on each cobbler. Return to oven for an additional 10 minutes. Remove from oven and allow to cool for at least 10 minutes before serving.

APPLE PIE
Plaza Inn
Main Street, U.S.A.   *DISNEYLAND Park*

Yield: 1 9-inch pie

Pastry

2 cups flour
½ teaspoon salt
6 tablespoons solid
vegetable shortening

2 tablespoons butter, chilled
½ cup (or as needed) orange
juice, chilled

Mix flour and salt in a bowl. Add shortening and butter. With a pastry blender or fork, cut butter and shortening into flour until crumbly. Gradually add enough of orange juice until dough holds together. Knead dough very lightly and form into 2 balls. Wrap in plastic wrap and refrigerate while preparing filling.

Filling

3 pounds baking apples
1 lemon, juiced
¾ cup sugar

1 teaspoon cinnamon
⅛ teaspoon salt
4 tablespoons butter

Peel and core apples. Cut into ½-inch slices and place in a large bowl. Sprinkle with lemon juice and mix with sugar, cinnamon, and salt. Let mixture sit for 10 minutes at room temperature.

Preheat oven to 425 degrees.

On a floured board, roll out one ball of pastry and fit into bottom of a 9-inch pie plate. Add filling and dot top with chilled butter. Roll out remaining pastry and cover apples, sealing edges carefully. Prick top of pie with the point of a paring knife to allow steam to escape.

Bake for 10 minutes. Reduce heat to 350 degrees and continue baking for an additional 40 to 50 minutes. Remove pie and allow to cool before serving.

APPLE STRUDEL WITH FILO DOUGH
Caffe Villa Verde
Disneyland Hotel

Yield: 1 strudel

**1 pound apples, thinly
  sliced**
⅓ cup sugar
**½ teaspoon cinnamon,
  ground**

5 sheets filo dough
½ cup butter, melted
**Whipped cream or custard
  sauce**

Preheat oven to 400 degrees.

Peel and core fresh apples. Cut each into four wedges, then into thin slices. Sprinkle with two thirds of cinnamon and sugar and mix lightly. Set aside.

On a clean kitchen towel, put a single layer of filo dough. Brush with melted butter. Place another piece of dough on top and repeat, until all five pieces of dough have been layered with butter. Place apple mixture on upper third of filo dough layers. Sprinkle with remaining cinnamon sugar and roll dough, using towel to lift dough, as tightly as possible around apples. Place rolled dough, seam side down, on a buttered baking sheet and brush top with remaining butter. Add a little more cinnamon sugar to top of roll.

Bake for 30 minutes, or until golden brown.

Serve hot with whipped cream or custard sauce.

BANANAS AND STRAWBERRIES FLAMBÉ
Special Events
Disneyland Hotel

Yield: 8 servings

2 ounces butter
½ cup powdered sugar
½ teaspoon cinnamon
¼ cup orange juice
  concentrate
1 ounce clear orange
  liqueur
2 ounces cognac, divided

1 pint strawberries,
  cleaned, washed
3 medium bananas, peeled,
  sliced
8 scoops vanilla ice cream
8 parfait glasses or
  stemmed glasses

In a medium-size saucepan, heat butter, powdered sugar, cinnamon, and orange juice concentrate. Bring to a boil and add clear orange liqueur and 1 ounce of cognac. Mix well and add sliced strawberries and bananas. When mixture is warm, pour into a chafing dish and add 1 ounce of hot cognac and light. Ladle over ice cream in decorative glassware.

BLACK FOREST CAKE
Biergarten
Germany   *EPCOT Center*

Yield: about 12 servings

Cake

5 eggs
3 egg yolks
⅔ cup sugar
¾ cup cake flour, sifted
6 tablespoons cocoa,
  unsweetened

¼ teaspoon baking powder
¼ teaspoon baking soda
1½ teaspoons vanilla
  extract

Preheat oven to 350 degrees.

Grease 3 8-inch round cake pans and line bottoms with waxed paper.

In a medium-size mixing bowl, combine eggs, egg yolks, and sugar. Beat until thick and light. Sift together flour, cocoa, baking powder, and baking soda. Gradually fold flour mixture into egg mixture. Add vanilla extract last and pour batter into 3 cake pans.

Bake for 18 to 20 minutes, or until tops spring back when pressed lightly with your finger. Cool on a wire rack for 10 minutes before removing from pan.

(continued on next page)

BLACK FOREST CAKE
(continued from previous page)

Syrup

⅓ cup water
½ cup sugar

3 tablespoons cherry
liqueur

Combine water and sugar in a small saucepan and bring to a boil. Remove mixture immediately and let cool. Stir in cherry liqueur.

Filling and Frosting

1¼ cups cherry pie filling
3 tablespoons cherry
liqueur

1 pint heavy whipping
cream, whipped
12 ounces semi-sweet
chocolate, shaved

Mix together cherry pie filling and cherry liqueur.

Put 1 layer of cake on a flat plate. Brush top of first layer with syrup. Spread a layer of cherry mixture over syrup, spreading evenly. Add a second layer of cake and spread with more syrup. Add another layer of cherry mixture, then a layer of whipped cream on top of that. Top with third layer of cake and brush with any remaining syrup. Frost top of cake with a thick layer of whipped cream, leaving sides exposed to show layers, and decorate with additional cherries. Sprinkle entire cake with shaved chocolate and refrigerate 1 hour.

BREAD PUDDING
Papeete Bay Verandah
Disney's Polynesian Resort

Yield: 10 servings

4 loaves bread, dry
4 cups half-and-half or milk
1½ cups sugar
1 stick butter or margarine,
melted
2 teaspoons nutmeg

2 teaspoons cinnamon
2 tablespoons vanilla
extract
6 eggs, beaten
Vanilla sauce
(see Sauces)

Preheat oven to 350 degrees.

Tear bread into 2-inch pieces. In a large bowl, add half-and-half, sugar, nutmeg, cinnamon, vanilla, and half the butter. Add eggs and mix well. Add bread and allow to sit 5 minutes.

Grease a 9 x 12 x 2-inch baking pan and add bread mixture. Dot top with remaining butter and bake for 1 hour.

Let cool and serve with vanilla sauce.

CARIBBEAN SAND BARS
Cinnamon Bay Bakery
Disney's Caribbean Beach Resort

Yield: 9 3-inch squares

1¼ sticks butter
1¼ cups light brown sugar,
  firmly packed
1 cup flour
½ teaspoon salt

1 teaspoon baking powder
2 eggs
1 teaspoon vanilla extract
1 cup walnuts, chopped
4 cups pecans, chopped

Preheat oven to 375 degrees.
Butter a 9 x 9-inch pan.
Sift flour, salt, and baking powder and set aside.
Cream butter and brown sugar until smooth. Add eggs, one at a time, and beat until smooth and creamy. Add vanilla and stir well. Add flour mixture and blend well. Fold in nuts and spread batter evenly in greased pan.
Bake for 25 to 30 minutes. Remove and cool completely before cutting.

Note: For maple bars, add 2 tablespoons maple syrup. For chocolate chip nut bars, reduce pecans by 1 cup and add 1 cup semi-sweet chocolate chips.

CHOCOLATE CHIP COOKIES
Farmers Market
The Land   EPCOT Center

Yield: 2 to 2½ dozen cookies

¾ cup sugar
½ cup shortening
¼ teaspoon salt
¼ teaspoon baking powder
1 teaspoon vanilla extract

1 egg
1 cup plus 2 tablespoons
  cake flour
1 8-ounce package
  chocolate chips

Cream together sugar, shortening, salt, baking powder, vanilla, and egg until light and fluffy. Fold in cake flour. Add chocolate chips, stirring just enough to mix evenly. Wrap cookie dough in plastic wrap, forming 2 2-inch rolls of dough. Refrigerate and chill thoroughly.
Preheat oven to 350 degrees.
To bake, cut dough into ½-inch slices and bake on an ungreased cookie sheet for 10 to 12 minutes.

CHOCOLATE AMARETTO MOUSSE
Caffe Villa Verde
Disneyland Hotel

Yield: 4 servings

1½ ounces almond paste
¼ cup almond-based
  liqueur
4 large egg yolks
¼ cup sugar
½ cup half-and-half
4 ounces dark chocolate,
  chopped

3 tablespoons cocoa powder
¼ cup cream cheese,
  softened
2 cups heavy cream,
  whipped
Mint leaves, fresh
Chocolate, shaved

In a medium-size mixing bowl, combine almond-based liqueur, egg yolks, sugar, and almond paste. Mix by hand with the back of a spoon until well blended. Set aside.

In a double boiler over medium heat, combine half-and-half and chopped chocolate. Heat only long enough to melt chocolate. When chocolate is melted, sift in cocoa powder and mix well. Increase heat and bring sauce to a simmer. Add a few tablespoons of chocolate mixture to egg mixture until both mixtures are combined. Return combined sauce to double boiler and cook for 3 to 5 minutes. Do not boil. Sauce will be creamy. Remove from heat and place top of double boiler in an ice bath and stir sauce until cool.

Whip heavy cream and fold into cooled chocolate mixture. Fill individual champagne glasses with mousse and refrigerate until firm.

Serve with additional whipped cream and garnish with fresh mint leaves and shaved chocolate.

CHOCOLATE CHIP PECAN PIE
Narcoossee's
Disney's Grand Floridian Beach Resort

Yield: 1 pie

3 eggs, lightly beaten
1 cup light corn syrup
1 tablespoon butter, melted
½ cup sugar

Pinch salt
½ cup chocolate chips
1 heaping cup pecan meats
1 unbaked pie shell

Preheat oven to 400 degrees.

In a mixing bowl, combine ingredients in order given. Mix well and pour into an unbaked pie shell.

Bake for 5 minutes. Reduce heat after 5 minutes to 300 degrees and continue to bake for 1 hour, or until filling is thick. Cool on a wire rack.

Serve at room temperature.

CHOCOLATE CHAMBORD
WITH RASPBERRY BAVARIAN CREAM
Ariel's
Disney's Beach Club Resort

Yield: 16 slices

Chocolate Genoise

7 eggs
1 cup sugar
½ cup cocoa
1 cup cake flour
⅓ cup cornstarch

1 tablespoon butter, melted
Raspberry Bavarian cream
  (recipe follows)
Raspberry topping (recipe
  follows)

Preheat oven to 375 degrees.

Grease and lightly flour a 10-inch spring-form pan and line bottom with waxed paper. Set aside.

Sift together cocoa, cake flour, and cornstarch and set aside.

In a glass or stainless steel mixing bowl, combine eggs and sugar. Mix well and heat over hot, not boiling, water, double-boiler style. When eggs and sugar are warm, not hot, beat by hand with a balloon whip or electric mixer until light and fluffy. Fold in melted butter and add flour mixture. Pour into prepared spring-form pan and bake for 30 to 40 minutes, or until center springs back when pressed with a finger.

Remove from oven and cool on a wire rack. Set aside and prepare raspberry Bavarian cream and raspberry topping before assembling.

(continued on next page)

CHOCOLATE CHAMBORD
WITH RASPBERRY BAVARIAN CREAM
(continued from previous page)

Raspberry Bavarian Cream

4 egg yolks
½ cup sugar
2 cups raspberry syrup or
  juice
2 cups heavy cream

4 leaves gelatin, (or 2
  tablespoons dry gelatin
  dissolved in ¼ cup warm
  water)
2 cups raspberries, fresh

With a balloon whisk or electric mixer, beat egg yolks and sugar until thick and creamy. Heat raspberry syrup and bring to a boil. Slowly add syrup to eggs and sugar, a little at a time, mixing well after each addition.

After all syrup has been added to eggs and sugar, place mixture in a double boiler and cook over low heat, stirring constantly.

Soak gelatin leaves in cold water. When softened, squeeze out as much water as possible and add leaves to hot sauce. Stir until completely dissolved. Remove from heat and strain through a fine sieve. Cool at room temperature. Whip heavy cream and fold into cooled sauce. Refrigerate for 10 minutes before assembling torte.

Raspberry Topping

½ cup raspberry jam
½ cup water

½ cup sugar

Combine all ingredients in a saucepan and heat over low heat until sugar is dissolved. Allow topping to cool before pouring over top of cake.

Assemble as follows:

Slice the chocolate genoise in 3 equal layers. Place one layer back inside the spring-form cake pan.

With a pastry bag, pipe rings of filling on top of the first layer, leaving ½-inch spaces of cake exposed between rings. Fill empty spaces with fresh raspberries. Place more filling on top of raspberries and spread smooth with a spatula.

Place the second layer of chocolate genoise on top of filling and repeat process. Replace top layer and refrigerate torte for a least 2 hours.

After 2 hours, remove torte from pan and place on a serving plate. Pour cooled topping over torte and serve with additional fresh raspberries and whipped cream.

CHOCOLATE MOUSSE
Boulangerie Pâtisserie
France   EPCOT Center

Yield: 3 cups

**5 ounces semi-sweet
  chocolate, melted
2 egg yolks, lightly beaten
¼ cup heavy cream**

**1 teaspoon vanilla extract
3 egg whites
¼ cup sugar**

Melt chocolate in a double boiler over warm water. Remove from heat. Combine egg yolks and cream and gradually add chocolate, stirring rapidly. Add vanilla.

Beat egg whites with sugar until stiff peaks form. Gently fold egg whites into chocolate mixture. Spoon mousse into a decorative mold or individual serving glasses and chill until firm (about 2 hours).

CHOCOLATE MOUSSE CAKE
Boulangerie Pâtisserie
France   EPCOT Center

Yield: 10 servings

This recipe is made in four parts. First make the genoise, or cake layer, then the rum syrup, the chocolate mousse, and finally the chocolate ganache.

Genoise

**⅓ cup flour
3 tablespoons unsweetened
  cocoa
3 eggs**

**½ cup sugar
3 tablespoons sweet butter,
  melted, cooled
½ teaspoon vanilla extract**

Sift together flour and cocoa and set aside. Blend eggs and sugar in top of double boiler. Put over hot, not boiling, water and stir constantly until creamy and warm. Remove pan from heat and beat egg mixture until thick and fluffy. Gently fold in one third of flour mixture. Dribble butter and vanilla over batter and fold in. Add remaining flour and fold that in also.

Preheat oven to 350 degrees.

Grease and flour a 9-inch springform pan and line with waxed paper. Add batter and bake for 15 to 20 minutes, or until top springs back when lightly pressed with a finger. Remove from oven and cool for 10 minutes before removing from pan. Cool completely on a wire rack.

(continued on next page)

CHOCOLATE MOUSSE CAKE
(continued from previous page)

Rum Syrup

½ cup water
1 teaspoon sugar

1 tablespoon rum

Bring water and sugar to a boil in a saucepan. Add rum and cool.

Chocolate Mousse

5 ounces semi-sweet
  chocolate, melted
2 egg yolks, lightly beaten
¼ cup cream

1 teaspoon vanilla extract
3 egg whites
¼ cup sugar

Melt chocolate in a double boiler over warm water. Remove from heat. Combine egg yolks and cream and gradually add chocolate, stirring rapidly. Add vanilla.

Beat egg whites with sugar until stiff peaks form. Gently fold egg whites into chocolate mixture. Blend well and refrigerate until ready to use.

Chocolate Ganache

8 ounces semi-sweet
  chocolate
½ cup milk
1 cup heavy cream

1½ tablespoons vanilla
  extract
3 tablespoons sugar

Melt chocolate over very low heat, stirring constantly.

Combine milk, cream, vanilla, and sugar in a mixing bowl. Beat until thick. Quickly mix cream mixture into melted chocolate. Cook for 1 minute and remove from heat. Allow ganache to cool slightly, stirring occasionally.

Assembly of chocolate mousse cake:

First trim top of genoise to form a flat top. Return trimmed cake to the springform pan to use as a mold. Brush trimmed top of genoise with rum syrup. Add chocolate mousse and spread evenly. Top with cooled chocolate ganache and refrigerate for 2 hours.

Remove from pan and serve with additional whipped cream and sliced almonds, if desired.

CHOUX FRITTERS
Royal Street Veranda
New Orleans Square   DISNEYLAND Park

Yield: 3 dozen

½ cup butter or margarine
1 cup boiling water
¼ teaspoon salt
1¾ cups flour

4 eggs
4 cups vegetable oil
Granulated sugar

Combine butter, boiling water, salt, and flour in a saucepan over moderate heat. Beat mixture vigorously until it leaves sides of pan and forms a ball. Remove from heat and cool slightly. Spoon into a mixer or food processor with a steel blade, and add eggs one at a time, beating well after each addition. When all eggs have been added and mixture is thick, it should hold its shape when lifted with a spoon.

Heat oil to 375 degrees. Dip a tablespoon first in hot oil, then in batter. Carefully drop tablespoonfuls of batter into hot oil and cook until brown on all sides. Remove from oil with a slotted spoon and drain on paper towels.

Sprinkle with sugar and serve hot.

COQUINA COOKIES
Cinnamon Bay Bakery
Disney's Carribean Beach Resort

Yield: 24 1-ounce cookies

3 egg whites
1 teaspoon cider vinegar
½ teaspoon salt

1 cup sugar
1 cup almonds, ground
1 cup mini chocolate chips

Preheat oven to 300 degrees.

In a large mixing bowl with an electric mixer, whip egg whites, cider vinegar, and salt until foamy. Add sugar, a tablespoon at a time, until stiff peaks form. With a spoon or spatula, fold in almonds and chips. Using a teaspoon, drop cookies onto an ungreased cookie sheet.

Bake for 40 to 45 minutes, or until golden brown and firm to touch.

When cool, cookies can be frosted with melted chocolate and pistachio nuts.

Note: Mixture may also be formed into shells before baking and used for fresh fruit or ice cream.

CROCKETT'S APPLE DUMPLINGS
Crockett's Tavern
Disney's Fort Wilderness Resort and Campground

Yield: 12 dumplings

12 medium cooking apples, Cortland or Northern Spy
½ pound butter
1 cup sugar
2 tablespoons cinnamon
12 cinnamon red hot candies

2 pounds pie dough (or enough for 12 6-inch circles), rolled to ⅛-inch thick
Cinnamon sugar syrup (recipe follows)

Core apples from top, three quarters of the way through apple, leaving about ¼-inch on bottom of apple.

Cream together butter, sugar, and cinnamon until smooth. Fill each apple with a tablespoon of butter/sugar mixture. Place a red hot candy on top of each apple and set aside.

Preheat oven to 350 degrees.

Divide pie dough into 12 equal pieces. Roll each piece into a 6-inch circle and place an apple in center of each piece of dough. Fold dough up around apple, sealing top. Place finished apple in a 12 x 12-inch baking dish and repeat process until all apples are complete.

Bake apples for 30 minutes. Remove from oven and cover with Cinnamon Sugar Syrup. Return to oven and bake an additional 30 minutes. Remove from oven and serve warm with whipped cream, if desired.

Cinnamon Sugar Syrup

4 cups water
4 cups sugar
2 tablespoons cinnamon

¼ cup cinnamon red hot candies

In a 2-quart saucepan, combine ingredients and boil for 20 minutes. Sugar will dissolve and sauce will reduce by one third. Set aside until ready to use.

DARK CHOCOLATE CAKE
Farmers Market
The Land   EPCOT Center

Yield: 1 cake

5 eggs
3 egg yolks
⅔ cup sugar
¾ cup cake flour, sifted
6 tablespoons unsweetened
   cocoa

¼ teaspoon baking powder
¼ teaspoon baking soda
1½ teaspoons vanilla
   extract

Preheat oven to 350 degrees.

Grease 2 9-inch round cake pans and line the bottoms with wax paper.

Combine eggs, egg yolks, and sugar in a mixing bowl. Beat until thick and light. Sift together flour, cocoa, baking powder, and baking soda. Fold into eggs. Add vanilla last, mixing well. Pour batter into cake pans.

Bake for 22 to 24 minutes, or until tops springs back when pressed lightly with a finger. Cool on a wire rack for 10 minutes before removing from pan.

To assemble cake, brush each layer with syrup and frost with butter cream frosting.

Syrup

⅓ cup water
½ cup sugar

3 tablespoons orange
   liqueur

Combine water and sugar in a small saucepan and bring to a boil. Remove from heat immediately and cool. When cool, stir in orange liqueur.

Butter Cream Frosting   Yield: 3 cups

1 cup sugar, divided
½ cup water
1 tablespoon light corn
   syrup

3 egg whites
1 cup sweet butter
1 teaspoon vanilla extract

(continued on next page)

DARK CHOCOLATE CAKE
(continued from previous page)

Combine ⅔ cup of sugar with water and corn syrup. Stir over low heat until sugar is dissolved. Increase heat and boil without stirring to 238 degrees on a candy thermometer, or until syrup forms a soft ball when dropped into cold water.

Beat egg whites until foamy, then slowly add remaining ⅓ cup sugar and beat until mixture forms soft peaks. Pour boiling syrup very slowly into egg whites, beating until stiff. Cool completely.

Cream butter until soft and fluffy. Beat cooled meringue slowly into butter. Blend in vanilla.

Note: For chocolate butter cream frosting, fold in 1½ ounces melted and cooled semi-sweet chocolate after vanilla.

COCONUT SQUARES
Papeete Bay Verandah
Disney's Polynesian Resort

Yield: 64 1-inch squares

¼ cup coconut cream
2 cups half-and-half
½ cup cornstarch
1 cup coconut, shredded

½ teaspoon cinnamon
1¼ cups coconut, toasted,
  for coating

In a medium-size saucepan, combine all ingredients except toasted coconut and mix well. Heat over medium heat, stirring constantly, until mixture leaves sides of pan. Remove from heat and place in a lightly greased 8 x 8-inch pan. Refrigerate at least 2 hours.

Cut chilled mixture into 1-inch squares and roll in toasted coconut, coating well.

DECADENCE CAKE
Disney-MGM Studios Theme Park

Yield: 1 cake

2 cups cocoa powder
1¾ cups granulated sugar
½ pound semi-sweet
  chocolate

1 cup butter
6 whole eggs
½ cup bourbon

Sift cocoa powder twice and set aside. Sift sugar separately and set it aside, also. Melt butter and chocolate in a double boiler over very low heat. Stir until smooth and set aside.

Place eggs in a mixing bowl and mix slowly on low speed, being careful to only blend eggs, not whip them. Add sugar and bourbon to eggs and mix just enough to blend. Add sifted cocoa powder and blend again to incorporate. Add melted chocolate and butter and mix thoroughly, scraping sides well. Blend for about 5 minutes on low speed. Do not whip.

Preheat oven to 325 degrees.

Lightly grease a 5 x 9-inch loaf pan, or one of similar size, with butter or non-stick coating, and line bottom with waxed paper.

Pour cake mixture into pan and set pan in a water bath large enough to hold cake pan. Bake for 1½ hours. When a toothpick inserted in center of cake comes out clean, cake is done. Cool completely and remove from pan.

Slice and serve with powdered sugar or whipped cream.

DEEP DISH APPLE PIE
Rose & Crown Pub & Dining Room
United Kingdom   EPCOT Center

Yield: 1 pie

4 large apples
¾ cup sugar
¼ teaspoon cinnamon
1½ tablespoons cornstarch
⅛ teaspoon salt

1 tablespoon butter,
  softened
Pastry for a 9-inch
  2-crust pie

Preheat oven to 350 degrees.

Core and peel apples. Cut each apple into 16 slices. Finely chop apple peels in a food processor with a steel blade. Arrange sliced apples in a buttered 2-quart baking dish. Combine sugar, cinnamon, cornstarch, salt, and apple peelings. Sprinkle over apples. Dot with butter and cover baking dish.

(continued on next page)

DEEP DISH APPLE PIE
(continued from previous page)

Bake for 20 minutes until apples are tender but not soft. Remove baking dish from oven and turn heat up to 425 degrees.

Spoon apples into bottom crust of a 9-inch pie shell. Roll out top crust and cover apples, crimping edges and cutting 2 small vent holes in top of pie to allow steam to escape. Return pie to oven and bake another 15 to 20 minutes, or until crust is golden brown.

FANTASIA CHEESECAKE
Plaza Inn
Main Street, U.S.A.   *DISNEYLAND Park*

Yield: 1 9-inch cheesecake

Graham Cracker Crust

1 cup graham cracker crumbs	4 tablespoons butter or margarine, melted
1 tablespoon sugar	

Grease bottom and sides of a 9-inch springform pan.

Combine all ingredients and blend well. Press crumb mixture into bottom of pan. Set aside.

Filling

4 8-ounce packages cream cheese	⅛ teaspoon salt
2 cups sugar	½ teaspoon lemon extract
	4 eggs

Preheat oven to 350 degrees.

Mix cream cheese, sugar, salt, and lemon extract until smooth. Add eggs, one at a time, blending well after each addition. Do not overmix batter. Pour into prepared cake pan and bake for 45 to 50 minutes, or until cheesecake is set. Remove from oven and cool on a wire rack for 30 minutes. Refrigerate for several hours.

Sour Cream Topping

1 cup sour cream	Fresh fruit or fruit pie filling, if desired
2 tablespoons sugar	Fresh whipped cream, if desired

Mix sour cream and sugar together and spoon over cheesecake. Decorate with slices of fresh fruit, canned fruit topping, or fresh whipped cream, if desired.

FRENCH FRIED ICE CREAM
Garden Gallery
The Disney Inn

Yield: 4 servings

1 pint vanilla ice cream
(flavor optional)
2 egg whites, divided
3 tablespoons almond paste
1½ cups graham cracker
crumbs
4 10-inch flour tortillas
Oil for frying

Walnuts, chopped
Mint leaves, fresh
Vanilla sauce
(recipe follows)
Sliced peaches, fresh or
canned
Strawberries, fresh

Scoop ice cream into 4 balls. Freeze until very hard.

Blend 1 egg white into almond paste until very smooth. Divide almond paste into 4 equal parts and roll out very thin with a rolling pin. Wrap around frozen ice cream ball until completely covered. Dip ice cream ball into remaining egg white and roll in graham cracker crumbs, coating well.

Ice cream balls can be stored in an airtight container in freezer up to this point.

When ready to serve, heat enough oil in a deep pot (about 3 inches deep) to a temperature of 360 degrees on a candy thermometer. Fry tortilla shells, one at a time, until golden brown. Remove immediately and place over the outside of a 6-inch bowl and shape while warm. The tortilla will hold its shape when it cools slightly.

Fry each ice cream ball in the same oil until golden brown (15 to 20 seconds). Remove immediately and drain. Place fried ice cream in tortilla shell and garnish with vanilla sauce, peaches, strawberries, walnuts, and fresh mint leaves.

Serve immediately.

Vanilla Sauce

2 tablespoons margarine
2 tablespoons flour
½ cup half-and-half

1 tablespoon vanilla extract
4 tablespoons heavy cream

In a saucepan, melt margarine. Add flour to make a roux. Cook 4 to 5 minutes. Add the half-and-half and vanilla slowly, until mixture thickens (2 to 3 minutes). Stir in sugar and add heavy cream. Simmer lightly for 15 minutes on medium heat.

Strain before serving.

FROZEN MOCHA PARFAIT
Top of the World
Disney's Contemporary Resort

Yield: 8 servings

12 egg yolks
8 ounces sugar
4 cups heavy cream

2 ounces semi-sweet chocolate
2 teaspoons instant coffee

Warm egg yolks and sugar in a double boiler until sugar dissolves. Stir constantly with a whisk to prevent eggs from scrambling. Remove eggs and sugar from double boiler and place in a mixing bowl. Whip on high until stiff.

Melt chocolate and set aside.

Dissolve coffee in 4 tablespoons of water and set aside.

Whip cream until soft peaks form. Fold in egg yolk mixture and divide into thirds. Flavor one third with melted chocolate and one third with instant coffee. Reserve one third plain.

In a standard 4 x 4 x 9-inch loaf pan, alternately layer the three flavors of cream, starting with chocolate, then coffee, then plain, repeating process with as many layers as desired, using all flavors. Refrigerate or freeze between each layer for 10 minutes to allow cream to set up. When all three flavors are finished, place in freezer for 4 hours. Dip pan in hot water to remove.

Should be served frozen, with your favorite sauce (chocolate, caramel, strawberry, etc.).

Note: This recipe can also be prepared in individual glasses, if desired.

FRUIT TARTS
Caffe Villa Verde
Disneyland Hotel

Yield: 4 large tarts (24 individual servings)

To assemble fruit tarts, first prepare pastry cream (crème pâtissière) and refrigerate until ready to use.

Have baked tart shells (rich flan pastry) ready and cooled.

First, evenly fill cooled tart shells with pastry cream. Decorate with your favorite fruits, fresh if available, and make sure that you alternate colors.

Refrigerate for 1 hour and serve.

For an optional glaze, mix apricot jam with a little water and warm until consistency of syrup. Brush onto fruit and allow to set while in refrigerator.

Pastry Cream—Crème Pâtissière

2 cups milk, divided
3 egg yolks
⅔ cup sugar
Pinch salt
¼ cup cornstarch

2 tablespoons unsalted butter, cold and firm, cut in eighths
1¼ teaspoons vanilla extract

Place 1½ cups of milk in a double boiler. Reserve ½ cup. Cook over moderate heat until scalded. Meanwhile, combine egg yolks, sugar, cornstarch, salt, and reserved milk and whisk until dissolved. When milk is scalded, slowly add scalded milk to egg mixture, whisking constantly. When all milk has been added, return mixture to double boiler and cook until mixture thickens. Stir constantly to prevent eggs from scrambling and lumps from appearing. Cook for 7 to 10 minutes, or until mixture is the consistency of mayonnaise. Remove from heat and whisk in butter and vanilla.

Pour into a clean bowl and cover with plastic wrap to prevent top from forming a skin. Refrigerate overnight. Whisk smooth before using.

Notes: For a richer, more refined cream, fold in up to 50% heavy cream or heavy whipped cream.

Pastry cream may also be flavored with additional vanilla, brandy, Kirsch, or a flavor of your choice. Flavoring should be added before other creams are folded in.

(continued on next page)

FRUIT TARTS
(continued from previous page)

Rich Flan Pastry—Pâté Sablée

3½ cups unsalted butter
2 cups powdered sugar
4 egg yolks
6 cups flour (sift before
   measuring)

1 lemon rind, finely grated
1 teaspoon vanilla extract
   (optional)

This recipe may be put together in a food processor or traditionally, on a board or marble table.

In a food processor:

Using a steel blade, place butter and sugar in processor. Pulse on/off for 10 seconds until well blended. Add eggs, one by one, until absorbed. Add flour, lemon rind, and vanilla. Mix quickly on pulse, just enough to blend dough. Overmixing results in a tough dough, which may be crumbly and cause shrinkage of crust.

On a board or in a large bowl:

Place flour on board or in a large bowl. Form a well in center of flour and add all remaining ingredients as follows: With your fingers, work together butter and sugar. Add eggs, one by one, until well blended. Then gradually push flour into mixture. When all of flour has been absorbed, knead dough only until it holds together.

For tarts, roll out dough ⅛-inch thick. Cut with cutter and line your favorite tart shells. Bake in a 350-degree oven until golden brown.

GERMAN CHOCOLATE CAKE
Plaza Inn
Main Street, U.S.A.   *DISNEYLAND Park*

Yield: 1 cake

1¼ cups sugar
½ cup shortening
2 eggs
¼ teaspoon salt
1¾ cups cake flour
2 tablespoons unsweetened
  cocoa

½ teaspoon baking soda
1 teaspoon baking powder
1 cup buttermilk
4 egg whites
¼ cup sugar

Grease and flour 3 9-inch round cake pans and set aside.

In a mixing bowl, combine sugar, shortening, eggs, and salt and blend until light and fluffy. Sift together cake flour, cocoa, soda, and baking powder. Add to shortening mixture alternately with buttermilk until thoroughly blended.

Preheat oven to 350 degrees.

Beat egg whites separately with ¼ cup of sugar until very stiff peaks form. Then gently fold egg whites into chocolate cake mixture. Divide batter evenly among the 3 cake pans and bake for 20 to 25 minutes, or until tops of cakes spring back when pressed lightly with a finger.

Cool layers on wire racks for 10 minutes before removing from pans. Cool completely before frosting.

Topping

1 cup evaporated milk
1½ cups sugar
1 cup butter, softened
3 egg yolks

¼ teaspoon vanilla
1½ cups pecans, chopped
1½ cups coconut, flaked

Combine milk, sugar, butter, and egg yolks in a saucepan. Cook and stir over medium heat until mixture comes to a boil and is thickened (about 10 minutes). Add vanilla, pecans, and coconut. Stir until cool and of smooth spreading consistency.

Frost the top of each layer generously with topping. Stack layers evenly, leaving sides uncovered.

APPLE-BLACKBERRY COBBLER
King Stefan's Banquet Hall
Fantasyland   *MAGIC KINGDOM Park*

Yield: 1 cobbler

1½ pounds Granny Smith
  apples
2 tablespoons butter
⅛ teaspoon nutmeg, ground
¼ cup sugar
1 teaspoon cinnamon
¼ cup light brown sugar

1⅓ cups water
½ teaspoon cornstarch
½ cup blackberries, fresh
  or frozen
Pie dough (recipe follows)
Egg wash (recipe follows)

Peel and core apples. Cut in quarters, then in ¼-inch slices. Add to a 3-quart saucepan with butter, nutmeg, sugar, cinnamon, brown sugar and 1 cup of water. Cook until apples are tender, but not soft. Stir occasionally to keep from sticking.

After apples have become tender, reduce heat. Mix ½ teaspoon of cornstarch with ⅓ cup of water and slowly add to apple mixture. Continue stirring until mixture thickens (3 to 5 minutes). Remove from heat and cool.

Preheat oven to 350 degrees.

Lightly butter 6 individual baking dishes or soufflé cups. Fill each dish with ½ cup of apple mixture. Top each cup with one tablespoon of blackberries. Cover blackberries with pie dough and brush top of each crust with egg wash.

Bake for 10 to 12 minutes, or until top of each cobbler is lightly browned. Remove from oven and serve warm.

Pie Dough

¾ teaspoon salt
1⅓ cups pastry flour
1 tablespoon sugar

½ cup vegetable shortening
¼ cup water
¼ cup milk

Sift into a 3-quart mixing bowl salt, pastry flour, and sugar. Add shortening and blend with a pastry cutter. Combine water and milk and gradually add to flour mixture, just enough to form a moist dough. Knead lightly and refrigerate for 1 hour.

Roll dough ¼ inch thick and cut to fit individual baking dishes, allowing enough extra dough to hang over sides of dish.

Egg Wash

1 egg, beaten

¼ cup milk

Combine egg and milk and brush on cobbler just before baking.

FUDGE MUD SLIDE
Beaches and Cream
Disney's Beach Club Resort

Yield: 1 sundae

1 brownie
3 tablespoons whipped
   cream
2 teaspoons chocolate
   syrup
1½ cups vanilla ice cream

½ cup hot fudge topping
1 Oreo® Cookie, crushed
¼ cup almonds, sliced and
   chopped
1 maraschino cherry

Place brownie in a large bowl or sundae dish. Add ice cream and top with hot fudge sauce and crushed cookie. Add whipped cream and drizzle with chocolate syrup. Sprinkle with almonds and top with a cherry.

GINGERBREAD MICKEY
Monorail Cafe
Disneyland Hotel

Yield: approximately 3 dozen cookies

¼ cup unsalted butter
½ cup brown sugar
½ cup dark molasses
3½ cups all-purpose flour
1 teaspoon baking soda
½ teaspoon cloves, ground
1 teaspoon cinnamon,
   ground

3 teaspoons ginger, ground
½ teaspoon salt
¼ teaspoon cardamom,
   ground
½ cup water

In a large mixing bowl, cream butter and brown sugar. Add dark molasses and blend until completely absorbed.

Sift all dry ingredients together and add to butter mixture in thirds, alternating with water. Blend completely.

Store dough, wrapped in plastic, in refrigerator until well chilled.

Preheat oven to 350 degrees.

Grease cookie sheet.

Roll dough on a lightly floured surface and cut into desired shapes. Bake on cookie sheet for 8 to 10 minutes, depending on size. Cool on a wire rack.

Cookies can be decorated before baking with nuts and candies, or when cool with royal icing.

(continued on next page)

GINGERBREAD MICKEY
(continued from previous page)

Royal Icing
Used for frosting gingerbread men and gingerbread houses

1 pinch (⅛ teaspoon) cream   3½ cups powdered sugar,
  of tartar   sifted
2 egg whites

Add cream of tartar to egg whites. Beat egg whites in a small bowl with an electric mixer at high speed until whites hold a soft peak. Reduce speed and gradually add sifted powdered sugar. Continue to whip frosting until a smooth, spreadable consistency is reached.

At this point, frosting can be separated into small bowls and colored with food coloring, as desired. Frosting will become very hard when dry.

Note: Before preparation of frosting, make sure all utensils are free of any grease or oil and egg whites are free of any yolk. Egg whites will not whip if mixed with any type of oil or fat.

GOURMET DOUBLE CHOCOLATE CHUNK COOKIES
Main Street Bake Shop
Main Street, U.S.A.   *MAGIC KINGDOM Park*

Yield: 2 dozen

1 cup butter   1½ cups flour
1 tablespoon brown sugar   ¼ teaspoon baking soda
1 cup white sugar   ¼ teaspoon salt
2 large eggs   1½ packages (18 ounces)
¼ teaspoon vanilla extract   semi-sweet chocolate
¼ cup cocoa powder   chunks

Preheat oven to 375 degrees.

Cream butter, sugars, vanilla, and cocoa powder. Stir in remaining ingredients and blend well. Refrigerate for 30 minutes.

Drop dough by rounded teaspoonfuls onto an ungreased cookie sheet about 2 inches apart. Bake until cookies are set (5 to 8 minutes). Cool slightly and remove from pan.

When making large cookies, press down slightly on cookie dough to help cook more evenly. Bake slightly longer (8 to 10 minutes).

HAWAIIAN CHOCOLATE BROWNIES
Caffe Villa Verde
Disneyland Hotel

Yield: 50 2-inch bars

2½ cups sugar
1½ cups unsalted butter
5 ounces bitter chocolate,
  finely grated

2 cups flour, sifted
6 eggs
1 cup macadamia nuts,
  chopped

Preheat oven to 350 degrees.

Line a 15 x 15-inch baking pan with parchment or waxed paper. Butter sides of pan and set aside.

In a medium-size sauce pot, melt sugar, butter, and chocolate together, just until chocolate melts. Blend in sifted flour, eggs, and nuts. Mix only until flour is moist and eggs are blended.

Spread batter evenly into prepared baking pan and bake for approximately 30 minutes. Remove from oven and cool completely.

Fudge Topping

1 cup heavy cream

12 ounces sweet dark
  chocolate, finely grated

Heat heavy cream to a boil. Reduce heat and add chocolate. Stir until chocolate melts and mixture becomes smooth. Cool thoroughly, then frost brownies.

Sprinkle brownies with additional chopped macadamia nuts, if desired.

HERMITS (Raisin Pecan Cookies)
Farmers Market
The Land   EPCOT Center

Yield: 5 dozen 2-inch cookies

½ cup margarine
1 cup brown sugar, firmly
    packed
2 eggs
1½ cups flour
2 teaspoons cinnamon

½ teaspoon baking soda
1 cup raisins
½ cup candied citron,
    chopped
1 cup pecans, chopped

Preheat oven to 375 degrees.
Grease cookie sheet.
Beat margarine, sugar, and eggs until light and fluffy. Blend together dry ingredients and add to margarine mixture, mixing well. Stir in raisins, citron and pecans.
Drop by rounded tablespoons onto cookie sheet about 2 inches apart.
Bake for 10 to 12 minutes, or until lightly browned.

KEY LIME PARFAIT
Coral Reef Restaurant
The Living Seas   EPCOT Center

Yield: 6 servings

1 14-ounce can sweetened
    condensed milk
4 egg yolks
3 to 4 ounces Key lime juice
8 ounces pound cake

½ cup whipping cream
1 teaspoon powdered sugar
6 whole strawberries
1 kiwi, peeled, sliced in
    6 slices

In a medium-size mixing bowl with an electric mixer, combine milk and egg yolks and blend at low speed. Slowly add lime juice and continue mixing until well blended.
Slice pound cake into 1-inch slices and cut to fit inside of a white wine glass. Pour Key lime filling over pound cake and refrigerate for at least 2 hours.
Whip whipping cream with powdered sugar and top each wine glass.
Garnish with a fresh strawberry and a slice of kiwi.

KEY LIME PIE
Chef Mickey's Village Restaurant
Disney Village Marketplace

Yield: 1 9-inch pie

1¾ cups sweetened
  condensed milk
4 egg yolks
6 tablespoons Key lime juice
1 9-inch prepared graham
  cracker pie shell

1½ cups heavy cream,
  whipped
¼ teaspoon vanilla
1 fresh lime, sliced

Preheat oven to 250 degrees.
Combine milk and egg yolks in a blender or food processor on low speed. Slowly add lime juice, mixing until well blended. Pour into pie shell and bake 20 minutes. Let cool and refrigerate. Top with whipped cream and a slice of lime.

MACADAMIA NUT PIE
Papeete Bay Verandah
Disney's Polynesian Resort

Yield: 1 9-inch pie

½ cup butter
½ cup brown sugar
½ teaspoon vanilla extract
⅛ teaspoon salt
¾ cup light corn syrup

3 eggs
⅔ cup macadamia nuts,
  coarsely chopped
1 9-inch pie shell, unbaked

Preheat oven to 400 degrees.
Cream together butter, sugar, vanilla, and salt. Blend in syrup. Add eggs slowly, stirring until well mixed. Fold in nuts. Pour into pie shell.
Bake for 10 minutes, then reduce heat to 325 degrees and bake an additional 45 minutes, or until center is firm and set.

MAPLE SYRUP PIE
Le Cellier Restaurant
Canada   *EPCOT Center*

Yield: 1 9-inch pie

½ cup butter, melted
1 cup heavy maple syrup
½ cup brown sugar, firmly
  packed
⅛ teaspoon salt

4 eggs, lightly beaten
1¼ cups pecan halves
1 9-inch pie shell, unbaked
Sweetened whipped cream

Preheat oven to 350 degrees.
Blend together butter, maple syrup, brown sugar, and salt. Stir in eggs, mixing until well blended. Add pecans and pour into unbaked pie shell.
Bake for 40 to 45 minutes until firm.
Serve with sweetened whipped cream

Note: For a less rich pie, reduce butter to ¼ cup.

MARBLE CHEESECAKE
Concourse Grille
Disney's Contemporary Resort

Yield: 1 9-inch cheesecake

4 8-ounce packages cream
  cheese, softened
1 cup sugar
2 teaspoons vanilla extract
¾ teaspoon lemon flavoring
4 eggs, lightly beaten

3 egg yolks, lightly beaten
¾ cup heavy cream
6 ounces semi-sweet
  chocolate, melted
½ cup milk

Beat cream cheese until smooth. Add sugar, vanilla, and lemon flavoring and mix well. Slowly add eggs, one at a time, mixing well after each addition. Add heavy cream and blend until smooth.
Lightly grease and flour a 9-inch springform pan.
Preheat oven to 400 degrees.
Remove 1½ cups of cheese mixture to a small bowl and stir in melted chocolate. Add milk to remaining cheese mixture and pour into springform pan. Add 1½ cups of chocolate cheese mixture to pan in spoonfuls dotted around top of cake. With tip of knife, run blade through cheesecake, swirling mixtures together.
Place springform pan in a water bath and bake for 15 minutes. Reduce temperature to 325 degrees and cook an additional 40 to 50 minutes, until center of cheesecake is set. Cool and refrigerate several hours.

NARCOOSSEE'S CHEESECAKE
Narcoossee's
Disney's Grand Floridian Beach Resort

Yield: 1 10-inch cheesecake

2 pounds cream cheese
¾ cup sugar
3 tablespoons heavy cream
3 tablespoons sour cream
6 eggs

2 teaspoons lemon juice
1 teaspoon vanilla
Pie dough, enough for the
    bottom of a 10-inch cake
    pan (about half a recipe)

Grease a 10-inch round cake pan. Roll out pie dough and line bottom of pan with the dough.

Preheat oven to 300 degrees.

In a mixing bowl, cream cream cheese and sugar. Add heavy cream and sour cream and continue to mix until smooth. Blend in eggs, one at a time, mixing well after each addition. Add lemon juice and vanilla. Mix until smooth.

Pour mixture into cake pan and bake in a water bath for approximately 2 hours, or until filling is set. Remove from oven and allow to cool at room temperature for 1 hour. Remove from pan and refrigerate.

Serve cold with fresh berries.

NEW YORK STYLE CHEESECAKE
Farmers Market
The Land   EPCOT Center

Yield: 1 9-inch cheesecake

New York Style Cheese Cake is made in three parts: the crust, the filling, and the topping, which is optional. Start with the crust.

Crust

1 cup graham cracker
    crumbs
1½ teaspoons sugar

¼ teaspoon salt
3 tablespoons butter or
    margarine, melted

Lightly grease sides of a 9-inch springform pan with butter or margarine.

Combine all ingredients and mix well. Press crust into bottom of pan. Set aside.

(continued on next page)

NEW YORK STYLE CHEESECAKE
(continued from previous page)

Filling

3 8-ounce packages cream
   cheese, softened
1 3-ounce package cream
   cheese, softened
10 ounces farmer cheese
1⅓ cups sugar
½ teaspoon salt

1¼ teaspoons vanilla
   extract
2½ tablespoons flour
5 eggs, lightly beaten
2 egg yolks, lightly beaten
¼ cup milk

Preheat oven to 400 degrees.

Blend cream cheese and farmer cheese until soft and fluffy. Add sugar, salt, vanilla, and flour. Beat until well mixed. Add eggs and egg yolks slowly, beating well after each addition. Add milk last and blend batter until smooth. Pour batter into springform pan over crust.

Bake cheesecake for 25 minutes. Reduce heat to 350 degrees and continue cooking for an additional 30 minutes. Remove from oven when center of cheesecake is firm to touch. Cool for 30 minutes and refrigerate for several hours. Top with fruit glaze, if desired.

Toppings for Cheesecake

Blueberry Sauce Topping
½ cup sugar
¾ cup water
1 cup whole blueberries,
   fresh or frozen

1 tablespoon cornstarch
1 tablespoon cold water

Heat sugar, ¾ cup water and blueberries in a small saucepan until boiling. Stir in cornstarch dissolved in 1 tablespoon water and simmer for 2 minutes. Cool for 20 minutes and serve on top of cheesecake.

Strawberry Topping
½ cup sugar
Pinch salt
¾ cup water
¼ teaspoon red food
   coloring
1 tablespoon cornstarch

1 tablespoon cold water
1 tablespoon strawberry-
   flavored gelatin
1 tablespoon lemon juice
1½ pints strawberries,
   hulled, fresh or frozen

Heat sugar, salt, and ¾ cup water until boiling. Add food coloring and cornstarch dissolved in 1 tablespoon water. Simmer for 2 minutes. Stir in strawberry gelatin and lemon juice. Cool. Add strawberries, coating well, and spoon topping on cheesecake. Refrigerate for several hours.

MEXICAN BREAD PUDDING
Monorail Cafe
Disneyland Hotel

Yield: 8 servings

1 cup brown sugar
1 cup water
½ teaspoon cinnamon
½ cup toasted pine nuts,
  sliced almonds, and
  chopped walnuts, mixed
1 cup raisins

½ pound Monterey Jack
  cheese, cut in ½-inch
  cubes
1 apple, peeled, thinly sliced
1 loaf French bread
Whipped cream

Grease a 9-inch baking dish.
Preheat oven to 350 degrees.
In a medium-size saucepan, boil water, brown sugar, and cinnamon for 2 to 3 minutes. Set aside.
Slice bread in thick slices and toast lightly; then break into large pieces. Place half the bread in a baking dish. Combine pine nuts, almonds, walnuts, raisins, and cheese. Layer half of nut mixture on top of bread in baking dish. Top with sliced apple and half of brown sugar mixture. Add remaining bread and cover with remaining nuts and cheese. Add remaining brown sugar mixture and cover with foil.
Bake for about 45 minutes.
Serve immediately with whipped cream.

MILKY WAY® CAKE
Beaches and Cream
Disney's Beach Club Resort

Yield: 1 cake

5 Milky Way® Candy Bars
1 cup butter
2 cups sugar
4 eggs, separated
2½ cups flour

½ teaspoon baking soda
1¼ cups buttermilk
1 cup pecans, chopped
2 cups semi-sweet chocolate
  morsels, melted

Grease and flour an angel food cake pan.
Preheat oven to 325 degrees.
In a small pot over low heat, melt candy bars with ½ cup of butter. Cream sugar with remaining ½ cup of butter until light. Add candy and blend well. Add egg yolks, one at a time, mixing well after each. Dissolve baking soda in buttermilk and add alternately with flour to candy mixture, ending with flour. Beat egg whites to stiff peaks and fold into candy mixture with chopped pecans.
Bake for 1 hour, 10 minutes.
Cool and frost with melted semi-sweet chocolate.

ORCHARD FAVORITE CRÊPE
The Land Grille Room
The Land   EPCOT Center

Yield: 12 crêpes

Crêpe Batter

⅔ cup flour
½ teaspoon salt

¾ cup milk
3 eggs, beaten

Combine all ingredients and beat until smooth. Let stand 30 minutes.

For each crêpe, pour 2 tablespoons of batter into a hot, lightly greased 8-inch skillet. Cook on one side only until underside is lightly browned and top is dry. Repeat until all batter has been used.

Filling

1 cup large-curd cottage
  cheese
½ cup sugar

2 cups strawberry slices
1 cup sour cream

Combine cottage cheese and sugar in a blender or food processor with a steel blade. Blend until smooth. Fold in strawberries and sour cream. Fill each crêpe with ¼ cup of cheese/strawberry mixture and top with any remaining filling.

PEACH COBBLER
Chef Mickey's Village Restaurant
Disney Village Marketplace

Yield: 4 servings

2½ cups sliced peaches,
  canned, drained
2 teaspoons apricot brandy
2 teaspoons unsalted butter
2 teaspoons vanilla extract
1 teaspoon cinnamon
½ cup sugar

2 teaspoons lemon juice
¼ teaspoon nutmeg
1 tablespoon cornstarch
2 teaspoons water
½ package pie dough, or 1
  ready-made pie shell

Preheat oven to 350 degrees.

In a 2-quart saucepan, add peaches, brandy, butter, vanilla, cinnamon, sugar, lemon juice, and nutmeg. Bring to a boil. Add cornstarch mixed with water and cook until mixture thickens. Place peach mixture in a deep-dish pie plate. Top with pie dough, crimping edges to seal in filling.

Bake for 45 minutes, or until crust is golden brown.

PUMPKIN CRÈME BRÛLÉE
Ariel's
Disney's Beach Club Resort

Yield: 6 4-inch tarts

Spice Short-Crust Pastry

1¼ cups pastry flour
¼ cup granulated sugar
1 egg yolk
½ cup butter, chilled

Pinch cinnamon
Pinch nutmeg
Pinch cardamom

In a large mixing bowl, combine flour and spices. Make a well in center of flour and add sugar and egg yolk. Cut chilled butter into small pieces and place around edge of bowl on flour. With a pastry cutter or knife, cut butter into flour/sugar mixture, just enough to moisten and combine all ingredients. Do not overmix, or dough will become tough when baked. Dough will remain crumbly and dry to this point.

Gather dough together with your hands and place on a clean, dry pastry board. Knead dough just enough to hold together. Wrap in plastic and refrigerate for 30 minutes.

Roll out pastry dough to ¼-inch thickness and cut out shapes to fit deep tart shells. Line tart shells with pastry and weight the dough with cupcake liners filled with dried beans or rice. Return to the refrigerator for an additional 30 minutes.

Preheat oven to 400 degrees.

Bake pastry shells with weighted cupcake liners for 8 minutes. Remove liners and finish baking until shells are nicely browned. Set aside to cool.

Note: Cupcake liners filled with dried beans or rice set on top of pastry keeps it flat in pan and prevents dough from puffing up.

Filling

6 extra-large egg yolks
1¼ cups sugar
3 cups heavy cream
1 cup pumpkin puree (or canned pumpkin)

Pinch nutmeg
Pinch cinnamon
Pinch allspice

Combine egg yolks and half the amount of sugar in top half of a double boiler over very hot water. Whisk until lemon-colored and the consistency of mousse. Remove from heat and set aside.

(continued on next page)

PUMPKIN CRÈME BRÛLÉE
(continued from previous page)

Place cream, pumpkin, and spices in a saucepan and bring to a boil. Immediately remove from heat once cream boils. Strain and slowly pour into egg mixture, whisking rapidly as you pour. Return to double boiler to heat and cook, stirring occasionally until it reaches consistency of very thick custard. Remove from heat and cool.

Fill pastry shells and refrigerate for 4 hours. When fully chilled and firm, remove from refrigerator and sprinkle 2 tablespoons of sugar over each filled shell. Place about 6 inches away from broiler flames for about 2 minutes, or until sugar caramelizes. Do not overcook, or cream will melt.

Serve immediately with caramel sauce.

FRANGIPANE (Rich Almond Batter)
Special Events
Disneyland Hotel

Yield: 1 cake

8 ounces almond paste
1¾ sticks unsalted butter
1 cup sugar
6 medium eggs

Peel from 1 lemon, grated
1 teaspoon vanilla
2¼ cups all-purpose flour
or cake flour, sifted

Combine almond paste, unsalted butter and sugar. Blend well. Add eggs, one at a time, mixing well after each addition. Add lemon peel and vanilla. Blend well. Mix in flour, only enough to incorporate. Overmixing creates a tough dough.

Preheat oven to 350 degrees.

Choose a decorative mold or cake pan. Grease well or line with sweet dough. Add batter and bake until a toothpick comes out clean (about 20 minutes). Cool and remove from pan.

Note: Batter can also be used for pastry tarts and shells.
Batter can be stored in an air-tight container for up to 7 days, refrigerated.

POIRES FRAMBOISES
(Pears in Raspberry Sauce)
Club 33
New Orleans Square   *DISNEYLAND Park*

Yield: 4 servings

Pears

4 pears, fresh   **1 cup white wine**
1 cup water   **1 cup sugar**

Peel pears and remove core from bottom, leaving stem intact.
Bring water, wine, and sugar to a boil in a saucepan just large enough
to hold pears. Simmer pears in syrup just until tender (about 5
minutes). Let pears cool in cooking liquid. Set aside.

Sabayon Sauce

2¼ cups Sauternes wine,   **1 whole egg**
**   divided**   **2 tablespoons cornstarch**
½ cup sugar, divided   **2 tablespoons pear liqueur**
1 egg yolk

Bring 2 cups of wine to a boil. Add ¼ cup of sugar and simmer on
low heat.

Mix remaining ¼ cup wine, ¼ cup sugar, egg yolk, whole egg, and
cornstarch until thoroughly blended and cornstarch is dissolved. Add
some of hot wine to mixture, stirring with a whisk, then gradually
add egg mixture back into remaining hot wine, mixing until sauce
returns to a boil. Continue whisking to prevent eggs from
scrambling. When sauce is thick, remove from heat and stir in
liqueur.

Raspberry Sauce

1 cup good raspberry   **1 cup raspberries, frozen,**
**   preserves**   **   thawed**

Combine preserves and thawed raspberries and beat well. Strain
through a fine sieve to remove seeds.

To serve, remove pears from syrup and drain well. Divide Sabayon
sauce in 4 dessert dishes. Stand pears upright in sauce and spoon
raspberry sauce over pears.

SHERRY TRIFLE
Rose & Crown Pub & Dining Room
United Kingdom   EPCOT Center

Yield: 6 servings

3 eggs
¼ cup sugar
⅛ teaspoon salt
2¼ cups half-and-half, or
   milk, heated
½ teaspoon vanilla extract
1 package strawberry
   gelatin (4-serving size)
1 cup boiling water
¾ cup cold water
¼ cup sherry
1 cup strawberries, fresh,
   sliced
8 ounces pound cake
½ cup heavy cream,
   whipped
6 whole strawberries
6 mint leaves

Combine eggs, sugar, and salt in a 2-quart mixing bowl. Whisk together. Slowly stir in heated half-and-half or milk. Strain cream mixture into a double boiler and cook over simmering water until custard coats a metal spoon. Stir constantly. Remove from heat and cool. Add vanilla.

Dissolve gelatin in boiling water. Stir well and add cold water. Chill until consistency of heavy syrup. Stir in sherry and whip until fluffy. Fold in sliced strawberries.

Cut pound cake into 12 slices, approximately ¼ inch thick. In a large decorative serving bowl, layer strawberry filling, cake and custard sauce in alternate layers, ending with strawberry filling. Refrigerate for 2 to 4 hours, or overnight.

To serve, spoon out into serving dishes, cutting deep into bowl to all three layers. Garnish with whole strawberries, whipped cream and fresh mint leaves.

RASPBERRY CHIFFON PIE
Ariel's
Disney's Beach Club Resort

Yield: 1 9-inch pie

1¼ cups raspberries, frozen
3 tablespoons sugar
1 tablespoon gelatin,
   unflavored

3 tablespoons raspberry
   liqueur
1¼ cups whipped cream
½ cup raspberry yogurt
1 9-inch pie shell, baked

In a medium-size saucepan over medium high heat, bring raspberries, sugar, and gelatin to a simmer. Cook until gelatin and sugar dissolve. Remove from heat. Pour into a large bowl and refrigerate for 2 hours, until gelatin has set.

Using a wire whisk, whip yogurt and raspberry liqueur into chilled raspberry gelatin mixture. Fold in whipped cream and blend thoroughly. Pour into a prepared pie shell and chill 3 to 4 hours before serving.

RASPBERRY FOOL
(Raspberries and Cream)
Rose & Crown Pub & Dining Room
United Kingdom   EPCOT Center

Yield: 6 servings

1 cup raspberries, fresh
   (or 1 frozen 10-ounce
   package)
¼ cup granulated sugar
2 cups heavy cream

1 tablespoon powdered
   sugar
½ teaspoon vanilla extract
1 tablespoon cherry brandy

Crush raspberries (if using frozen raspberries, thaw and drain first).

Place crushed raspberries in a small saucepan and add granulated sugar. Simmer raspberries and sugar over medium heat until a thick syrup forms (about 5 minutes). Force raspberries through a fine sieve to remove seeds. Allow to cool.

Combine heavy cream, powdered sugar, and vanilla and beat until thick. Combine cooled raspberry syrup and cherry brandy and fold into whipped cream mixture. Chill at least 1 hour.

Serve with additional whipped cream.

THE DAREDEVIL
Disney Village Resort Club
Disney Village Resort

Yield: 4 servings

8 2½-inch brownie squares
1 pint vanilla ice cream
¾ cup hot fudge sauce

1 cup strawberry sauce
1 cup freshly whipped
cream

In a glass bowl or on a plate, place one brownie. Scoop one quarter of pint of ice cream onto brownie. Top with another brownie square. Add hot fudge sauce, strawberry sauce and ¼ cup whipped cream.

ANGEL FOOD CAKE
The Land Grille Room
The Land   EPCOT Center

Yield: 1 cake

1¾ cups egg whites
1¾ cups granulated sugar
1½ teaspoons cream of
   tartar
½ teaspoon salt
1¼ cups cake flour

⅛ teaspoon vanilla extract
⅛ teaspoon lemon zest
   (grated from lemon rind)
Strawberry coulis (recipe
   follows)

In a large mixing bowl, whip egg whites until stiff peaks form. Combine sugar and cream of tartar and add to stiffly beaten egg whites. Sift cake flour and salt and add to egg whites in thirds, mixing well after each addition. Finally, add vanilla and lemon zest, folding carefully so as not to break down batter.
Preheat oven to 375 degrees.
Pour mixture into an ungreased angel food cake pan and bake 40 to 50 minutes, or until crust is golden brown.
Allow cake to cool upside-down on a bottle, so that no pressure is on cake. Cool approximately 2 hours.
Serve with fresh berries and strawberry coulis.

Strawberry Coulis

2 cups strawberries, fresh
½ cup granulated sugar

1 cup strawberry jam
½ cup water

Puree all ingredients in a blender or food processor and pass through a large sieve. Serve with angel food cake.

TIRA-MI-SU
Flagler's
Disney's Grand Floridian Beach Resort

Yield: 12 servings

2 cups mascarpone cheese　　3 tablespoons coffee liqueur
3 cups heavy cream　　　　　1 teaspoon instant coffee
¼ cup powdered sugar　　　　1 10-inch sponge cake
½ teaspoon vanilla extract　　¼ cup cocoa powder

　Combine mascarpone cheese, cream, sugar, vanilla, coffee liqueur, and instant coffee in a mixing bowl and whip until stiff.
　Split sponge cake in half, creating a top and bottom layer. Spread cream mixture on bottom layer and replace top half of cake. Refrigerate for 1 hour.
　Just before serving, dust top of cake with cocoa powder.

S'MORES
50's Prime Time Cafe
Disney-MGM Studios Theme Park

Yield: 4 servings

2 whole graham crackers　　　15 large marshmallows
　(4 sections)　　　　　　　2 tablespoons chocolate
1 1.65-ounce milk chocolate　　　syrup
　bar

　Place graham crackers on an oven-proof plate. Top with milk chocolate bar and heat briefly under broiler or in a hot oven.
　Cut marshmallows in half and place over melted chocolate bar. Broil marshmallows until golden brown.
　Drizzle chocolate syrup randomly over marshmallow and serve immediately.

WHITE CHOCOLATE CHEESECAKE
Ariel's
Disney's Beach Club Resort

Yield: 1 10-inch cheesecake

8 ounces white chocolate, melted
3 pounds cream cheese
1¼ cups sugar

½ cup flour
6 eggs
1 cup heavy cream
1 tablespoon vanilla

Grease 2 10-inch springform pans.

Preheat oven to 300 degrees.

Place cream cheese, sugar, and flour in a mixing bowl and cream until light and fluffy. Add eggs, one at a time, mixing well after each addition. Scrape down bowl and add melted white chocolate. While mixer is running on very low speed, slowly add vanilla and heavy cream. Blend well.

Pour mixture into springform pans. Place cheesecake pans in a water bath filled with warm water. Bake for 50 to 60 minutes, or until center of cheesecake is just firm.

Cool at room temperature for 1 hour. Refrigerate until set before removing from pan.

Sauce for Topping

1 cup heavy cream
2 cups white chocolate, finely chopped

2 ounces orange liqueur

Place heavy cream in a saucepan and bring to a boil. Pour over white chocolate and stir with a wooden spoon until melted. Add orange liqueur and continue stirring until incorporated. Pour over chilled cheesecake and serve.

NOTES

SAUCES

SAUCES

BORDELAISE SAUCE
Chefs de France
France   EPCOT Center

Yield: 2½ cups

1 cup butter, divided
2 tablespoons shallots,
  chopped
¾ cup Burgundy wine
4 mushroom stems, diced
2 tablespoons parsley,
  chopped
5 peppercorns
1 sprig thyme, fresh (or ⅛
  teaspoon dried thyme)

½ stem tarragon, fresh (or
  ⅛ teaspoon dried
  tarragon)
1 bay leaf
3 tablespoons flour
1½ cups beef stock or broth
Salt
Pepper, freshly ground

Heat ½ cup butter in a skillet and sauté shallots for 2 minutes. Add Burgundy, mushrooms, parsley, peppercorns, thyme, tarragon, and bay leaf. Simmer on medium heat until reduced by half. Set aside.

Heat remaining butter in a saucepan. Add flour and cook until lightly browned. Stir constantly. Add beef stock and bring to a boil, stirring with a whisk. Reduce heat and simmer, covered, for about 30 minutes.

Strain wine mixture into beef stock. Bring sauce back to a simmer and adjust seasoning with salt and pepper, if necessary.

CHAMPAGNE SAUCE
Disney-MGM Studios Theme Park

Yield: 3¼ cups

¼ cup butter
¼ cup flour
2½ cups chicken stock or
  bouillon
¼ cup champagne

Salt
Pepper
½ cup heavy whipping
  cream

In a 3-quart saucepan, melt butter and add flour. Cook 5 to 7 minutes, forming a roux. Do not brown.

Heat chicken stock and add to roux. Stir well to blend and continue cooking approximately 10 minutes. Add champagne and heavy cream and season with salt and pepper to taste. Simmer for an additional minute and strain through a fine sieve.

CHICKEN DIJON® SAUCE
Special Events
Disney's Yacht and Beach Club Resorts

Yield: 1 cup

⅔ cup heavy cream
⅔ cup chicken stock or
  broth
2 tablespoons Dijon®
  Mustard
½ teaspoon garlic, minced

½ teaspoon salt
½ teaspoon white pepper
¼ teaspoon chives, fresh,
  chopped

In a heavy skillet, over medium heat, simmer chicken stock for 10 minutes. Reduce liquid by one third. Add heavy cream and simmer for 1 minute over low heat. Add Dijon Mustard, garlic, salt, pepper, and chives and continue to simmer for 2 to 3 minutes more.
Serve immediately.

CHILE SAUCE
Special Events
Disneyland Hotel

Yield: about 1¼ cups

6 whole green chile
  peppers, fresh
3 cups hot water
¼ cup tomato paste
1 clove garlic, minced

¼ cup oil
1½ teaspoons salt
1 teaspoon oregano
¼ teaspoon cumin

Preheat oven to 400 degrees.
Place peppers on a sheet pan and bake for about 5 minutes. Remove from oven and allow to cool only long enough to handle.
Cut peppers open and remove any seeds and soft flesh from inside of each pepper. Rinse under cold water. Repeat process until all peppers have been prepared. Cover peppers with hot water and let stand for 1 hour.
After 1 hour, remove peppers from water, reserving one cup of water, and place in a blender or food processor with a steel blade. Add reserved chile water and remaining ingredients. Blend well until peppers and sauce are smooth. Place mixture in a saucepan and simmer for 15 minutes. Stir occasionally to blend flavors.

LOBSTER BUTTER SAUCE
Coral Reef Restaurant
The Living Seas   *EPCOT Center*

Yield: 1 cup

¾ cup white wine
2 tablespoons white vinegar
1 tablespoon shallots,
  minced
½ cup heavy cream

10 ounces unsalted butter,
  softened
1 ounce lobster paste
Salt
Pepper

In a heavy saucepan, combine white wine, white vinegar, and shallots. Reduce over low heat until only ¼ cup remains. Stir in heavy cream and reduce over low heat until only ⅓ cup remains. Slowly add butter and whisk continually. Strain sauce and add lobster paste and salt and pepper to taste. Blend well and serve.

MARINARA SAUCE
Disney-MGM Studios Theme Park

Yield: 2½ cups

1 tablespoon olive oil
1 teaspoon garlic, minced
⅓ cup green bell pepper,
  diced
⅓ cup celery, diced
⅓ cup onion, diced
¼ teaspoon oregano, dry

¼ teaspoon thyme, dry
¼ teaspoon basil, dry
¼ teaspoon black pepper
3 cups tomatoes, canned,
  diced, with juice
1 teaspoon sugar
1 whole bay leaf

In a medium-size saucepan, heat olive oil. Add minced garlic, green pepper, celery, onion, and spices. Sauté about 5 minutes, until vegetables become transparent. Remove from heat and transfer to a food processor with a steel blade. Add canned diced tomatoes and sugar and puree until smooth. Place mixture back in saucepan and bring to a boil. Add bay leaf and simmer 15 to 20 minutes. Adjust seasoning and remove bay leaf.

MADEIRA PEPPERCORN SAUCE
Garden Gallery
The Disney Inn

Yield: 1¼ cups

Pan drippings from roasted
  chicken
2 shallots, peeled, chopped
¾ cup chicken stock or
  canned broth, divided
½ cup Madeira wine

1 tablespoon green
  peppercorns in brine,
  drained, crushed
1 tablespoon cornstarch
Salt
Pepper

Skim any remaining fat from roasting pan and scrape browned pan drippings into a 1-quart saucepan. Add shallots, half cup of stock, Madeira wine, and peppercorns. Simmer over low heat for 5 minutes. Mix cornstarch with remaining ¼ cup of stock and slowly add to saucepan, stirring rapidly. Season with salt and pepper to taste and simmer an additional 5 minutes.

MONTEGO BAY MARINARA SAUCE
Royale Pizza and Pasta Shop
Disney's Caribbean Beach Resort

Yield: 2 quarts

2 small Spanish onions,
  diced (about 2 cups)
2 cloves garlic, crushed
2 teaspoons olive oil
2 16-ounce cans plum
  tomatoes, diced
2 16-ounce cans tomatoes,
  crushed

1 cup red wine
2 teaspoons oregano
2 teaspoons basil
1 teaspoon thyme
2 teaspoons parsley
2 teaspoons white pepper
2 teaspoons kosher salt

In a 4-quart sauce pot, heat olive oil and sauté onion and garlic until tender. Add remaining ingredients and cook, lightly covered, on medium heat at a light simmer for 2 hours.

NEW ORLEANS BARBECUE SAUCE
Cafe Orleans
New Orleans Square DISNEYLAND Park

Yield: 3½ cups

1 cup tomato ketchup
1 cup chili sauce
½ cup currant jelly
¼ cup Dijon® Mustard
½ cup brown sugar
¼ cup red wine vinegar
1 tablespoon
   Worcestershire sauce
2 tablespoons steak sauce

1 teaspoon dry mustard
¼ cup honey
1 teaspoon black pepper,
   coarsely cracked
Salt
Pork spareribs or beef
   short ribs (allow 1 pound
   per person)

Combine all ingredients, except ribs, and blend well.

Cut ribs into serving-size pieces and cover with barbecue sauce. Marinate in refrigerator for several hours or overnight.

Grill ribs over low coals for about 1 hour, basting occasionally with additional sauce. Turn ribs frequently.

Refrigerate any leftover sauce.

SAUCE FOR ORIENTAL PORK RIBS
Tahitian Terrace
Adventureland DISNEYLAND Park

Yield: 3 cups

2 cups tomato ketchup
¼ cup soy sauce
¼ cup pineapple juice
¼ cup pineapple, fresh or
   canned, crushed
¼ cup orange juice, fresh
1 teaspoon orange rind,
   grated

½ cup brown sugar
1 tablespoon wine vinegar
3 whole cloves
Pork spareribs (about
   1 pound per person)

Combine all ingredients except ribs, and blend well. Allow mixture to stand in refrigerator overnight. Strain before using.

Preheat oven to 275 degrees.

Cut ribs into serving-size pieces. Place on a rack in a roasting pan. Bake, basting with sauce often, for 2 to 2½ hours, or until meat separates easily from bone.

Refrigerate any leftover sauce.

SAUCE VERDE
Special Events
Disneyland Hotel

Yield: 1 quart

¼ cup scallions, chopped
2 cups mayonnaise
⅓ cup frozen chopped
  spinach
1 cup parsley, chopped
½ teaspoon garlic powder

½ teaspoon salt
2 teaspoons sugar
1½ teaspoons tarragon
¼ cup water
¼ cup red wine vinegar
½ teaspoon white pepper

Combine all ingredients in a blender or food processor and blend until mixture is smooth.

Note: This sauce is best served with broiled fresh fish.

STRAWBERRY DIP FOR FRUIT
Tony's Town Square Restaurant
Main Street, U.S.A.   *MAGIC KINGDOM Park*

Yield: 1½ cups

8 ounces strawberry yogurt
  (or any flavor desired)

¼ cup honey
⅔ cup ricotta cheese

In a medium-size mixing bowl, blend all ingredients with a wire whisk until smooth. Refrigerate until ready to use.

TOMATO-BASIL SAUCE
Coral Reef Restaurant
The Living Seas   EPCOT Center

Yield: 2 cups

1 teaspoon vegetable oil
2 shallots, diced
1 cup fish stock or bouillon
Salt
White pepper

2 teaspoons cornstarch
   (more, if necessary)
2 teaspoons water
12 plum tomatoes, chopped
2 tablespoons basil, fresh,
   chopped

In a medium skillet, heat oil and sauté shallots until transparent. Add fish stock and bring to a boil. Add salt and white pepper to taste. Dissolve cornstarch in water and add to fish stock. Simmer 3 to 5 minutes until thickened. Add an additional teaspoon of cornstarch dissolved in water for a thicker sauce, if desired. Add tomatoes and basil. Simmer an additional 3 to 5 minutes and check seasonings.

VANILLA SAUCE
Disney-MGM Studios Theme Park

Yield: 2 cups

½ cup butter
¼ cup flour
3 cups half-and-half

1 teaspoon vanilla (more
   if desired)
½ cup sugar
Pinch salt (optional)

Melt butter in a small saucepan. Add flour and cook on low heat for 7 to 10 minutes, or until a nutty aroma develops. Do not brown or color roux. Remove from heat and let cool.

In a separate saucepan, heat half-and-half with sugar and bring to a boil. Add roux and stir until thickened. Reduce heat and continue cooking an additional 5 minutes to prevent sauce from breaking. Stir constantly. Remove from heat once sauce has thickened and stir in vanilla. Strain through a fine sieve and serve.

YAKITORI SAUCE
Yakitori House
Japan   *EPCOT Center*

Yield: 2½ cups

¼ cup sake wine
1 cup mirin wine
1 cup soy sauce

1 tablespoon sugar
2 tablespoons cornstarch
⅓ cup water

Combine sake and mirin wines in a medium-size saucepan and bring to a boil. Add soy sauce and sugar. Simmer, covered, for 30 minutes.

Dissolve cornstarch in water and add to boiling mixture. Cook and stir until mixture thickens.

Serve hot over baked, broiled or roasted chicken.

INDEXES

RESTAURANT INDEX